QUEER YOUTH SUICIDE, CULTURE AND IDENTITY

Blending beautifully extant research with analyses of media representations, Rob Cover shows us that queer youth do not seek death, but an end to the pressure of making their sexual identities coherent, alongside shame, vulnerability, homophobia and the cultural politics of coming out. We must have a genuine interdisciplinary dialogue if we are ever to comprehend queer life as resilient.

Katrina Jaworski, University of South Australia, Australia

Informed by post-structuralism, queer theory and a transdisciplinary ethos, this highly accessible text demonstrates the relevance of culture studies to a topic dominated by psychological and sociological analyses. Introducing debates on sexuality and suicidal risk while questioning the explanatory frameworks and prevention strategies that might be applied to issues of vulnerability and queer youth suicide this book is an important marker in the emerging field of queer youth suicide.

Katherine Johnson, University of Brighton, UK

Queer Youth Suicide, Culture and Identity
Unliveable Lives?

ROB COVER
University of Western Australia, Australia

ASHGATE

© Rob Cover 2012

Published by
Ashgate Publishing Limited
Wey Court East
Union Road
Farnham
Surrey, GU9 7PT
England

Ashgate Publishing Company
Suite 420
101 Cherry Street
Burlington
VT 05401-4405
USA

www.ashgate.com

British Library Cataloguing in Publication Data
Cover, Rob.
  Queer youth suicide, culture and identity : unliveable lives?.
  1. Gay youth--Suicidal behaviour. 2. Gay youth--Psychology. 3. Suicide in mass media.
  I. Title
  362.2'8'086642-dc23

Library of Congress Cataloging-in-Publication Data
Cover, Rob.
  Queer youth suicide, culture and identity : unliveable lives? / by Rob Cover.
     p. cm.
  Includes bibliographical references and index.
  ISBN 978-1-4094-4447-3 (hbk. : alk. paper) -- ISBN 978-1-4094-4448-0 (ebook)
  1. Gay youth. 2. Gay youth--Suicidal behavior. 3. Youth in mass media. 4. Suicide in mass media. I. Title.

  HQ76.27.Y68C68 2011
  362.28086'642--dc23

                                                    2011049790

  ISBN 9781409444473 (hbk)
  ISBN 9781409444480 (ebk)

MIX
Paper from
responsible sources
FSC
www.fsc.org   FSC® C018575

Printed and bound in Great Britain by the
MPG Books Group, UK.

Contents

Acknowledgements

I would like to thank many people across several cities and eras for their contributions, both social and intellectual, towards the development of ideas around youth, sexuality, suicide and subjectivity that inform this book: in Melbourne – Elizabeth Dean, Tessa Keegel, Stephen Pritchard and Daniel Marshall; in Adelaide – Katrina Jaworski, Rosslyn Prosser, Veronika Petroff, Mandy Treagus, Barbara Baird and Keren Yi; in Sydney – James Duncan; in New Zealand – Shona Hill; and in Perth – Elena Jeffreys and most importantly Jeff Williams. Thanks are also due to Shona Hill and Sarah Moody, both of whom undertook research assistant work for various parts of this project. At the University of Adelaide, the Fay Gale Centre for Research on Gender provided funding that supported the writing of one chapter; a research grant from Victoria University of Wellington helped with the writing of another. This book is for those I know and those I have never known who are lost, who felt their lives were unliveable and for whom we must grieve. I hope that in some unforeseeable way this small contribution can help to make the lives of all young people liveable.

Preface

In late 1997, while a postgraduate student at Monash University in Melbourne, a few friends from the student queer organisation had been out to dinner and were later listening to music and chatting at my flat. A call came through on one someone's mobile, and we learned that a young student, James, had in the previous week committed suicide. As a member of the queer group he was known to some of us, and had occasionally come out socialising. While everyone was upset at the news, there was a certain, unspoken feeling in the room that can only be described as 'resigned expectation'. No one had thought James was suicidal – he was quiet, sometimes a little shy, but could be a lot of fun and had a good sense of humour. There was just no distinctive indication of his feelings or intentions, and of course that was one of the things we spoke about at length that evening. What remained tacitly agreed among us, however, was that there was somehow no real surprise about a young queer male killing himself. Over the following weeks and months I thought about this 'resigned expectation'; I worried that as a community and even as activist queer students we were either complacent, or that the problem of queer youth suicide was so overwhelming that we could not really imagine queer lives untouched by suicide, or that contemporary culture had forged such a strong link between non-heterosexuality and suicide it felt 'natural' to lose a young queer friend in that way. Ultimately, I was angry that we did not react with, indeed, greater anger and greater curiosity and inquisitiveness about the nature of queer youth suicide. Although youth suicide was not among my primary research interests I wrote a little about it over the few years afterwards. And over time I stopped writing about it – perhaps out of the very complacency I had earlier criticised, but also out of a growing sense that there seemed to be less evidence that queer youth were as vulnerable as they had been, particularly as eradication of inequitable same-sex age-of-consent laws in Australia (and elsewhere) was legislated, as media representation of queer youth was increasing, especially after the late 1990s.

In September and October 2010, a spate of sexuality-related suicides which occurred in the United States was reported on widely and internationally, much of the reportage focusing on the ways in which different forms of bullying had driven young school-aged or university students to attempt suicide. The news was predominantly about eighteen year-old Tyler Clementi, a young Rutgers University student who jumped from the George Washington Bridge after his roommate had remotely used a webcam to capture footage of Clementi during an intimate encounter with another male and broadcast it live. The roommate was charged with invasion of privacy for using the camera to view and transmit a live image. Within a month of Clementi's suicide, there were international reports of several youth suicides in which taunting over non-heterosexuality was frequently discussed as the cause or reason. These additional suicides involved two nineteen year-olds, one fifteen year-old and two thirteen year-old boys. While there is a range in ages here, the relative youth of the youngest boys was considerably alarming, even though it indicates some of the shifts over the past fifteen years in how younger persons are accessing information about sexuality, forming sexual subjecthood or being perceived to have non-normative identities at relatively younger ages than, say, only one or two decades ago. Importantly, the series of reports began to alter the focus on causal reasons for queer youth suicide from queer vulnerability to institutionalised bullying in school (and other) environments. The reports also sparked a wholly new phenomenon in the way in which queer youth suicide is addressed in public discourse – the development of the *It Gets Better* website in which thousands of people have uploaded videos about queer youth suicide, taking the dialogue out of the psychological, sociological and health sciences and policy development, and generating a public interest in tackling this issue.

During October 2010, I found the act of reading this wave of reports on queer youth suicides to be both distressing and strangely familiar. It evoked the same uneasiness about the feelings of 'resigned expectation' that occurred after James' suicide over a decade earlier, prompting for me some urgent and necessary questions: Why it is that young queer men are still killing themselves? What has and has not changed over time? What new ways are available for thinking about queer youth suicide, and what contribution can cultural studies and critical theory make towards fostering change? In particular, I began wondering to what extent the work I do around sexual subjectivity through poststructuralist queer theory, and the research I undertake in media, digital media and culture from a cultural studies perspective, might allow for some re-thinking on queer youth suicide from angles which are rarely discussed in either socio-medical literature, policy or queer community debate. That is how this book came about – the need to address the striking similarities and yet vast cultural and generational differences that were apparent to me between James' suicide in 1997 and all those of late 2010. I was thus compelled to put aside some other projects in favour of the ethical urgency this topic demands, and to consider how some of the theoretical and analytical tools I use in other work might be lent to the project of preventing young queer people from killing themselves. Naturally, I am aware as to how small a contribution it is compared with those made by people who work every day in the field, who work personally with queer youth in intervention and prevention roles and who actively devote the majority of their time to averting unnecessary loss.

This return to researching, thinking and writing about queer youth suicide has had two aims or, really, two fields of inquiry. Firstly, it is important to understand how that sense of 'resigned expectation' is culturally produced and governs various responses to youth suicide today: what is it in contemporary culture that makes suicide continue to seem like a logical outcome for queer youth? In what ways is a link between non-heterosexuality and suicidality forged and maintained in popular culture, news media, some strands of academic research and, more recently, in online digital media forms? How does that link make all queer youth *appear* to be automatically vulnerable because of their sexuality alone, and what does that actually do for queer youth? What is it that makes it culturally 'comfortable' for people to see a young queer life as an unliveable life? Secondly, it is necessary to think about queer youth suicide from the perspective of queer theory and cultural studies approaches, which have not to date been deployed as a means of interrogating why some queer youth might, indeed, be more vulnerable than heterosexual younger persons or than other queer younger persons. That means asking: in what ways does the formation of sexual subjectivity contribute to the conditions that make queer youth suicide possible? How does the materialisation of the queer subject through shame operate to create tensions, risks but also resilience? And how does the persistence of heteronormativity in western societies, including those that have slowly begun to tolerate and even protect non-heterosexuality, relate to the conditions that make suicide a thinkable path for some queer youth? By examining the field of queer youth suicide from the two perspectives of culture and identity it is hoped that communities, policy-makers and those who work in intervention and prevention will have access to some alternative perceptions that might help not only to prevent further suicides and self-harm, but also prompt a broader number of people to shift away from the 'resigned expectation' that a queer life is an unhappy one, that queer youth are vulnerable and, instead, to see that queer youth can and do indeed have lives that are very much liveable.

Introduction

Queer Youth Suicide, Vulnerability and Unliveable Lives

Figures, Statistics and Risk: Queer Youth Suicide Research

For over twenty years, publications in policy, psychology, sociology, paediatrics and other fields have often stated that non-heterosexual younger persons are at greater risk of suicidal behaviour, ideation, thoughts and acts than youth identifying as heterosexual (Gibson 1989, King et al. 2008, Hegna and Wichstrøm 2007). Indeed, the link between non-heterosexuality and youth suicide is well-represented in contemporary news media, popular culture, policy and research (Cover 2005b, Igartua et al. 2009). While there have been some improvements in the social situations and environments for younger non-heterosexual persons that had previously been thought to contribute to suicidality, particularly in the areas of media representation (Padva 2004), legal protections against discrimination (Almeida et al. 2009: 1002), protections against homophobic violence and bullying (Espelage and Swearer 2008: 157), the prevalence of suicide among non-heterosexual youth remains high (Almeida et al. 2009: 1001, Ryan et al. 2009: 346, Zhao et al. 2010: 104), and there is a demonstrated and ongoing need to continue qualitative research and theorisation of the relationship between sexuality and suicidality (McAndrew and Warne 2010: 93). That is, while public attitudes continue a liberal shift towards new forms of tolerance for non-heterosexual behaviours, representations and personages across a range of institutions, the continuing higher frequency of suicide attempts among current queer youth across a range of countries is a matter of ongoing concern (Hegna and Wichstrøm 2007: 22), requiring further research, new theorisation and innovative approaches. As institutional homophobia, media representation, queer invisibility and stigma have changed (and in some ways diminished) in recent years, continuing suicides indicate that some of the older ideas, reasons and causes no longer explain why young queer persons would kill themselves.

But what does the research to date tell us about *why* queer youth are at greater risk of suicidal behaviours? What is it that makes queer youth more vulnerable than straight youth (to be very narrowly categorical), and what makes *some* queer youth at greater risk of suicide than other queer youth? Much of the framework through which queer youth suicide is understood in research occurs through a risk discourse, which often is derived from assumptions which drive quantitative research and statistics that have formed such a significant part of the methodological work of suicidologists. Queer youth suicide statistics have been widely disseminated in public sphere discussions, news reports and policy submissions, not always unproblematically. In almost all cases throughout the 1990s and 2000s, research and public discourse have cited Paul Gibson's (1989: 110) chapter on lesbian and gay suicide in the United States Administration's *Report of the Secretary's Task Force on Youth Suicide* and the statements that 'gay youth are 2 to 3 times more likely to attempt suicide than other young people' and that they 'may comprise up to 30 per cent of completed suicides annually.' Subsequently, these statistics have at times been updated through a variety of data-gathering and reporting methods, producing some variances although the queer/heterosexual comparative rate remains high. In one piece of research, queer youth were estimated to have a suicide ideation rate ranging from fifty per cent to seventy per cent, and an attempt rate from thirty to forty-two per cent, being three times that for heterosexual youth (Rutter and Soucar 2002: 290). Hegna and Wichstrøm (2007: 22) reported a rate for queer youth as being 'at three to four times greater risk of attempting suicide than heterosexual young people.' More recently, Zhao and colleagues (2010: 104) reported that queer adolescents have a suicide attempt rate of between twenty and forty per cent, which is two to six times greater than that of non-queer adolescents. These high rates have been questioned in a number of ways, with claims of under-reporting (that is, queer youth who may have attempted or thought about suicide but not discussed their sexuality openly) and over-reporting (samples drawn from queer support groups compared with more general samples of heterosexual-identifying youth not accessing support of any kind). This is in addition to the difficulties in obtaining data on sexuality through psychological autopsies and coronial reports (Plöderl, Kralovec and Fartacek 2010: 1412).

In terms of contemporary knowledge frameworks, what the circulation of statistics giving rates for queer youth suicide attempts or completions does is present a 'suicidal script', linking non-normative sexualities with *prevalence* for suicide in a relatively simplistic and rigid manner (Russell 2003: 1251–1252). There is, of course, a statistical link between non-normative sexualities and higher risk of suicidal behaviours, but the factors which make the link tenable tend to be debatable, particularly in terms of understanding the complexity of reasons why sexual non-normativity is implicated in increased susceptibility to self-harm (Dorais 2004: 14). Where the link between queer sexuality and suicide is presumed to be causal – that is, youth are at risk if they are non-heterosexual *per se* – the field of research on queer youth suicide relies on assumptions that limit the possibilities for exploring how notions of vulnerability are fashioned in contemporary culture. In producing an exclusive link between non-normative sexuality and suicidal behaviours, the reliance on queer suicide statistics frequently fails to contextualise the environmental, social, cultural and institutional setting in which suicide becomes thinkable, particularly in 'snapshot' public communication and policy dialogue.

None of this is to suggest that statistical research does not contribute to knowledge and solutions for queer youth suicide, nor is it to claim in any way that queer youth are less vulnerable than has previously been indicated in some of that research. Rather, it is to question the ways in which the circulation of those commonly-cited statistics present an impression that *all* queer youth are vulnerable, and that of this vulnerable population a percentage are *likely* to attempt suicide. The 'vulnerabilisation' of queer youth is not uncommon in research on queer sexuality. Although they indicate heterosexism as a significant factor in making non-heterosexual persons at-risk of reduced health, wellbeing and resilience, Fenaughty and Harré (2003: 18), for example, argued that queer youth sexuality itself was uniformly a risk factor with all queer youth at risk of suicide due to growing up within a heterosexist society. Queer youth are thus perceived in this framework to be universally at risk of suicidal behaviours, and it is not just some but, as they put it, *all* – or at least all who have not yet been helped to develop special resiliencies necessitated by being categorised a sexual minority. In this framework, the risk of suicide for queer youth is perceived as internal to the non-normative subject, whereas resilience is external and to be fostered socially.

There are two issues for ongoing research into queer youth suicide that emerge from this particular formation which posits non-heterosexuality itself as a suicide risk factor. Firstly, there is the assumption that vulnerability to suicidal behaviours for queer youth is the result singularly of sexuality, rather than looking to the fact that sexuality is one facet of identity – albeit an important and sometimes fraught one for adolescents in general – located within a complex of other elements of a multiply-constituted subject. In other words, there is a tendency to view minority sexuality as the only significant part of queer youth's subjectivity (Fuss 1989: 116), thereby missing the opportunity to think through the conditions of queer youth as one in which there is interaction between different facets of identity, or other cultural, contextual and environmental factors. Positing a sub-population as vulnerable because they are in a minority has the tendency to remove any sense of agency from that group as a whole (Meyer 1996: 102), leaving the subjects at-hand as knowable only though that vulnerability. While there are some shortcomings, there has been a notable shift in the ways in which the field contextualises minority identity, with greater emphasis on the role of social reception factors such as heterosexism as a risk factor for suicide, moving away from the problematic conception that minority identity is the risk itself (White 2009: 3–4). The academic need to refigure causality away from minority identity and examine instead the role of other social factors in causality has begun to be acknowledged in more recent youth suicide research, although this is yet to filter into the public imagination of the ways in which queer youth are depicted and positioned.

Secondly, in thinking about why queer youth might be at risk of suicide, the popular reliance on such statistics tends to disavow a more important question, which is to ask why some queer youth are more resilient than others. Ritch Savin-Williams (2001) has argued against the unwitting pathologisation of queer youth by pointing out that young queer persons have indeed demonstrated a significant ability to cope with complex concepts and situations related to non-normative sexuality. Young queer lives are *often* (but not always) more difficult than the lives of those living in sexual normativity due to a range of social factors such as persistent heteronormativity, bullying, forms of shame and instances of marginalisation or exclusion, and this does currently involve increased risks that may lead to suicide and self-harm. However, to avoid depicting queerness as a risk itself, the way in which we attempt to understand the sociality of being queer must occur through a lens that focuses on youth resilience, agency, changing cultural forms and new or alternative understandings of sexuality. That is, queer younger persons are not vulnerable *because* they are queer; rather, there are greater risks of vulnerability resulting from social, cultural and psychological factors that may be a result of the heteronormative environmental context in which that person is having, feeling or expressing non-normative sexual desires or behaviours. In other words, risk cannot be ignored, but we should avoid indulging the view that the risk is produced simply by the existence of queer persons, which ultimately reinforces some of the same heteronormativities that produce an environment for difficult lives in the first place. Providing some alternative means for understanding how such difficulties, vulnerabilities and risks are culturally-produced in complex ways that do not place queer sexuality at the start of a causal chain is one of the aims of this book.

More recent research has, indeed, taken steps to respond to the problems of locating suicidal causality in sexual minority status, looking more to the risks that emerge in the social situation and setting for queer youth, and this has begun the process of shifting risk from queerness to the specificities of being queer in certain contexts. However, risks identified by many researchers are generally formulated through a psycho-social discourse in which they are depicted as factors understood to be 'internalised' by the suicidal subject. These include: distress and depression leading to suicide ideation (Almeida et al. 2009: 1001); low self-esteem and reduced capacity for social integration (Hegna and Wichstrøm 2007: 32); anxiety, alcohol and drug abuse (Hegna and Wichstrøm 2007: 22); social hostility, discrimination, social stigma (King et al. 2008: 83); experience of victimisation (Kloos et al. 2007: 91); a sense of hopelessness resulting from an early awareness of same-sex attraction or desire (Hershberger, Pilkington and D'Augelli 1997: 479); heterosexism leading to isolation and/or family rejection (Suicide Prevention Resource Centre 2008); experiencing violence or physical abuse (Friedman et al. 2008: 892). Many of the risk factors are presented as singular causes co-opted from the external environment into the psyche – the result of the emphasis in more recent queer youth suicide research on psychiatric, psychological and psycho-social causality, often in combination with quantitative methodologies that depend on articulating *measurable* risks (McDermott, Roen and Scourfield 2008: 816–817). Problematically, this ignores for queer youth what is widely regarded in other areas of youth suicide research: that suicide ideation and attempt is the result of a broad range of types and motivations, which may include mental illness and clinical depression (but not in all suicides), an attempt to send a message or gain a particular outcome, or an attempt to end unmanageable psychological pain resulting from despair, shame, loss or guilt (Commonwealth of Australia 2008: 11). Multiple risk factors for youth suicide interact in complex ways, 'making it impossible to describe a singular profile of a "typical" suicidal youth' (White 2009: 3). Yet, in the case of queer youth suicide, there is a tendency to begin with the factor of queerness/non-heterosexuality, and either look for or present an image of a reductively typified suicidal queer young man. This clouds the capacity of suicide research to seek out the reasons why some queer youth are vulnerable, but vulnerable in complex ways.

Through the ways in which the common risk factors are seen to operate at the interface between the personal-psychological and the social-situational, vulnerability is produced in the *extent* to which situational risks such as discrimination or homophobia are internalised, thereby disavowing the breadth of diversity of both social situation and self-resiliency among queer youth overall (Cloud 2005). As Savin-Williams has pointed out (2001: 5), this often simply calls attention to the difficulties younger queer persons do indeed face, rather than investigating how such difficulties are overcome, thereby again maintaining the perception both publicly and in research of queer youth as victims. In asking, then, what makes queer youth more vulnerable to suicidality than non-queer youth, it is obviously necessary to avoid reducing *all* queer youth to a depiction of sameness, whether that is the social experience of being queer or the ways in which negative elements of that social experience are taken on-board.

Refiguring Vulnerability: Youth, Sexuality and Suicide

None of the above is to meant to suggest that queer youth are *not* more vulnerable than heterosexuals in contemporary culture; rather it is to point out that the diversity of experience and the ways in which different persons deal with different aspects of experience, sex, sexuality, identity and discord are pivotal in furthering our understanding of that vulnerability. Despite the statistical work around queer youth and the deployment of risk discourses to understand causality, then, it still remains unclear what it is that puts queer youth at greater risk of suicidality than non-queer younger persons. To begin to unpack this idea involves asking first what is meant by queer youth. While the use of the term is sometimes controversial, in this book I use the label 'queer' as short-hand for persons whose identifiable sexuality, desire, behaviour, attractions or identity are non-heterosexual. In this sense, it is a cover-all term for gay, lesbian, bisexual, transgendered, intersexed or otherwise queer – sometimes given as GLBTIQ. It may at times include youth who identify as straight but engage in same-sex attractions and behaviours. It is also a word often associated with younger homosexuals in opposition to the ideological and conceptual identities of an older generational 'gay' (Buchbinder 1997: 150). As short-hand for non-heterosexual identifying or behaving persons, queer in this usage is distinct from how I use the term 'queer' of 'queer theory'. Queer theory is not merely the study of non-heterosexuality or lesbian/gay identities but the deployment of poststructuralist theories in the field of gender and sexuality. While often confused, the two uses of the term queer do in fact have separate histories arising in two contexts: academic debate resulting particularly from discussions at Gay and Lesbian Studies conferences in the late 1980s held at UC-Santa Cruz, Yale and other American universities and, without relation, reclaiming a negative term as the banner for a new United States lesbian/gay activist organisation, *Queer Nation*. De Lauretis stated as early as 1989 that there was in fact very little in common between the advents of both theory and organisation (presuming co-incidental parallels in the use of 'queer'), though queer theory and queer movement/community have frequently been conceived as related 'wings' of the same discursivity. The ambiguity has been productive for both queer theory and queer culture (Jagose 1996: 96–97), although the popularity of the term has involved its up-take as an umbrella term for a range of non-heteronormative sexualities and genders, and it is this to which I refer when I use the term queer youth. Important to note here is that, in referring to young persons expression non-heterosexual attractions, behaviours, identities or desires in some form, the term queer is frequently given as gender-neutral. There is always the risk that the persistent rearticulation of such gender neutrality erases young women from the argument. Indeed, queer male youth are, according to many studies cited in this book, at much greater risk than queer young women, however that is not to suggest that there is no lesbian or queer female suicidality at all. Nor is to state that there are distinctions that make a topic for a separate study. Rather, I have, for the most part, been very deliberate in using the term queer both to be inclusive of all possible genders in discussing suicidality and, at the same time, to acknowledge the fact that for young women the socio-cultural mechanisms that make life unbearable are frequently very different from those experienced by young men. For example, the pressures even on queer male youth to perform a masculine *inviolability* present circumstances very different from those of young women who are better positioned – at least sometimes – to articulate their own vulnerability in peer contexts in order to achieve support and connectivity. The gender distinctions in experience and yet the unwillingness to present gender as essentialist are deliberately figured in the choice to use the term queer.

In the context of this work, the term 'youth' refers to persons aged eleven to twenty-five years. Youth itself is not, however, a simple category determined only by age demographics, but is a construct which has significant implications not only for how we think about important topics such as youth suicide and self-harm, and for how younger persons themselves are placed within framework in which suicide and self-harm are enacted. Often the term youth is produced through a discourse of generationalism that frequently reduces younger persons or minors into being depicted through notions of deficiency or lack of reason and radical difference from earlier generations (Davis 1997). However, there are generational differences that are often considered to be subcultural (Hebdige 1979: 17) and these distinctions between older and younger persons are partly the result of divergences in experience and partly the product of the culture in which one is transformed through ageing. At times, youth are depicted through a discourse of *crisis* – a concept which depends on a list of the problems that supposedly affect youth, of which they are at risk, of which they are sometimes at fault and to which they are sometimes subjected unwittingly (Maira and Soep 2004: 252). Other discourses frame 'youth' as a transitional period for individuals as opposed to a set of ideas about a group or group culture. This is a process of transition from 'normal childhood to normal adulthood' (Kelly 2001: 24). Such framing of youth through transition often depicts individuals as being in a persistent state of emotional upset while shifting from a childhood marked by immaturity, emotional and economic dependence on parents to emotional and economic autonomy and ties with an adult partner and children. This view tends to see all individuals as potentially 'at risk' during a period that is represented through a concept of turbulence. While there are competing discourses that constitute the category 'youth' differently, it is necessary to remain aware in its usage here that it is a cultural construct produced through contemporaneity and a diverse range of cultural conditions.

Where 'queer youth' is a constructed category built on linking the two demarcations of age and sexuality, it is important that those thinking about queer youth suicide do not fall into the trap of imagining that vulnerability is endemic simply to that combination of the two terms, for this not only replicates older stereotypes around young people expressing non-heterosexual attractions or behaviours, but discursively produces the vulnerability it seeks to describe. The idea of same-sex attracted youth, queer youth or lesbian/gay youth as being particularly different from heterosexual youth is not the only perspective in youth risk studies. According to Savin-Williams, 'youth with same-sex attractions are similar to all youths, independent of sexual desire. That is, an adolescent is an adolescent is an adolescent. This should be our basic assumption – but rarely is' (Savin-Williams 2001: 6). In examining queer youth suicide, there is thus a need to re-focus on the 'youth' element of identity rather than sexuality, given the fact that many adolescents in general have difficulty grasping the gravity of suicide and the impact of succeeding in a suicide attempt, as well as being subject to social pressures to balance a relatively broad range of demands in a number of contextual environments: school, family, peers, media and other 'measures' of normality (Tefft 2000: 67–69). This is not to argue for the radical diversity of queer youth on the one hand and the homogenisation of *all* youth on the other, but to suggest that it might in fact be more appropriate not to attempt to imagine a distinction between queer youth and straight youth and instead focus on subcultural elements in generational terms such as the ways in which *all* sexualities come to be constituted in teenaged years might be produce forms of youth vulnerability (rather than vulnerability being seen as a particular trait of a particular demographic).

Recent work by theorist Judith Butler has taken to task the ways in which we construct and view vulnerability in general, and this usefully informs some of the ways in which we can attempt to understand how the category 'queer youth' is produced in vulnerability, but also how vulnerability is produced for different persons in different ways. Butler (2004: 31) notes that vulnerability is a trait shared by all persons – a condition common to human subjectivity which emerges with life itself. This has led her to call for an ethics that is built on the recognition of the vulnerability of the other. In the context of our relationality with others, knowing and seeing that another is vulnerable is an ethical responsibility of all subjects, but not an automatic occurrence: it requires a moment of recognition in order to be seen and understood and for the situation of vulnerability to be altered or reversed; such recognition is, of course, never guaranteed (Butler 2004: 42–43). This common vulnerability is not, however to suggest that all persons are *equally* vulnerable. Rather, Butler points out the ways in which different persons are positioned into having to negotiate different forms of vulnerability at different times, including sudden, unprecedented and unexpected forms of being made exposed or made weak. For Butler, these also include being vulnerable to particular forms of violence – physical, emotional, psychological – for which persons may be required to respond by wishing for death as a 'vain effort to pre-empt or deflect the next blow' (Butler 2004: 42), thereby indicating the relationship between subjectivity, pain and vulnerability that can lead to suicidality. Within this framework of vulnerability and the ethical relationships that might yet emerge from its recognition is the question as to whose lives are liveable and whose are *rendered unliveable* through the foreclosing violence of silence about their 'unbearable vulnerability' (Butler 2004: xi). This is significant in the ways in which I am trying here to formulate a perception of queer youth suicidality as that which is the response to the conditions of unbearability experienced by the most vulnerable of queer youth without wanting at any stage to suggest that all or even most queer youth are suicidal, vulnerable in the same way or victims.

Unliveable Lives: Discerning Suicide

Although the very idea of suicide has its roots in ancient culture and has been determined through a range of discourses over the past two thousand years, the idea of suicide remains ultimately the unknowable. We do not really know why a person chooses death over life, for those who complete a suicide are not available to communication or make their reasons intelligible. While suicide notes are common, they are the reductive trace of a reason, governed by processes of writing and narratives of finality, and these do not present reasons either. In other words, understanding either the suicide of an individual, identifiable groups or just suicide in general is something which occurs through reading suicidality through available systems of knowledge – there is no truth that can be discerned. At the same time, any search for a singular cause or formula for suicides generally or for the suicides of an identifiable group is fruitless, as causes are multiple, manifold and diverse. Thus history has not produced a clear definition of suicide. Medieval Christian rhetoric equated suicide with sin and subsequent ethical systems, until recently, likewise framed definitions of suicide within the status of the taboo and the unspeakable (Battin 1995: 19–20). Durkheim's work is perhaps still the most comprehensive and foundational of texts on suicide. For Durkheim, suicide is 'pre-eminently the desperate act of one who does not care to live' (Durkheim

1952: 44). This is a very brief introductory definition in his own view, but his summary statement is as follows:

> We may then say conclusively: the term *suicide is applied to all cases of death resulting directly or indirectly from a positive or negative act of the victim himself, which he knows will produce this result.* As attempt is an act thus defined but falling short of actual death (Durkheim 1952: 44, *original emphasis*).

Where Durkheim viewed suicide as a reasoned and deliberate act, conversely the psychiatric, medical and psychological disciplinary frameworks typically posit suicide as the emanation or result of a mental illness (Battin 1995: 6). This makes some amount of sense for those of us who bear witness to the suicides of others: one *must surely* be mentally ill to give up on life. However, where this either ignores social factors or relies on the notion of internalisation of those factors, it leaves aside ways in which both mental illness and suicidality can be understood as co-morbidity resulting from the same social, subjective or environmental factors through which a subject is constituted, as well as the fact that similar suicides do not always result from the same causes. In that sense, suicide can be argued to be neither a fully rational act nor fully the unintelligible outcome of mental illness; rather, causes can be said to be diverse and multiple. What appears unintelligible to those who bear witness is not necessarily irrational to the suicidal subject; the reverse may also be true.

For Michel Foucault (1990), suicide is embedded in a deployment of discursive power/knowledge relations. It is not simply the *taking* of life, but the *talking* about life that is at stake. He indicated that the ancient right either to take life or let live was replaced in the Nineteenth Century by a disqualification of death, a loss of rituals which accompany death, and a discursive system which deploys the procedures of power onto the field of death. Foucault pointed out that:

> Suicide – once a crime, since it was a way to usurp the power of death which the sovereign alone, whether the one here below or the Lord above, had the right to exercise – became, in the course of the nineteenth century, one of the first conducts to enter into the sphere of sociological analysis; it testified to the individual and private right to die, at the borders and in the interstices of power that was exercised over life (Foucault 1990: 138–139).

The question of death is linked to biopower, and speech on death is as much a manifestation of that governmental framework as is the national census. The biopolitical mechanisms utilised as a form or technology of power in contemporary governance often result in the over-determination of suicide as an object for measurement through quantification and statistics, intersecting with the role of coronial investigation into deaths. This effectively produces a contemporary policy environment driven by the biopolitical governance arrangements that emerged in the nineteenth century, in which suicide becomes knowable by the degree to which it occurs, and thus a matter for intervention or prevention determined predominantly by rates and figures.

As a construct, then, suicide is made intelligible through a range of competing – but not mutually exclusive – discourses that range across the religious, the ethical, the psychiatric, the psychological and the social. A definition of suicidality that works well in the context of queer youth suicide and the approaches I am taking here follows the work of Edwin Shneidman. In 1968, he proposed three types of suicide: the *egotic* which occurs through an internal struggle between elements of the self and in which all socio-environmental factors such as the existence or presence of significant others are disregarded by the victim as a source of support; the *dyadic*, whereby seeking death relates to deep, unfulfilled needs within the social and intrapersonal, may relate to conflict and may involve excessive frustration, hate, anger, disappointment, shame, rage or rejection; and the *ageneratic* which involves the ways in which a subject relates to and is integrated within generational and social groupings. Later, Shneidman (1985) began to collapse the three types under the *egotic*, indicating the ways in which psychic conflict and the social are both integrated within the experience of suicidality. Important in his approach is that suicide is not understood as a self-conscious and voluntary movement towards death, but an attempt

> to put an end to suffering by stopping the unbearable flow of consciousness. This last is the igniting element that explodes the mixture of the previous three components. In this context, suicide is understood not as a movement toward death (or cessation) but rather as a flight from intolerable emotion (Shneidman 1985: 36).

Suicidality, then, involves a range of behaviours, but a suicide attempt is about a flight from the psychic pain that emerges from the ways in which the subject is located or, indeed, constituted within sociality. Such emotional pain might be the result of stigmatisation, breakdown in the coherence of identity, an inability to fulfil the cultural demands for intelligible subjectivity, a perception of an incapacity to belong in any context, intolerable shame, unbearable exclusion. None of these necessarily need to occur within the context of actual social acts of others: exclusion can be purely perceived, marginalisation or stigmatisation may not necessarily be the result of the homophobic act of a person or a group, and a breakdown in subject coherence may not necessarily be knowable to one's self. In that sense, it is possible to suggest that a suicidal queer youth does not seek out death *per se*, but seeks to *escape* from the complex tensions that are produced in subjectivation. Suicide can then be understood as an act that is somewhere between being a reasoned choice and a non-rational act. Both social and psychic factors may compel a subject to enact suicide as a means of escaping the unbearability of living, but if suicide is the articulation of a performative self, it is constituted culturally for that particular subject as a coherent, intelligible and logical means by which to escape the unliveability of living.

Subjective Frameworks: A Queer Cultural Studies Approach

The approach to understanding sexuality, suicide, subjectivity and selfhood that I take in this work draws on the poststructuralist work of Foucault and Butler. That, for me, means paying attention to the fact that competing regimes of power work with a range of discourses which produce the objects – in this case, vulnerable queer youth – they purport to study or represent. As the general domain of statements as well as specific utterances produced through institutional knowledge (Mills 1997: 6), discourses operate within disciplinarity and biopolitical technologies of power to shape knowledge and expertise (Foucault 2004b: 38). This is also to say that discourse, as both language and that which extends beyond it, *is* contemporary culture (Spivak 1999: 353). A Foucauldian cultural studies approach not only considers culture to be the everyday lived experience of specific groups within broader social contexts (Williams 1976: 80–81), but also understands culture as an ongoing process (Williams 1981: 10), which includes the ways in which conditions that discursively govern and make known the knowable differ in generational and communication contexts for younger persons. Fundamental shifts in how queer youth, for example, are represented in culture have taken place, much of this around the inclusion of younger queer characters in broadcast film and television (Cover 2000; Padva 2004). Not all of this is entirely positive, and that is what cultural studies seeks to investigate – not just to assume progress and take a linear approach to representations, changes and developments but to explore how such developments have emerged and the implications they have for changes in sociality, identity and culture. This approach governs much of what I do in the first half of the book, where I explore some of the ways in which queer youth suicide has been represented in popular entertainment, academic research and online communication, from the perspective of the ways in which queer youth suicide knowledges are produced and change over time.

At the same time, I strongly utilise queer theory, which is a poststructuralist academic enterprise that seeks to de-naturalise common cultural assumptions about gender and sexuality. Queer theory takes to task the 'common sense' evidence of classes of sexuality categorised through a hetero/homo binary, understanding that sexualities and sexual behaviours classified in this way are discursively imagined into being. In other words, while there are heterosexual behaviours and identities and homosexual behaviours and identities, they are neither 'natural' nor 'foundational' but are produced in and understood though discursive regimes. This does not, of course, mean that they are any less valuable or meaningful to those who practice or self-define by those sexual categories, only that they are always contingent and historical, and open to cultural change and transformation.

The 'queering' of queer youth suicide that is undertaken here demands attention to a number of elements that are common to both sections of this book but that are rarely discussed in research and public dialogue addressing issues related to queer youth. Firstly, media and communications: important within this analysis is the role of contemporary digital media, whereby online communications technologies are understood as having the capacity for broad, fundamental shifts in how queer youth in particular relate to themselves and others, particularly in terms of the availability of information and resources and the potential for building new forms of community and culture (Hillier and Harrison 2007: 83). With younger people utilising online media for exploring aspects of identity through concepts and discourses that might not otherwise have been accessible (Green 2008: 2–3), for 'practising' ways in which to perform non-heteronormative identities (Hillier and Harrison 2007: 88, 95) or for coming out to others in the relatively safe environment of digital communication (Cloud 2005), new media has significantly changed the cultural environment for queer youth over the past decade. This leaves us with the need to ask what disjunctures and continuities in communications technologies impact on how queer youth identity and knowledges around suicidality are formed today.

Secondly, I focus to some considerable extent on the role of stereotypes throughout much of this work. Stereotypes are not discussed nor analysed at great length today, partly because those with the cultural and media literacy to do so are able to recognise the falsity of a stereotype as a piece of reductive knowledge about a group (usually a minority). That does not, however, change the fact that stereotypes are available to be read by those with less cultural knowledge or the experience derived through age, as 'truth' – a potentially damaging truth to oneself or to others. Stereotypes link an identity category with a set of attributes and are communicated, often in media texts, as a short, recognisable 'byte' of information (Cover 2004). That is, they are used in film, television and media imagery to avoid having to explain the background about a character or event: a queer person can be recognisable by certain attributes, which might be tastes, aesthetic appreciation, particular looks and glances, ways of moving or holding the body, ways of speaking, career choices or other behaviours. While there is nothing wrong with that in itself, stereotypes tend to be reductive in the sense that they frequently risk conveying the idea that this is how *all* persons of that category act. It does not need much explaining to see how suicidality can be presented in some texts as recognisable traits of queer youth, thereby implying that this is 'how' queer youth can or, worse, *should* behave in order to be coherent and intelligible subjects to selves and others. I will address several aspects of this throughout. Stereotypes are notoriously difficult to eradicate from cultural knowledge (Rosello 1998), meaning that part of the task here is to find ways in which to make the continuing circulation of reductive stereotypes less harmful. As contemporary media and communications become ever more reliant on the stereotype as a 'byte' of easily-packaged information about identifiable groups, it is necessary to pay increasing attention to stereotyping as a major element in the cultural field in which queer youth identity and sexual subjectivity is constituted.

Thirdly, the question of identity is absolutely core to the work here. One of the key arguments in the second half of this book is that the ways in which sexual subjectivity is constituted in discourse is central to understanding and addressing queer youth suicide. For Foucault (1998: 10), the subject is not a substance but a *form*, one constituted in and by discourse and dependent on a contextual relationship (such as the political subject or the sexual subject). The power of discourse over bodies and their behaviour is effected, in his analysis, through a series of regulatory controls (Foucault 1990: 139). Overturning the previously-held liberal notion of power as the power which represses sex and sexualities (Foucault 1990: 85), Foucault's *History of Sexuality* (1990) provides queer theory with a foundational argument in which power, as deployed through discourse and discursive formations, produces the coherent sexual subject. This occurs historically and only in specific periods. In Foucault's genealogical history, homosexual (and hence heterosexual) subjectivities become possible in the Nineteenth Century as a result of specific juridical, medical and criminal discourses (Foucault 1990: 43). From a Foucauldian perspective, there is no subject driven by an inner psyche or a pre-determined desire (as in psychoanalysis). Instead, such subjectivity is produced in and through the power/knowledge network of discourse as it writes or scripts the subject into subjectivity.

Canonical queer theorist Judith Butler has been central in extending Foucault's analysis in ways which can, indeed, be remarkably pragmatic for understanding queer youth in the context of suicidality and vulnerability. Her theory of performativity has usefully complexified how we can understand sexual identity in ways which overcome the core assumption in much queer youth suicide research that heterosexual and homosexual identities are natural, mutually-exclusive and innate. Instead, this allows a focus on how the process of subject formation for youth is implicated in the tensions and pressures that make suicide a logical outcome of flight from emotional pain. Butler projects the most useful post-structuralist discussion of subjectivity by suggesting that the subject is constituted by repetitive performances in terms of the structure of signification that produces retroactively the *illusion* of an inner subjective core (Butler 1990: 143). Identity/subjectivity becomes a normative ideal rather than a descriptive feature of experience, and is the resultant effect of regimentary discursive practices (Butler 1990: 16, 18). The sexual subject, then, is performatively constituted by the very 'expressions' that, in everyday life, we usually assume to emanate from an inner self (for example, desires, behaviours, tastes and attitudes). As Butler writes, 'performativity must be understood not as a singular or deliberate "act," but, rather, as the reiterative and citational practice by which discourse produces the effects that it names' (Butler 1993: 2). As performativity is tenuous, so too is queer subjectivity. Its contingency has, as I discuss in later chapters, both positive and negative implications for suicidality.

Finally, it is also important to point out that a thread that runs through all parts of this work is a desire to overcome some of the disciplinary impasses that have constrained the ways in which queer youth suicide can be understood. In particular, the distinction between sociological work on the one hand and medico-psychiatric or psychological work on the other is notable, as both fields play dominant roles in queer youth suicide research. However, there remains in force a tendency for these disciplinary areas, like many others, not to communicate with each other. This work is not, however, interested in identifying shortcomings, as all disciplines have them; likewise, all disciplines make valuable contributions to knowledge in their own ways. What I am interested in doing is overcoming the medico-psychiatric/psychology and sociological disciplinary impasse not through socio-psychology; rather, the task is to do so through cultural theory by figuring suicide not as either the outcome of depression and other mental health issues, nor as the product purely of socio-environmental factors, such as homophobia and discrimination, but as the flight from unbearable pain for which some young queer persons are vulnerable in terms of a vulnerability produced socially but which can produce mental health concerns that sit alongside suicidality – mutual symptoms, not necessarily in a chain of causality. This also involves acknowledging that all subjects are multiply-constituted, and competing discourses may produce different forms of vulnerability, resilience and suicidality in the same subject; in other words, a shift away from deterministic and linear patterns of causation without eradicating the ways in which the psychic and the social are implicated.

The over-determination of mental health issues has been noted in some suicide research on queer youth (McAndrew and Warne 2010: 93), although other studies on queer youth suicide restore mental illness and depression as the primary causal factors through a process in which 'internalizing negative life events and victimization in the social environment' leads to depressive symptoms and thus suicidal ideation (Ryan et al. 2009: 346). The concept of internalisation sits uneasily within a queer theory framework, as it separates the subject from sociality – a subject who 'takes in' particular negative experiences in the social and, injection-like, these are seen to re-figure an otherwise individually-determined subject. Such a view is often articulated through the term 'gay-related stress' as a set of stressors specific to queer youth – homophobia, disclosure of homosexuality, internalisation of stigma (Hegna and Wichstrøm 2007: 24, Suicide Prevention Resource Centre 2008: 20, Russell 2003: 1248). This is to ignore the ways in which the subject is produced already in relationality and sociality, such that there is in fact no 'pure' subject who suddenly experiences socio-environmental stresses, internalises these and develops suicidality, either with mental health factors or not. Instead, the relationship between mental health/illness and suicidality is a highly complex one. Some recent research showed that while psychosocial disorders increased in populations over a thirty-year period consistently across men and women, suicide rates for men rose while those for women remained relatively static, indicating that the experience of mental health concerns is gendered, and the ways in which suicidality is produced can depend more on gender identity and relationality than on mental illness (Smalley, Scourfield and Greenland 2005: 139–140). In the context, then, of queer youth, the ways in which sociality produces the subject as a queer subject is highly implicated in the production of some queer people as vulnerable, as having mental health concerns and as suicidal. And it is through queer theory and cultural studies approaches to subjectivity that we come at some of the possibilities for complexification of cause-and-effect around suicide as I will show in later chapters.

Overview

Following from the above descriptions of queer youth suicide, risk and vulnerability, ways of perceiving suicidality and the need to investigate alternative approaches to how some queer youth are positioned as vulnerable, the following chapters draw on cultural studies and queer theory approaches as means of re-thinking sexuality and suicidality. The book is divided into two parts: the first three chapters investigate some of the ways in which queer youth suicide has been depicted across three mediums: popular film and television, academic writing, and online Web 2.0 digital and participatory media environments. This framework is not, of course, intended to suggest that representations of youth suicide are governed purely by medium, since they do inform each other, drawing on a range of 'available' discourses that give sense and intelligibility to the topic. This analysis is undertaken by examining some of the themes, representations and depictions that emerge across these forms of communication, while always acknowledging that audiences read, engage with and interact with these discourses in diverse ways. By showing how different ways of conceiving queer youth suicide operate at different times and in different contexts, the aim is to provide an overview as to how queer youth suicide has become 'knowable', how different forms of knowability produce ideas of suicide causes and, through textual analysis, how solutions to queer youth suicide can be understood and developed.

The second section of the book reads a number of suicide cases and texts as reported in media, news, and online forms from the perspective of queer theory. It takes suicide knowledges to task by investigating queer youth suicidality in the context of poststructuralist theories of subjectivity and sexuality. Chapter 4 provides an overview of the ways in which non-heteronormative sexual identities are produced in teenaged years through an 'authorised' encounter with discourses of sexuality, effectively 're-constituting' the child subject as a sexual subject. It is argued that the re-constitution and stabilisation of identity can produce forms of vulnerability which, using Durkheim's approach to suicides that result from regulatory practices, are implicated in suicidality and self- harm. By examining the process by which the non-normative subject is formed within contemporary sexual regimes, it is possible to understand ways in which certain lives can be made unliveable through regulatory practices that position a subject beyond normativity. Chapter 5 examines the concept of shame, which has a long history in the cultural knowledges around both sexuality and suicide. Recent work by a number of theorists has shifted how shame is understood as an emotion or affect, and how it is implicated in the formation of the subject. Following this, it is argued here that shame operates to create 'tensions' between self and the expectations of significant others, between private desires and public identification, and between the self and the perception of others through conceptions of non-normative bodies in public space. The ways in which shame continues to be implicated in sexuality-related suicide is opened up through readings of a number of texts on queer youth suicide. Finally, Chapter 6 takes a slightly different view on suicide, using a model known as 'relative misery' in which groups and individuals who perceive their circumstances to be worse off than their peers are made vulnerable or put at risk of suicide. Exploring this in the context of queer youth sexuality, I ask what role is played by queer community in its contemporary 'homonormative' formation – and the way in which it is represented in popular media and entertainment – in producing norms and exclusions which establish a context in which some queer youth will not develop a sense of community belonging. Where queer community is often depicted as a 'saving refuge' for queer youth in a predominantly heteronormative society, there is the argument that the community is, much like all minority groupings, exclusive and, for some, inaccessible, thereby doubling the vulnerability of the already vulnerable. This is not, of course, to place 'blame' on any community group or organisation, but to show some of the ways in which the context of varieties in queer youth belonging are not inseparable from the processes by which some youth are made more vulnerable than others.

Where there remains a relatively persistent marginalisation of the topic of queer youth suicide in both queer research and in queer community politics (Cover 2010), we have not only a gap in inquiry nor only the sidelining of a health policy issue. For Butler, silencing is tied in with forms of discursive de-humanisation that occur through an unwillingness to recognise vulnerability or a disavowal of the commonality of vulnerability. It is a violence against those who are seen to be not quite living, not quite worthy of attention – a situation produced in sociality and mandated by the mutual and reassuring identifications of those who are not positioned as living unliveable lives (Butler 2004: 36). Part of the problem in prompting an ethical reflection on queer youth suicide emerges from the question of suicide itself. For completed suicides, there is no vulnerable human to be recognised (Jaworski 2008: 784); one mourns but the ethical response is more difficult to make because there it can only be to a construct of the deceased subject's memory, or a recognition of the commonality of vulnerability and the precarious nature of life itself, perhaps even a response to a call for justice. These are markedly more difficult forms of recognition and response to negotiate than those that can be made for a suicidal younger person, received as a cry-for-help and as an injunction to act to save a (known) life, a life by its knowability that is deemed liveable, and must be made to live. In deploying cultural studies and queer theoretical critique in the study of queer youth suicide, it is possible to develop an ethical position for responding to the liveability of certain lives without reinforcing subjection as vulnerable victims.

Chapter 1

Queer Suicide Representations
in Popular Media

Popular entertainment media, which includes plays, film and television, has long associated suicidality with gay men and lesbians and with sexual non-normativity. Texts such as Tennessee Williams' *Cat on a Hot Tin Roof* or the 1970 film *The Boys in the Band* among the more well-known accounts, although the idea that non-heterosexual persons are prone to suicide has also been depicted in countless fleeting references and characters (Remafedi 1994: 7–14). As Larry Gross (1991: 28) points out, of thirty-two films with major homosexual characters released between 1961 and 1976, thirteen feature gay suicide. Queer youth suicide is made knowable in a range of media depictions from supporting characters in television series and fleeting references to unseen characters in films and self-help talkback shows interviewing the mothers or siblings of vulnerable queer youth. Social and cultural knowledge of the connection between queer youth and suicidality is as much forged in popular culture as in news and policy documents, texts on mental health, psychology, sociology, self-help manuals and in queer community political rhetoric.

The persistence of the link between non-heterosexuality and suicide is, on the one hand, remarkably useful in drawing attention to an issue that in other contexts and situations is often forgotten (Howes 1993: 800). At the same time, however, disseminating the relationship between non-heterosexuality and suicide in popular culture has its risks, given the capacity of entertainment media to reinforce stereotypes of queer persons (Cover 2004). What makes even a brief, throwaway reference to queer suicide in popular non-fictional media significant is that it reiterates and puts into further circulation the notion that suicide is not only what gay men and lesbians *have done* but what they *will do*. This serves to strengthen the existing discourse that links non-heterosexuality with suicide as a logical outcome for the more vulnerable and at-risk younger queer persons.

'Suicidal queer youth' is not, of course, the dominant image of non-heterosexual youth in entertainment media today. The mid-1990s saw a renaissance in lesbian/gay film and television representation, with a significant change in the frequency and tone of non-heterosexuality on-screen: these include mass-circulation films such as *The Opposite of Sex* (1998), *But I'm a Cheerleader* (1999), and television series such as *Queer as Folk* (USA and UK) and *Buffy the Vampire Slayer* (USA). Even more recently, depictions of even younger lesbian and gay youth have been more frequent in television, with series such as *Glee* (2009–), *Gossip Girl* (2007–), the re-booted *90210* (2008–) and *Skins* (2007–) depicting mostly male same-sex attracted younger persons as major characters with significant storylines. Contrasting with earlier films such as *This Special Friendship* (*Les Amities Particulieres,* 1964) and *Another Country* (1984) which portray non-heteronormative sexualities and behaviours explicitly in connection with suicide, recent films and television series do not represent minority sexualities as suicidal and they do not present risk behaviour or self- harm as the narrative 'stumbling blocks' which young lesbians and gay men must overcome in order to become fully-coherent sexual selves. However, they do frequently represent non-heterosexual characters as vulnerable (Padva 2004), which does not entirely overturn the stereotypical relationship between queerness and suicidality. At the same time, it is important not to presume that just because new entertainment productions do not explicitly make a sexuality-suicide link that the trope is eradicated from popular culture altogether. Stereotypes of homosexual suicidality remain in circulation in *repeated* television series and older films broadcast on cable networks, overshadowing the often more positive and visible portrayals of queer persons in film and television (Davis, Saltzburg and Locke 2009: 1030). Earlier films and series remain in circulation – no matter how dated some of their concepts might be – through television repeats and video-cassette and DVD availability (Mulvey 2006: 21), and these serve to re-circulate and reinforce stereotypes of sexual minority suicidality. Period pieces such as Tom Ford's *A Single Man* (2009), based on Christopher Isherwood's novel and set in the early 1960s likewise represents suicide as a 'thinkable' outcome for a gay man suffering loss and depression, despite the efforts to locate the story in the context of its time.

This chapter examines some of the broad trends in the representation of queer suicidality in popular film and television media with a view to presenting a typology for comprehending the knowledge framework that associates non-heterosexual behaviours, erotics and identities with suicide. Important here is the need to theorise some of the ways in which these changing frameworks contribute to the popular cultural knowledge that sexual minorities are inherently connected with concepts of suicide, are at risk of suicide ideation and suicide attempts, and/ or that suicide is the likely outcome for at least some sexual minority youth. This is significant for the formation of a culture in which queer youth suicide emerges and continues: in contemporary western culture, it is primarily through various media forms, technologies, spaces and geographies that discourses on sexuality and sexual identities are communicated, disseminated, and given varied weightings of value. Indeed, adolescents in the later twentieth century and early twenty-first century encounter discourses of sexuality – and make sense of sexual identity – not through the institutions of family, church or education, but predominantly through film, television and magazines (Ashcraft 2003, Greenburg, Brown and Buerkel-Rothfuss 1993). Four different ways of representing queer suicide are identifiable in films and television series that address or mention queer youth and adult suicide: (1) stereotypes of shame and melancholia in the representation of the queer male as 'fated' towards a suicidal outcome; (2) queer youth and the various relationships between mental illness and suicide; (3) isolation and rejection from social participation and belonging as a causal factor for queer youth suicide; and (4) stigma, homophobia and the 'cry for help' suicide model. Naturally, an exhaustive survey of every reference to queer suicidality in film and television is neither feasible nor useful; rather, by undertaking textual analyses of a number of representative films and television series it is possible to tease out some of the ways in which the social perceptions of both queer youth and queer youth suicidality are formed in popular culture.

Popular Culture and the Constitution of Queer Youth Suicide

Much literature on sexuality-related youth suicide has referred to a debilitating lack of media representation of lesbian/gay personages (Gibson 1989: 133, Morrison and L'Hereux 2001: 44–45, Dorais 2004: 68), although this view has increasingly become outdated since the mid-1990s (Becker 2006). While it is true that popular media culture in general maintains heteronormativity by mirroring social expectations that everyone is heterosexual unless indicated otherwise, there has been a vast increase in the number of representations and voices on, about and by lesbians and gay men including those depicted in dozens of films and television series centring on queer lives. Likewise, the incidental or sideline lesbian/gay characters that have become fixtures in much television drama today are also among the significant voices and often are seen as sympathetic or positive depictions of non-heterosexuality; these range from Willow, Tara and Kennedy in *Buffy the Vampire Slayer* and David Fisher in *Six Feet Under* to Mitch in *Skins* and Kurt in *Glee*.

Within the study of popular culture, mass media forms such as television are understood to homogenise a community by posing as an extension of a perceived common self, such as heterosexuality, and by confronting audiences with images of what they are not expected to be, such as non-heterosexuals (Day 1990: 8–9). Stories of heterosexual romance and homosexual otherness are part of the sexual narratives that make up our contemporary culture, and what different sexual personages *do* are depicted in these narratives. As Kenneth Plummer has pointed out, the modern western world has become cluttered with sexual stories:

> We have moved from the limited, oral and face to face tales told throughout much of history in epic poems, songs and narratives; through the development of a public print inscribing sexual stories in limited text, first for the few and then for the 'masses'; and on to a contemporary late modern world where it seems that 'sexual stories' know no boundaries (Plummer 1995: 4).

These popular cultural stories tell us, then, not only about common, recognisable and expected sexual lives, but also the sexual lives of the less-common, the less well-reflected, the less-recognisable to broader audiences. It certainly remains true that images of sexual minorities sell media texts (Case 1995: 41), and this includes the depiction of the suicidal gay man or teenager in the past as much as today it is in the depiction of the gay man as connoisseur of fashion, culinary taste and decorative style as represented in, say, *Queer Eye for the Straight Guy* (2003–2007). Although such representations often commodify queer identity as that which can be produced through conspicuous consumption, it does not make them any less real or informative for different audiences: policymakers, researchers, community activists and queer youth themselves.

In that sense, representations of queer suicidality matter. In some important work on the uses by adolescents of popular media, Catherine Ashcraft points out that popular culture is 'an increasingly important site of struggle where adolescents' sexual identities are produced and where dominant discourses of sexuality are reinscribed and/or transformed – often in ways that are more meaningful to or effective with youth' (Ashcraft 2003: 38). If we are to be concerned with the ways in which suicide might be understood by the more-vulnerable as an 'expected behaviour' or logical solution to a seemingly unliveable life, then the role of entertainment media in providing that expectation must not be underestimated, for it is here that expectation is accessed and encountered first and most-readily by younger persons today, whether that be in the re-distribution of older texts or in the intertextual knowledges of a suicide-homosexuality link disseminated in more recent ones. Jane Pirkis and Warwick Blood (2001) have noted that media portrayal of suicide does *not* have a clear, linear causal relationship with actual suicide attempts or completions. That is, there is no evidence that in consuming such texts an audience member will be driven to attempt suicide. However, what these depictions do is contribute to and reinforce the broad, existing cultural knowledge that *associates* non-normative sexuality with self-harm and suicide. This is not to suggest that queer youth suicide should not be depicted on-screen, rather it is to say that understanding how popular media has modelled sexuality-related suicide in different ways at various times is important in understanding the cultural framework that makes sexuality-related youth suicide possible and thinkable.

Sexuality, Shame, Stigma and Fate

It was once a common narrative function of texts involving lesbian and gay characters to invoke suicide in some way in order to provide non-heterosexuality with a 'melancholic quality'. This is typically related to older film and literary stereotypes of the male homosexual as the 'sad young man' (Dyer 1993: 22, 42, 73–92). The melancholic representation of homosexual males in film reached its peak in the mid-1970s, best represented by films such as *Zee and Co.* and *Boys in the Band*, both of which combined the presentation of sexual non-normativity, camp theatrics and melancholic dispositions as storytelling devices. The swing between camp enthusiasm and melancholic sadness or depression for the gay man or lesbian's solitary, sidelined existence represents what Dyer suggests are familiar narrative functions that repeat and reinforce existing stereotypes: a woman's gay male best friend or the threatening, psychopathic and self-destructive lesbian bent on destroying another woman's marriage, neither of which leads to happiness but to increased melancholia and self-destruction (Dyer 1993: 22). Such depictions resulted partly from the traditions of the Motion Picture Association of America Production Code which, between the 1930s and 1968, insisted that no sympathy for the violation of human, natural and divine laws should be presented. The homosexual was to have been depicted only as a sad or pathetic creature; unhappy and suicidal (Russo 1981: 121–122). The fact that the code was overturned and abandoned by the 1970s did not, of course, prevent the repetition of this trope in film and television of the following decades. *Another Country*, for example, reinforces melancholia through a historical portrayal of British boarding-school life, in which a boy caught in a same-sex erotic act with another boy hangs himself. Young gay men are likely to be lonely and stigmatised; the lesbian monster must be destroyed. In this category of popular media representation, non-heterosexual identity or behaviour is represented as always *fated* towards a suicidal outcome: a fate against which one can struggle, but a fate of which one is always vulnerable.

To be fated to take one's own life has its non-queer precursors, of course. For Emile Durkheim, fatalistic suicides appear predominantly in what he sees as 'primitive' societies, and they fall into three categories: the suicides of men on the threshold of old age or illness, those of women on their husbands' death, and those of servants or followers on the death of their chiefs. Such persons kill themselves not because it is an assumed right of agency over their own lives, but because it is their responsibility to do so (Durkheim 1952: 219) – a subject has lost the authority to be an ongoing, liveable life. While Durkheim does not extend his analysis into the field of identity and identity-related behaviours or expectations, there is a clear pattern of subjectification that can be drawn out from his delineation of fatalistic suicide. The sick elderly, the widowed wife, and the bereaved follower are not only dishonoured or punished for the failure to kill themselves under culturally-sanctioned customs, but are expected to do so because that is the linear, performative pattern dictated by the label or category of identity.

In a similar way, the representation of queer persons for whom suicide is an expected outcome operates within a framework of the non-normative person's life as an unliveable life, compelled to suicide because the person is not productive (or, indeed, reproductive). The responsibility to suicide is not explicit as in the cultural traditions alluded to by Durkheim (1952: 227), but the narrative functions that produce the melancholic, sad queer person in such representations present an implicit statement that suicide is the expected *outcome* of such a life. The concept of fatalistic suicide thus draws a link between the notion of a specific identity or category of subject and the expectations that such identities in specific, perhaps extreme, circumstances perform suicide. In contemporary western culture in which sexual preferences and behaviours constitute discrete identities (hetero or homo), subjectivity is upheld by a range of performances that are coherent and intelligible to that identity (Butler 1990). Suicide and suicidality in this respect are among a range of performances that are coherent, intelligible and recognisable for the non-heterosexual subject. In this particular understanding of suicidality, one is fated towards suicidality as a direct result of one's sexual non-normativity: one must die not only *from* it but *for* it.

The portrayal of queer personages as fated towards suicide communicates and recirculates a set of stereotypes. Stereotypes are a node of communication which present 'recognisable' information about an identity category – albeit reductive, simplistic and usually not representative of genuine diversity and the broad complexity of subjectivity. As a form of language or a 'byte' of information, stereotypes associate a set of behaviours, attitudes or dispositions with an identity category, and this is typically the case for minorities and non-heterosexual persons (Cover 2004). Stereotypes find their persistence over time not in the extent to which a culture might dispute them, but in the ease by which they are circulated and repeated, thereby reinforced even when disavowed (Rosello 1998). Thus in films such as, for example, *Consenting Adult* (1985) where only the passing mention of a gay male suicide is made by Martin Sheen's character, or in the TV Movie *An Early Frost* (1985) where the (unsuccessful) attempt at suicide is made by a closeted gay character recently diagnosed HIV-positive, or *Wonder Boys* (2000) in which young queer student James (Tobey Maguire) demonstrates a fascination with celebrity suicides, the stereotype that queer persons are fated towards suicidality is reinforced through popular cultural repetition to become a coherent and recognised 'social fact'.

The classic film *The Boys in the Band,* based on Mart Crowley's play and directed by William Friedkin, is a good case in point as to how homosexuality has been depicted as fated towards suicide. Although the characters are on the outer edge of being classified queer youth – noting the relative absence until the early 2000s of younger non-heterosexuals on screen – the film is significant in that it infuses a narrative about gay men with a sense of suicide as a *likely* outcome for them all. Set at a party of a number of youngish gay men in their late twenties and early thirties, the dialogue among the characters swings between camp frivolity and angry melancholia, with frequent references to suicide. As the men become intoxicated and bitchy, Michael (Kenneth Nelson) taunts his friend Harold (Leonard Frey) over his suicidality:

> And the pills: Harold has been gathering and storing and saving up barbiturates for the past year like a squirrel. Hundreds of nembutals, hundreds of seconals, all in preparation for – and anticipation for – the long winter of his death. Well, I'll tell you something Hally, when the time comes you won't have the guts. It's not always like it happens in plays. Not all faggots bump themselves off at the end of the story.

Significantly, Michael's speech draws attention to the stereotype of queer suicidality and to Harold's location within the fatalism that is communicated by it. Disavowing the truth or fate of the stereotype, he effectively continues its circulation in popular culture. He does, however, confirm by the end of the film the truth that not all gay men kill themselves, reacting in horror to its symbolism when offered a valium to calm him down. What is made explicit is the notion that the theatrics of manipulation, exuberance and consumption are tools of public self-identification which attempt to obscure the melancholia of homosexual selfhood but effectively reveal it; hiding one's melancholic 'nature' is depicted here always to fail.

While a melancholic and suicidal disposition forms part of the recognisable stereotype circulated by this film, on closer examination we can see that it is actually produced in the text as a fated or cultural expectation resulting from inherent and indelible shame. This is not shame over being homosexual but, rather, *unavoidable* shame over the failure to be heterosexual. Shame, of course, figures within Durkheim's categorisations of suicide as an 'obligatory altruistic suicide' (Durkheim 1952: 221); the suicide that results from the loss of honour, although this is rather different from the form of shame and self-deprecation that has marked sexual non-normativity throughout much of the Nineteenth and Twentieth Centuries. Queer theorist Michael Warner refers to the ways in which shame figures in the articulation, determination and discourses of sex and sexuality. For Warner, gay culture is 'marked by a primal encounter with shame', both embraced in the cultural production of identities within lesbian/gay communities and latched onto by moralists pointing to shame in gay life 'as though it were proof of something pathological in gay people' (Warner 1999: 8). Shame operates here, then, not as affect or emotion but as a manifestation of the permanency of stigma, marking the homosexual as fatalistically shamed in such a way that the shame must be turned on oneself:

> The shame of a true pervert – stigma – is less delible; it is a social identity that befalls one like fate. Like the related stigmas of racial identity or disabilities, it may have nothing to do with acts one has committed. It attaches not to doing, but to being; not to conduct, but to status (Warner 1999: 28).

In the framework through which queer subjects are categorised as perverse, shame infuses being as stigma such that life becomes not only dishonourable but unliveable. What might be added to Warner's account, however, is the point that a stigmatised shame has often been culturally represented in pre-1990s media as that which not only *does* but *must* permeate all aspects of the homosexual self. Shame is implicated within an identity and is thus portrayed as inseparable from subjecthood.

This stigma, which is what shame becomes when impossible to alleviate, underpins the stereotype of the self-hating homosexual (Altman 1982: 27). Self-hatred produced through stigma and shame permeates the characters in *The Boys in the Band*, thereby constructing an environment in which death and suicide are figured as the logical fate of queer identity. Indeed, the film is framed by the self-deprecating humour of the young men at the party which leads to demeaning each other and ultimately to Michael's breakdown in the final scenes:

MICHAEL: [sobbing uncontrollably and drunkenly] I won't make it! I won't make it! I won't make it!

DONALD: I'll give you a valium, I've got some in my pocket.

MICHAEL: No! No pills or I'll die.

DONALD: I'm not going to give you the whole bottle!

MICHAEL: I feel like old man river. I'm tired of living and I'm scared to die … If we could just not hate ourselves so much. That's it, you know. If we could just learn not to hate ourselves quite so very much.

DONALD: I know, I know.

MICHAEL: Who was it who always used to say: you show me a happy homosexual, and I'll show you a gay corpse.

Suicide, as scholar Edwin Shneidman has pointed out, is often depicted as a flight from such intolerable pain (Shneidman 1985: 36). What the fatalistic suicide of *The Boys in the Band* articulates is that the suicidality of non-heterosexuals is produced through an attempt to flee the pain of unavoidable self-hatred that cannot be separated from the performativity of queerness due to the discursive operations of stigma and shame. The alternative to a life of shame or fated towards an abrupt ending in suicide is not cultural transformation, radical liberation or social change, but, as Michael indicates, the need to learn to reject individual self-hatred and thus struggle against the fatalistic force of stigma as a permanent existence in shame.

Fatalistic representations of gay suicides in popular media, however, develop alongside a growing culture of gay liberation (the 1969 Stonewall rebellion in New York being an official marker of the beginning of the counter-rhetoric of 'gay pride'). From the mid-1990s, the depiction of the queer young man who is led from shame to suicide continues, however these depictions are predominantly a narrative device to present a contrast to alternative pride and self-affirmation discourses. The 2009 film *Prayers for Bobby*, articulates the ways in which residual social institutions such as Christianity can make life unbearable through persistent interpellation of a young queer subject as fated not only to stigma, shame and death in this life, but in the afterlife also. Based on Leroy Aaron's (1995) book of the same name, it narrates how Mary Griffith (Sigourney Weaver) learns to overcome her religious and naïve views on non-heterosexuality as indelibly shameful subsequent to the suicide of her son Bobby (Ryan Kelley). Following filmic conventions, the narrative stumbling block is her religiously-inspired homophobia articulated through her determined shaming of Bobby, with order restored in the end as she participates actively in the a pride parade to affirm queer life as liveable. As such, it draws attention to the figure of the sad young man as that which is out-of-step with contemporary liberal perceptions of queerness, pointing out that retreating from homophobic views is necessary to avoid producing stigma and hence suicidality.

Other films produced since the mid-1990s likewise draw attention to the debilitating effects of stigma but do so through setting up a comparison with forms of political anger. The 1995 film *Stonewall* retrospectively indicates this shift by illustrating the suicide of the closeted and melancholic businessman Vinnie (Bruce MacVittie) against the backdrop of younger homosexuals preparing to fight back against homophobia and police brutality in accord with a shame-eradicating radical pride articulated through rebellion. Even more recently, the British *Queer as Folk* (1999–2000) mini-series indicates the disjuncture between the fatalism of the melancholic young man and those whose identity is forged within either pride or rebellion. Alexander (Antony Cotton) attempts suicide not long after discovering that his estranged father is dying and that his disapproving, homophobic mother has requested he sign documents preventing him from making a claim on his father's will. While his household are preparing for a night out, it is revealed he has called an ambulance, indicating his familiarity with the 'routine' of a suicide attempt by displaying the bottle of pills he has taken and describing the foods and drink he has ingested. Accompanying him to the hospital, his landlady, Hazel (Denise Black), declares 'He's only gone and done it again!'. Of all the series' characters, he is the most camp, the most ostensibly frivolous and the most sad and melancholic, using his wit and flamboyance in stereotypical form to cover over his 'sad young man' stylisation.

Despite being one of the younger characters, Alexander can be read as an *older model* of the gay young man akin to the characters in *The Boys in the Band*. His response to his parents' persistent stigmatisation is to attempt suicide, although the series' narrative sets this up to contrast emphatically against his friend Stuart (Aidan Gillen), who intervenes first by making threatening gestures to the mother and then, after the suicide attempt, blowing up her car. A stylistic and generational gap is thus articulated in which an older form of playing out one's sexual minority status is to accept homophobia in sadness, melancholia and the suicidal fate (while 'covering up' through camp behaviour); the newer and 'queer' response is to refuse to accept shame and fate not in favour of community and self-pride but of anger and rage. This more recent account of a queer suicide is one which locates it in a 'passing': Alexander represents the sad young man of the past who is in the process of being replaced by those who refuse stigmatisation and suicide as queer fate and instead express their fury at the continuity of the cultural conditions that, however residual, persist in framing suicide as the outcome of queer being. From one perspective it can be said that rather than representing and reinforcing the 'sad young man' fatalistic motif, it is showing how that popular-cultural figuration of sexuality-related suicide is out-of-sync with more recent formations of queer youth vulnerability as I discuss them below.

Mental Illness, Perversion and Psychiatry

A second framework through which the link between sexual minorities and suicide is fashioned in popular culture is found in the location of suicide as a mental health issue. The fatalism of the earlier accounts of queer suicidality in *The Boys in the Band* and depicted as a cultural residue in *Stonewall* and *Queer as Folk* against the backdrop of queer political struggle presented suicide as the flight from pain rather than the product of psychological or mental health concerns such as depression. Although the idea of suicide as the result of psychological or psychiatric mental illness is not the only model, it is increasingly significant in discourse on suicide and the mental health of younger queer persons has recently begun to be investigated, particularly around questions of socially-induced stress and suicidal risks related to depression (Hegna and Wichstrøm 2007, Ryan et al. 2009, Walls, Freedenthal and Wisneski 2008, Davis, Saltzberg and Locke 2009). Depression is understood as a serious but treatable mental illness that, in extreme cases, can result in suicide.

However, the depiction of queer youth suicide from a mental health perspective has often been obscured in both queer politics and media accounts, and this is for a number of reasons. Discussing mental health concerns around queer youth suicidality often risks re-invoking the now-disparaged idea that homosexuality is itself a symptom of mental illness, allowing a return to the idea of homosexuality as a psychological problem that itself can be treated. Lesbian/gay culture has long maintained a deep suspicion of psychological formulations or (misread) constructionist approaches in order better to combat the still-powerful religious right and conservative rhetoric that seeks to re-criminalise or marginalise lesbian/gay sexual behaviour for being a freely-chosen 'lifestyle' or 'sin'. The American Psychiatric Association (APA), which first drew up its classification of diagnoses in 1952, categorised homosexuality as a sociopathic personality disturbance. In a 1968 revision of the classification document, it revised the entry on homosexuality but continued to characterise it as a mental disorder. It was only in 1973 that the APA declassified homosexuality as a disorder *per se*, although it did allude to homosexuality-related psychological problems (Murphy 1997: 51). Certainly, the APA classification has remained strong in the cultural memory of lesbian/gay discourse; opposition to any psycho-pathologisation of homosexuality is thus equally as strong, resulting in the avoidance of mental health issues in relation to the topic of non-heterosexuality.

Recent entertainment media has thus sometimes deliberately sought to avoid connections between sexuality and mental illness: it is rumoured that *A Beautiful Mind* (2001), telling the story of a real-life mathematical genius suffering from severe schizophrenia and paranoia, avoids mentioning the character's sexual orientation in order *not* to imply a link between mental illness and homosexuality. This has not always been the case, but has been significant in combating the extreme connections made between non-heterosexuality and dangerous psychopathology leading to serial killing in *Silence of the Lambs* (1991), *Hannibal*

(2001) and *Butterfly Kiss* (1995) and in the cultural fascination with the spectacle of the Jeffrey Dahmer and Andrew Cunnan 'queer' serial killings. Although these are extreme depictions of psychiatric illness, they have risked establishing a link between non-heterosexuality, mental illness and living an unliveable life through rage against sociality that manifests in the killing of others, or making other lives not only unliveable but no longer living.

While any film depicting non-heterosexual characters (with or without suicide) is usually available to be read, problematically, as representing non-heterosexuality as the product of mental illness, there are a very small number of films over the past two decades which address queer youth suicide as a mental health concern. The popular French film *Come Undone* (*Presque Rien*) (2000), however, frames a queer youth suicide attempt caused by mental health concerns within a narrative about a summer sexual awakening. Eighteen year-old Matthieu (Jéréme Elkaïm) meets Cédric (Stéphane Rideau) while vacationing at the beach; the two begin a relationship despite Matthieu's problematic relationship with his family which includes a distant father, an over-bearing sister and a mother who suffers from long-term clinical depression subsequent to the loss of a child some year earlier. The two boys' romance develops, and Matthieu makes the decision to leave his family to move in with Cédric and study at the university in nearby Nantes. In flash-forwards to the winter of two years later, however, we discover that the relationship remained solid until Matthieu became inexplicably depressed and attempted suicide. The flash-forwards narrate the story of the few weeks after his suicide attempt and clinicians' and Cédric's struggle to understand why it occurred. Subsequent to having his stomach pumped, Matthieu's psychiatrist tries to determine the cause of his overdose:

> You don't want to talk? Fine. Let me tell you what's going to happen. If you want, only if you agree to it, you can stay here for eight days. That's the usual procedure when people come to the hospital. We try to keep them for eight days to find out what's wrong. See what made you do what you did … and try to find some answers. I'm a psychiatrist, I'm here to help you. You are safe here. You can get yourself together.

The temporal distance of two years between the summer and the flash-forward winter scenes indicates that his suicidality is the not the result of youthful isolation, loneliness or sexual shame, given the passionate and relatively stable relationship that developed during the summer and the growing integration into a queer community through patronage of bars and clubs and participation in Cédric's small network of gay friends.

Although Matthieu has left Cédric, his former lover wants to help and hunts him down to where he is now living in the basement of his parents' empty vacation home. Cédric visits the psychiatrist who likewise is searching for reasons:

PSYCHIATRIST: He may have felt the need to hide it from you … How were things between you? I mean, were there any sexual inhibitions?

CEDRIC: No, not really. But this past month he hasn't wanted to. He accused me of cheating.

PSYCHIATRIST: It wasn't true?

CEDRIC: No … Just once, but it was nothing.

PSYCHIATRIST: Otherwise things were good?

CEDRIC: … Yeah fine. We argued, like everybody.

What is uncovered is that Matthieu's queer sexuality was not causal in that the relationship was relatively ordinary in and of itself. Nor is it implied that Matthieu's non-heterosexuality is a mental health concern coterminous with his depression and suicidality. Rather, the point is made that in some cases a queer youth suicide attempt may be about matters *other* than sexuality and that clinical depression may be a cause wholly separate from sexual non-normativity, isolation or shame as the conversation between the psychiatrist and Cédric reveals:

PSYCHIATRIST: Why do you think he did it?

CEDRIC: I don't know. Shouldn't you tell me?

PSYCHIATRIST: It's hard to say, exactly. I think it's a combination of things. In any case, it's not about you.

CEDRIC: So why the letter saying he wouldn't see me anymore?

PSYCHIATRIST: Depression doesn't leave much room for others.

Indeed, given the earlier focus on his mother's clinical depression, her treatment with pharmaceuticals during the earlier summer and her distancing herself from her children and husband, there is an implication that Matthieu's depression may be congenital. *Come Undone* thus breaks a number of assumptions about queer youth suicidality that have been circulated elsewhere in popular entertainment, effectively cautioning against any assumption that suicidality is the fated outcome of non-heterosexual behaviour or identity. Importantly, this particular category of representing queer youth suicide aims to re-frame the cause from shame and fate that was derived through much older narratives and instead to demonstrate that queer youth can be subject to mental health issues that have nothing to do with sexuality at all. Ultimately, it depicts queer youth suicidality through the complexity and diversity of subjectivity, distancing itself from stereotypes and repetitive narratives and instead articulating the idea that the multiply-constituted subject may have multiple events, feelings, emotions and problems that have little to do with the positively-depicted queerness of being.

Rejection, Isolation and Individuation

A third framework through which non-heteronormative sexualities and suicidality are associated in popular entertainment media involves the broad theme of isolation, whereby a sense of isolation from others is represented as an unbearable pain leading to suicidality. This can be geographic isolation from other same-sex attracted persons, isolation through an inability to come out, marginalisation within a broader heteronormative community or temporary isolation from significant others, such as friends, lovers and supportive peers. Isolation plays a significant role in the traditional theorisation of suicide, and the portrayal of such isolation as a causal factor of youth suicide can be read through Durkheim's 'egoistic' suicide. Egoistic suicide is that which occurs due to excessive individuation outside of integration in society (Durkheim 1952: 221). What Durkheim identified as a lack of integration of the individual into society that leads to self-harm (Durkheim 1952: 170) is reproduced in these accounts along the lines of an integration/isolation binary; it is therefore to see such suicides as a form of cessation due to a particular type of pain brought about by isolation, but at the same time to acknowledge that the isolation or dis-integration from collectivity is multiple and not necessarily grounded in sexual diversity. This integration/isolation binary is not a strict either/or dichotomy, but one which acknowledges the varying degrees to which a subject experiences isolation, alienation or marginalisation in different contexts and environments.

Isolation has thus been fundamental in understanding sexuality-related suicide through sociological approaches, and is a concept that emerges in popular cultural accounts of queer youth suicide in at least three ways. Firstly, it is characterised as an isolation that has been endemic to gay men and lesbians (and the otherwise sexually-diverse) for centuries. This is built upon the myth of the 'eternal homosexual identity' which presumes that gay men and lesbians have always existed as discrete, pre-discursive sexual subjects, only recently overcoming endemic loneliness, silence and invisibility through the development of subcultural community in the latter half of the twentieth century (D'Emilio 1992: 4–5). The 'eternal homosexual' myth is deployed to utilise the notion that 'community' is a gathering of individuals of fixed identity rather than a discursive or symbolic force that constitutes the identities of those claims to gather (Cohen 1985). The resulting representation of the contemporary isolated homosexual, then, is one who has been 'left behind' in this organising, who has not yet become capable of joining a community in a face-to-face capacity or, importantly, who is too young to access an inner-urban network of homosexuals built on adult social activities such as drinking alcohol.

One portrayal of isolation in popular media is that which centres on the failure or non-capacity to 'come out' and self-declare as a lesbian/gay or queer person, usually thereby being unable to participate in queer community. Coming out is, as Esther Saxey has pointed out, a culturally-expected activity for *every* lesbian, gay man or bisexual; with a correlate reflective story that acts as a 'tale summing up their own journey to sexual identity and showing how their nature made itself known to them despite a hostile environment' (Saxey 2008: 2). What this motif often entails is that one is isolated if one remains closeted and thereby unable to participate in lesbian/gay community, thereby at risk of suicide. An ironic and critical example of suicidality resulting from the isolation brought about by an inability to come out is shown in the cult classic film *Heathers* (1989). When Veronica (Winona Ryder) and JD (Christian Slater) murder two bullying, homophobic high-school football jocks and set the scene to look like a suicide, they leave behind the following fake suicide note:

> Ram and I died the day we realised we could never reveal our forbidden love to an uncaring and un-understanding world. The joy we shared in each other's arms was greater than any touchdown, yet we were forced to live the lie of sexist beer-guzzling jock assholes.

It references the clichéd cultural knowledge that homosexual teenagers attempt to conform within the authorised roles but suffer great isolation in not being able to 'reveal' themselves and come out. The irony presented in the plot is that the false note gave the two brash and homophobic characters undeserved depth and sensitivity. The fact that Veronica and JD reinforced the 'repressed homosexual' suicide pact scene by leaving beside the bodies a Joan Crawford photograph and mascara highlights the way in which the connection between isolated and closeted homosexuality and suicide had been previously written as a dated queer cliché. Importantly, *Heathers* makes the point that their community's overwhelming willingness to accept this fictional evidence demonstrates the power of older and inaccurate stereotypes not attributable to late-1980s queer youth to obscure the reality, depth and complexity of contemporary secondary school life.

This category of suicide depictions has also represented isolation in ways different from the motifs of endemic alienation or closetedness of queer youth, instead invoking a *temporary isolation* that reveals a broader sense of despair, aloneness or inability to articulate selfhood through social, political or cultural integration. An example is found in Gregg Araki's 1993 film *Totally Fucked Up* (subtitled 'another homo movie by Gregg Araki' and thus indicating both its place inside lesbian/gay culture and its critical distance from lesbian/gay narrative norms). The film begins with a shot of a magazine column which states the following:

Feelings of failure run deep among gay adolescents. Suicide Rate High Among Gay Teens. The National Institute of Mental Health said that 30 percent of teenagers who commit suicide are gay. Authorities explain that gay youths readily become despondent over their failure to succeed as heterosexuals while betraying their feelings of homosexuality because of society's prejudice. Two 15-year-old boys in Milwaukee recently committed what was a double suicide after becoming despondent over their families [sic] decision to move apart.

This snapshot news story provides a set of explanatory reasons for queer youth suicide in terms both of failure and the impact of discrimination. However, the two boys' reasons are immediately given as *otherwise* – separation and isolation from one another. Araki here presents 'queer youth suicide' not as a product of stigma or of failure to be heterosexual, but suggests that the common explanations themselves are dangerous by focussing on sexuality as causal rather than on other issues such as isolation.

In the final scene of the film, Andy (James Duval) poisons himself while alone, not long after he has been rejected by a boyfriend and, in attempting to find solace, has found all his friends' phones are engaged. A temporary if painful disappointment and a breach of immediate access to one's community or peer network forms the background causal reasons for his suicide. The inability to contact his peers is catalytic, and the suicide can be read as a response to his relationship breakdown. However, both are depicted as representative of a deeper, core isolation experienced by non-heteronormative youth; a particular brand of *felt* disconnection from the socially real and the 'really authentic' that is understood to affect and inflect the lives of postmodern youth (Latham 2002: 243). As Andy puts it: 'All I really want is to be happy for, like, one second. Be able to look around and not just see shit.' In the midst of a momentary crisis and isolation from his peers that reinvokes the separation he feels from contemporary sociality, it is the cessation of cognition and consciousness Andy seeks, what Shneidman refers to as the 'insight that it is possible to put an end to suffering by stopping the unbearable flow of consciousness' (Shneidman 1985: 36).

This category of queer suicide depictions in film and television therefore draws on forms of common, cultural knowledge about the experience of queerness as marked by an unbearable aloneness. While the older stereotype of the isolated queer young man (or couple) is markedly outdated, it does in fact continue as a concern for suicide risk in a number of forms, not the least of which is represented by Araki's attempt to complexify queer suicidality by indicating the ways in which a sense of isolation is not eradicated by the act of coming out, finding a lover or participating in queer community in some form or another. Rather, temporary isolation or the inability to reach one's peer network traumatically articulates a more endemic isolation that is common to all human beings but is more marked in those whose current lives have been built on forms of marginalisation, difference or non-normativity.

Discriminatory Cultures and the Cry for Help

The argument that suicide attempts are a 'cry for help' is a contemporary belief that suicidal behaviour is an elaborate device aimed at drawing attention to the pain or suffering an individual might be in. In this theory, suicidality is 'a kind of communication or interpersonal action' (Battin 1995: 8), neither the result of fate, nor mental illness or depression, nor excessive individuation or isolation, but a means by which to change painful circumstances where other options have failed or are unavailable. The representation of sexuality-related suicide in popular culture can often be read through the cry for help model, particularly when related to the existence of barriers to changing intolerable circumstances experienced by younger persons, such as lack of independent income or mobility. The narrative structure of much popular film and television, of course, enhances the cry for help representation, as a suicide attempt can thus be established as an obstacle that must be overcome in order for the narrative to achieve eventual closure. Suicide, of course, is never quite that simple. The cry for help model belongs also to a set of somewhat problematic cultural myths that see suicidality and suicide attempts not as serious acts requiring intervention and circumstantial or social change, but as an act of attention-seeking (Miller and Eckert 2009: 159). However incompatible with current thinking in interventionist strategies, this model presents us with a fourth framework for making sense of fictional accounts of queer youth suicide, whereby suicidality is represented as a call for help in the face of discrimination, marginalisation and seemingly unbearable difference.

The queer youth suicide film *Trevor* (1994), which is connected with the suicide resource website *The Trevor Project* (http://www.thetrevorproject.org/) and won the 1995 Academy Award for Best Short Film, is an important example of the ways in which queer youth suicide has been depicted as a cry for help in the face of homophobia and heterosexism. Thirteen year-old Trevor (Brett Barsky) is initially unaware of any clear sexual orientation or preference; likewise he is unaware that his intense fandom of Diana Ross, his interest in musical theatre and his otherwise camp behaviour are indicators to others of an apparent stereotypical gayness. In spoken diary entries, he identifies his unpopularity at school with the prejudice Diana Ross experienced in her early career, and cements that identification with a decision 'to be' Diana Ross for Halloween.

Early in the film, he becomes best friends at school with the popular and sporty Pinky Faraday (Jonah Rooney), significantly changing his own social status. Trevor's crush becomes obsessive, and the friendship sours as Pinky distances himself from Trevor's increasingly camp behaviour; at the same time, others have warned Trevor his devotion to Pinky might be evidence of a future 'perversion'. Indeed, the timing of his crush coincides with an awakening to sexual selfhood, an understanding among himself and his peers of 'proper' gender performances, a new attentiveness to his mannerisms and tastes and the ways in which all of these centre around codes of belonging and exclusion within a heterosexist school culture. The convergence of these is represented by a letter Pinky writes to Trevor telling him he is a 'fairy, a weak person and maybe didn't even deserve to live.' The discovery of homophobia here is a loss of innocence which, Trevor relates in class in a verbal report, is an experience of hurt involving a spontaneous reaction. Indeed, for Trevor, the loss of innocence that comes with the awakening to sexuality, romantic feelings and a sense of how place, belonging and selfhood operate within social norms is one which, in fact, involves not loss but the acquisition of knowledge as to the framework through which a dominant sexual regime orders the proper and the improper, the acceptable and the intolerable.

Trevor's reaction to the pain of discovering this knowledge is to see himself as 'a person with no future' and thereby to attempt suicide (by overdose of aspirin). However, the suicide attempt is not spontaneous as Trevor has a strong familiarity with the theatrics of suicide. Indeed, the film opens with Trevor's parents discovering him playing dead (badly) in a number of attempted suicide scenes. He complains in a spoken diary entry that his parents' lax and unbelieving reactions to his dramatised suicide scenes indicate they do not care enough about him. In a series of comic scenes, Trevor has rehearsed his funeral and familiarised himself with suicide methods, long before any sexual awakening.

Where Trevor's suicide attempt differs from Andy's in *Totally Fucked Up* is that it is not a response to Pinky's rejection, nor a sense of aloneness or isolation. Indeed, in the scenes leading up to the failed suicide attempt, it is not Pinky on which he has focused but his place in a culture in which he knows – or at least feels – he will be rejected: 'Everybody at school's saying that I'm a gay. It must be showing. But I look at myself and I don't see anything that's different . I tried to cure myself, but nothing worked.' Thus it is neither shame nor isolation nor depression which prompts his more genuine suicide attempt. Rather, it is a reaction to a culture in which his cry for help is a demand for change. The suicide stressor here is, of course, the possibility of ongoing stigmatisation through the 'anticipation of negative social reaction' known to cause psychological distress of suicidal proportions (Skidmore, Linsenmeier and Bailey 2006: 687).

In this framework of queer youth suicide representation, then, we see for the first time a very young character – aged thirteen – rather than the more common older teenager or young adult, demonstrating a continued shift towards depicting queer youth suicide as a problem for younger persons rather than queer adults. While Trevor's suicidal behaviour is to be taken seriously, the broader theme of the film is not an individual suicide but the 'discovery' of intolerance, heterosexism and homophobia that makes not only Trevor vulnerable but also his friends whose masculinity depends on disavowing non-normative difference. It might therefore be argued that while this film depicts suicide as a cry for help, it is a more sophisticated representation than found in the three earlier categories, given the ways in which it points not only to the need for awareness of very young queer persons' vulnerability, but simultaneously to the social factors which create that vulnerability in the first instance.

Conclusion

In the depiction of sexuality-related suicide in popular culture, what we witness are a series of shifts across four ways of making sense of queer youth suicide. These frameworks – the fated sad young man, the mental illness model, egoistic isolation and the cry-for-help – alter throughout the history of recent contemporary popular culture depending on both the relative tolerance or acceptance of non-heteronormative sexuality as well as the relative attitude to suicide. Much as they do indeed overlap, each step or change indicates the development of attitudes towards non-heterosexual personages and suicide. The notion of the sad young man fated to suicide *because* the failure to be heterosexual is a forbidden or shameful failure operates to connect suicide and divergent sexualities and works within a moral code which affirms the logic of suicide. By depicting shame over non-heterosexuality or sexual non-conformity as timeless and ahistorical, suicide is presented as the only option for homosexual men, women and youth to avoid the stigma that enfuses the living and can only be overcome by ceasing to live. The fact that such a perspective pre-dates counter-shame reasoning such as GLBT Pride discourses or radically-positive queer diversity has not prevented this fated-to-suicide stereotype from continuing in popular entertainment. The mental illness model in which both non-heterosexuality and suicidality are available to be read as illnesses disavows non-heterosexuality as a legitimate and stable form of subjective expression, but seeks to prevent the suicide by preventing its cause (mental illness). Although sympathetic to a so-called 'plight' of non-heterosexual persons, the model unwittingly pathologises the homosexual subject. Nevertheless, texts such as *Come Undone* which separate queerness from mental illness but retain a link between suicidality and clinical depression counter this stereotype. Finally, under a regime of increased sexual tolerance and lesbian/gay cultural representation, the idea that sexuality-related suicide results from one or several forms of isolation points to sociality as a factor in self-harm, leading to the possibility of investigating ways in which that form of suicide can be prevented by forms of overcoming isolation through community integration. That is, the suicide problem is latterly understood to be formed in cultural conditions that are available within constructs of change and flux.

As an addendum, it should be noted that the cliché of the suicidal gay or lesbian teen has also been addressed in popular entertainment in ways which help to delineate the stereotypes and undo the frameworks through which queer youth suicide is produced as a cultural logic. Part of the narrative of *Queer as Folk*, for example, has the fifteen year-old gay teenager Nathan (Charlie Hunnam) desperate to belong to the inner-urban lesbian/gay community in Manchester, U.K., where the greatest difficulty of access is not age or lack of knowledge but his school-work and his household chores. He threatens a litany of cliché acts of risk behaviour and self-harm thought to be those of the isolated queer teenager, only to be mocked by the other characters. Whether the humorous treatment of queer youth suicide helps to undo the myths or, on the other hand, work against the gains made in bringing this significant issue to light, will depend on the cultural knowledges through which such texts are read and, of course, no particular reading is ever guaranteed.

Chapter 2
Histories and Genealogies of Suicide Research and Sexuality

Operating in sometimes distinct ways, various discourses together construct and disseminate the idea of queer youth suicide. The chapters in this first half of the book explore some of the ways in which queer youth suicide is understood, disseminated and made public in popular culture, media and more recently in online videos. One field important to examine is that which provides a knowledge framework for suicide and sexuality in academic writing and research. Academic writing on queer youth suicide is relatively new, in the sense that not a great deal of work addressing sexuality and suicide occurs before the mid-1980s, although there has been a significant increase in research on queer youth, suicidality and self-harm since the beginning of the 2000s. As with all research and academic writing, there are certain genealogies of concepts which have governed the emergence of the current state of the field, at times constraining research from exploring alternative approaches to sexuality and at other times producing important insights that have significant potential for intervention and prevention. Academic research is a relatively distinct field that does not often intersect with popular culture or public debate. However, it does have a bearing on public sphere discourse, particularly in the areas of policy, youth affairs and health, and should thus not be considered wholly separate from the ways in which queer youth are publicly perceived as vulnerable or suicidal in non-academic communication.

Research on homosexuality and suicide prior to the late twentieth century was, as Kathleen Erwin (1993) has cogently pointed out, significantly restricted by a number of problematic assumptions and ideological perspectives. She pointed to four historical understandings of queer youth suicide. Firstly, a religious perspective which understood the suicide of sexual minority personages to be a 'second immoral act' subsequent to the shame of the initial immorality in sexual sin (Erwin 1993: 440). A second approach emerging in the nineteenth century tended to pathologise homosexuality and suicide simultaneously, understanding both to be not manifestations of immorality but of abnormal nervous systems (Erwin 1993: 441). The subsequent psychoanalytic approach, particularly as it was reconstituted within North American ego-psychology, presumed that both homosexuality and suicide were the result of psychopathological arrangements determined by individual characteristics (Erwin 1993: 442–443). Finally, these three approaches were de-centred by twentieth century sociological models, particularly in the 1980s, which tended initially to combine anti-homophobic polemic with research which aimed to draw on the experiences of younger queer persons. Developed through the work of queer activists and medical professionals who recognised that lesbian/gay persons suffered from high rates of suicide and self-harm, this last phase of research effectively re-figured sexuality-related suicide as a social fact in Durkheim's terms by suggesting that social intolerance and homophobia were internalised, thereby leading to self-hatred and self-destructiveness (Erwin 1993: 443). Of course, such categories are not simply replaced one after the other in a linear framework towards a more enlightened ideological governance of research but, to varying degrees, elements and parts of each continue to operate simultaneously to form contemporary research-based analyses of sexuality-related suicide and self-harm. For example, much of the field works between clinical and sociological models by pointing both to the ways in which social intolerance and environmental factors produce psychological issues that are known to lead to suicidality such as depression and other mental health stresses.

Writing on queer suicide became significant in the early 1980s, with Eric Rofes' *I Thought People Like That Killed Themselves* (1983) which contributed to shifting opinion from the idea that homosexuality was essentially abnormal, instead introducing the ways in which a number of factors were causal in the suicides of gay men, including shame resulting from blackmail and exposure, pressures around coming out and closetedness, isolation and ostracism. This work began to set the tone for public perceptions of suicide within queer communities, particularly emphasising the need for cultural change, political engagement with homophobic cultural environments and arguing for the development of queer community institutions which could provide resources and support for queer youth.

Similarly influential on the early development of the field was the foundational work that is Paul Gibson's chapter on 'Gay Male and Lesbian Youth Suicide' in the 1989 United States *Report of the Secretary's Task Force on Youth Suicide*. Gibson's thirty-two page chapter drew together scarce previous research to provide an account for investigators, social workers and policy-makers. He usefully re-located sexuality-related youth suicide in a culturalist framework and shifted the articulation of risk from one which pathologised homosexuality to an approach acknowledging that causal factors are constituted at least in part through cultural formations, forms of sociality and politico-cultural arrangements. It is Gibson's foundational work that is the source of the frequently cited statistics on queer youth suicide. Drawing on previous writings, he stated that 'gay youth are 2 to 3 times more likely to attempt suicide than other young people' and 'may comprise up to 30 per cent of completed suicides annually' (Gibson 1989: 110). Such has been the influence of this report that, more than two decades old, the document and the statistics it states have continued to be cited in news media, political statements and policy documents and, until only recently, in academic research. The significance of the report comes not from its compilation of previous ideas but from the *frequency* by which it is cited in subsequent research. The vast majority of written documents, articles and theses on queer youth suicide between 1990 and 2004 cite Gibson's piece and utilise it as a founding statement on sexuality-related youth suicide research. By way of example, some published research in which Gibson's report is cited include: Remafedi 1994, Muehrer 1995, Shaffer et al. 1995, Rotheram-Borus and Isabel 1995, Emslie 1996, Macdonald and Cooper 1998, Kulkin, Chauvin and Percle 2000, McDaniel, Purcell and D'Augelli 2001, McBee-Strayer and Rogers 2002 and Russell 2003. This is not to say that Gibson's insights are always uncritically accepted and repeated, for there are mixed perspectives. Russell (2003), for example, used Gibson's position on the relationship between sexuality and suicide but was critical of the lack of peer-review processes that might have produced more robust findings that could be utilised subsequently in the field more strongly; he also expressed concerns that the statistics might be overstated due to the sampling problems in the original texts. He did, however, affirm Gibson's underlying assumptions about the *conditions* of queer youth and reiterated intact the list of suicide risk factors suggested in the report (Russell 2003: 1241–1242).

Those conditions identified by Gibson as endemic risk-factors for individual queer youth have, however, changed markedly since the report's publication, and it remains important to address some of the ways in which they have changed, and to do so particularly in light of the idea that continued research must be undertaken to re-locate youth suicide in terms of new sexual cultures and new youth cultures. That is to say, the research field needs broadly to move beyond the dominant framework by refocussing on the current and changing conditions of younger non-heterosexual persons, particularly as those changes have developed through new media representations and new communications technologies. As contemporary western culture becomes increasingly media-saturated and media-savvy, and as new media and communications forms, representations and technologies emerge, the cultural fields that provided the social context for many sexuality-related suicidal behaviours in the 1980s are no longer the same as those in which the continuing high rate of queer youth suicides occurs today.

This chapter critiques some of the field of academic work on queer youth suicide by identifying and investigating four assumptions about sexuality, youth, identity formation and culture that are predominantly derived from the work of Rofes and Gibson in the 1980s and continued to be represented in more recent work, not always reflecting the changing cultural conditions of queer youth over the past twenty years. However, there are variations on the way the themes play out in later writing, and it is these that are also important to identify. Published research on queer youth suicide has grown dramatically over the last decade, and is often located in a range of disciplinary areas from paediatrics to clinical psychology to sociology and queer studies – with that in mind, it is not fruitful to present an exhaustive survey of this work, but to focus on a number of representative examples that demonstrate how these early assumptions are retained and how they change or are critiqued within the overall knowledge framework that academic writing on queer youth suicide produces.

Assumption One: Homophobia as Primary Causal Factor

Early research on sexuality-related suicide was often written from a political-activist stance with the goal of putting issues of non-heterosexuality into both the fields of suicide research and the discourse of broader health and intervention policy. In many ways, this resulted in research which by necessity drew on and elucidated relatively simple concepts in order to explicate the conditions of non-heterosexual youth within the health sciences as well as among policy-makers. The notion of homophobia as a direct cause of individual suicides is such an example of a politically-motivated but under-theorised reasoning found particularly in earlier work, and the trace of which carries through into more recent writings as well. Different from heterosexism or heteronormativity, homophobia is depicted in the study of suicide as a causal factor in both its formation as open hostility towards perceived non-heterosexual persons (Walton 2006: 14) and represented as the means by which legislative, institutional or religious marginalisation of non-heterosexuals is motivated. As a suicide risk factor, it becomes articulated through the production of what has been referred to as 'minority stress' or 'gay-related stress' (Russell 2003: 1248). Although he did not utilise the term homophobia to any great extent in his study, Rofes posited two central causes for queer youth suicidality: the 'result of societal pressure against homosexuality' and the 'minimal resources for support in the time of crisis ... largely because of the place of homosexuality in the society' (Rofes 1983: 46). Both of these, for Rofes, are the result of homophobia in its form as severe, socially-embedded negative attitudes towards non-heterosexual persons. The concept of homophobia in earlier works usually refers to an idea of socially-legitimated institutional homophobia whereby common institutions such as family, school and church to which a straight younger person can turn during a period of crisis are unavailable as resources and coping mechanisms for non-heterosexual youth and unaccepting of sexual difference.

Gibson likewise identified homophobia as a social risk factor which must be removed in order to reduce the number of queer suicides, arguing that homophobia occurrred at institutional, legislative, familial and individual levels:

> Legislation should guarantee homosexuals equal rights in our society. We need to make a conscious effort to promote a positive image of homosexuals at all levels of society that provides gay youth with a diversity of lesbian and gay male adult role models. We each need to take personal responsibility for revising homophobic attitudes and conduct. Families should be educated about the development and positive nature of homosexuality. They must be able to accept their child as gay or lesbian (Gibson 1989: 110).

The use of the concept of homophobia as it was emerging in the 1980s made it quite correct for Gibson to identify it among the risk factors impacting on queer youth in both politico-cultural and local/familial terms. However, the social and political environments in which homophobia occurs has altered significantly over the past twenty years. While there is still negative stigmatisation, harassment and bullying of persons perceived to be non-heterosexual, homophobia as outright hatred of homosexuals is no longer a barrier to legislative and policy change but – where those barriers continue – it is through the positing of *heteronormativity* and the continuing representation of heterosexuality as a more legitimate sexuality than others. That is, rather than the deployment of homophobia as a mechanism to enforce a notion of homosexuality as intolerable, a broader range of tolerated sexualities has emerged, but through heteronormativity, straight, coupled sexualities are advanced as the *most* normative on a broader curve of possibilities, desires and attractions.

Later published research on the topic of suicide ideation among adolescent gay men and lesbians has continued to frame either study or polemic in terms of the conclusions offered by Gibson, namely that sexuality-related suicide is a specific *type* of suicide manifesting as a direct response to intense homophobia (Macdonald and Cooper 1998: 23, Emslie 1996: 39). Indeed, a picture of a supposed 'typical' lesbian or gay young person is drawn in almost all ethnographic and speculative research on queer youth suicide over the past two decades as one who is either subject to homophobic abuse directly and personally or as one who is at risk of 'internalising' homophobia through identification with political, policy and legislative structures which de-value homosexuality (Fenaughty and Harré 2003: 4). For example, Kulkin, Chauvin and Percle (2000: 3) concluded that young gay males and lesbians face an enormous challenge in the need to develop a 'positive self-identity/self-image as a homosexual person in a homophobic society', arguing that there is a general lack of empowerment among this population to do so. For these authors, the common factor which ties together all other risk factors – such as early coming out, isolation, self-esteem and the role of religion – is homophobia, defined as irrational negative attitudes towards homosexuals and the internalisation of those attitudes, and seen to have 'infiltrated many aspects of society and young gay and lesbian lives' (Kulkin, Chauvin and Percle 2000: 12). Using Erving Goffman's (1963) theory of stigma, the authors suggest that ongoing social processes reduce the quality of life for young non-heterosexual persons, and thereby require greater coping mechanisms, increasing dysfunctionality, and leading to large numbers 'choosing suicide rather than deal with the stressors … they may have to confront' (Kulkin, Chauvin and Percle 2000: 13). Produced genealogically through citation and incorporation of earlier research, other writers in the early 2000s similarly added homophobia uncritically to lists of suicide causal factors whereby homophobia is understood as part of the standard social situation for young gay men and lesbians (Lebson 2002: 113, McAndrew and Warne 2010: 93, 96–98).

In a more recent example, McDermott and colleagues find that the extreme stress leading to self-destructive behaviours in young LGBT people results from their having to 'negotiate homophobia in their everyday interactions and manage being positioned as "deviant"' (McDermott, Roen and Scourfield 2008:

817). However, in this case the notion of homophobia appearing in the research is something which is constructed at least partly by the research participants themselves as a social formation that seeks to punish subjects for 'the transgression of heterosexual norms' (McDermott, Roen and Scourfield: 821). Where homophobia includes bullying and deliberate acts of marginalisation and shaming, this is somewhat distinct from the earlier work which focused homophobia on institutional, legislative and policy forms as the manifestation of social intolerance and discrimination. Another element that is notable in the body of research from 2000 onward is a significant reduction in the use of the term homophobia to describe social conditions, mirroring a trend in politics, policy, queer community dialogue and academic writing on sexuality in other fields. Usefully, this has opened the possibility of increasing the capacity of queer youth suicide research to consider the ways in which heteronormativity operates to constitute the unliveability of vulnerable queer lives. Heteronormativity is, indeed, a more prevalent concern as it continues to relegate non-heterosexuality to otherness despite public and private articulations of tolerance and institutional anti-discrimination policies. In a social environment, then, in which legislative and policy-driven homophobia is no longer an undisputed norm, it is important for queer youth suicide research to look to the ways in which risk-inducing discriminatory and harassing behaviour are motivated by factors other than outright negative perceptions of non-heterosexualities, particularly at the level of working towards broader social change while simultaneously providing preventative measures in the shorter term. At the same, further understanding of the ways in which younger queer persons develop and manage resilience within a persistently heteronormative culture is beginning to emerge is some strands of research (Savin-Williams 2001, Hatzenbuehler 2011); again, it would be beneficial for such a focus to be incorporated further into studies of queer youth vulnerability from the perspective of continuing heteronormative social discourses.

Assumption Two: Isolation and Media Invisibility as Risk Factors

Youth social isolation is often discussed as a formation resulting from loneliness, the inability to communicate with other younger persons of diverse sexualities, the unlikelihood of seeing face-to-face another person of sexual minority, or the inability to access lesbian/gay institutions such as clubs, bars, venues, youth groups or arts and cultural establishments due either to age or geographic distance. This has often been further marked for youth living in non-urban and rural areas who are understood to have had to face that sense of isolation in a notably more hostile or discriminatory environment (Roberts 1996: 57–60) or an environment that excessively reinforced and policed the discursive link between gender performance and heteronormative desire in which the capacity to perform sexual identity is framed by persistent self-surveillance and whereby failure to conform to a narrow heterosexuality can put the subject in danger of more explicit isolation and social exclusion. Isolation takes a number of forms in the study of youth suicide, and may be experienced as psychological isolation resulting from the risk of harassment or assault, an inability to share experiences with peers (Smalley Scourfield and Greenland 2005: 144) or a lack of relevant information or role models (Zhao et al. 2010: 105).

As with the assumption of homophobia as causal, queer youth isolation was, likewise, identified by early writers on the topic. In 1983, Rofes suggested that 'estrangement from the traditional support systems within our culture' was one of the major factors contributing to lesbian/gay suicides (Rofes 1983: 47). The resulting argument was that a greater access to lesbian/gay-specific social institutions, venues, support groups, cultural practices and media representation provides means for developing resilience against situations that prompt suicidal thinking. Gibson followed this with the assertion that social isolation is one of the most critical factors in suicide attempts by youth (Gibson 1989: 128). He pointed out that 'Gay youth frequently do not have contact with other gay adolescents or adults for support' (Gibson 1989: 128). Other studies have suggested that sexually-diverse youth are at risk of self-harm or identity instability due to a 'perceived sense of isolation' that may expose gay youth to a greater risk of suicidal behaviour (Nicholas and Howard 1998: 29). Gibson and Rofes' early points are similarly echoed by numerous other commentators on minority sexualities (e.g., Emslie 1996, Greenburg, Brown and Buerkel-Rothfuss 1993, Gross 1991, Kendall and Walker 1998, Macdonald and Cooper 1998, Morrison and L'Heureux 2001) – the basis for this social isolation being that while racial, ethnic and other minority youth are generally raised in a family, community or cultural environment in which their 'identity facet of difference' is neither objectified nor made to seem abject, youth experiencing or articulating non-heterosexual behaviour or desires are generally not within a family, educational or cultural environment in which such behaviours or desires are normative. What, at this stage, needs to be questioned is the extent to which lesbian or gay self-identifying youth are today 'lonely, afraid and hopeless', as Gibson put it (1989: 133).

One thread running through some of the subsequent writing that utilises the trope of isolation focuses on a lack of media representation and the invisibility of queer characters, themes or depictions in mainstream film and television. It has been commonly stated that limited or no access to media forms representing non-heteronormative sexualities and romantic behaviour, exacerbates the feelings of isolation and social ostracism from other non-heterosexual persons (Saulnier 1998), resulting in added psychological distress. For Gibson, such isolation resulted from a lack not of media representation *per se*, but of positive role models, criticising 'images of homosexuals as sick and self-destructive' (Gibson 1989: 126) and arguing that the 'only images of homosexuals that society provides them with are derisive stereotypes of lesbians who are like men and gay men who are like women' (Gibson 1989: 117). More recent accounts of suicide ideation and risk factors often replicate the 'queer media invisibility' motif and likewise relate low levels of media representation of minority sexualities with isolation that increases the risk of suicide. This was exemplified by Richard Roberts' claim that there are no 'positive role models' of lesbian and gay persons in mass circulation as the media in general provide 'anti-gay' messages (Roberts 1996: 57, 59–60). Erwin (1994), likewise, suggested in the early 1990s that the only role models available for younger lesbian/gay persons are those of the media's negatively-stereotyped effeminate men or masculine women, both sick and sinful. Nicholas and Howard similarly made the following statement: 'Exposure to gay role models is limited and stereotypical, with gay men often portrayed by the media as effeminate or "drag queens"' (Nicholas and Howard 1998: 31). Other studies of sexuality and suicide maintained an identical stance by reiterating statements on a lack of media representation of queer identities (e.g., Morrison and L'Heureux 2001: 44–45). Russell likewise expressed concern about the dangers eminent in that most youth 'rarely hear adults talk openly about sexual minority status' (Russell 2003: 1249).

While it is certainly true that there was once an invisibilisation of non-heterosexual behaviours, identities and attractions in mainstream film and television media (Gross 1991: 21, Gross 1998: 91) or that homosexuality was heavily coded and recognisable only to those 'in the know' (Russo 1981); this view has become markedly outdated since the mid-1990s renaissance in queer media representation (Cover 2000, Padva 2004). Gibson's claim that young people suffer from limited access to positive representations of lesbian/gay/bisexual sexualities was thus appropriate for its time but is clearly no longer the case. However, this notion has been repeated in the more recent work on suicidality and isolation. For example, Michel Dorais suggested that both news and entertainment media present 'few positive images of gay individuals' (Dorais 2004: 68) and asserted that the 'media norm includes "fag" jokes and a generalized view of homosexuality as either tragic or comic' leading to the death of young gay and bisexual males 'because they are so alone, often feeling that their fate is shared by no one else' (Dorais 2004: 6). Such views constrain the possibility of examining how the conditions by which youth suicide becomes a social logic have changed over the past two decades, and how we might approach (positive) media representations from the perspective of understanding the continued high rate of queer youth suicide.

This is not to suggest that the role of media depictions of non-heterosexual characters, themes and behaviours should now be considered a non-issue. Rather, it is important to interrogate what impact this changing mediascape has on both the psychological and social environments of queer youth, the extent to which these representation provide resources for self-esteem or that mitigate a sense of vulnerability, the ways in which they are accessed and interpreted, the degree to which these depictions regiment non-heterosexuality or maintain stereotypes even in positive ways and the value these depictions have for younger persons. Fenaughty and Harré have pointed out, for example, that many of the young men interviewed in their ethnographic study of sexuality and youth suicide noted the positive portrayal of lesbian/gay/bisexual persons and issues in mass media, and were keenly aware that these representations were useful to individuals in reducing a 'sense of isolation and alienation' (Fenaughty and Harré 2003: 8). Future studies need to focus more on the complexity of representation and the ways in which identity formation and subjectivity occur within intricate relationships of audience reception, subjectification, normalisation and cultural demands for identity intelligibility.

The idea that media representations of lesbians and gay men provide not only visibility but can or should be framed as positive role models is a polemical position which ignores the ways in which role-modelling might, indeed, be a call to represent oneself simply through the one identity factor of sexuality (Fuss 1989: 116) rather than through the complexity that is human subjectivity. Where Olson and King (1995) have suggested that a key factor in identity stability is through reframing an idea of difference to a self-concept that has positive overtones, we might respond by asking what it is that will constitute positive and negative, different and sameness, good and bad representations in contemporary media environments and in contemporary youth culture. What is required, then, is that research which focuses on youth isolation as a risk factor needs to be cautious not only of repeating older notions of media invisibility that are no longer the social condition of queer youth in western countries, but also to remain critical of the media visibility/invisibility and positive/negative role models approaches in order to pay greater attention to the ways in which media representation is implicated in the constitution of sexual identity, vulnerability and suicidality as well as resilience and self-esteem.

Inaccessibility of media representation is not the only form of isolation from which we can draw a genealogical line from Rofes and Gibson through to more recent research. Isolation from other same-sex attracted peers is a major theme in discussions of queer youth suicide causal factors. While institutionally-available and geographically-located forms of peer support are enormously useful in overcoming a sense of isolation and mitigating suicide risk (Hatzenbuehler 2011), the most significant factor that has affected the rate, quality and form of isolation of younger non-heterosexual persons today is found in the development of new media and communications technologies – particularly the utilisation of the Internet as a communicative and participatory media tool. Digital media, particularly the Internet, are in part constitutive of new youth cultures and this very much includes the cultural context in which queer youth are raised today. Digital media forms are significant for being conceptually available to young people all their lives, unlike those born in the 1970s and early 1980s who witnessed the introduction of these technologies. But they are not merely a tool of which teenagers today have significant capacities to use, but in complex ways are both interrelated with youth culture and working to define it. As Rob Latham points out, these technologies represent 'a convergence of commodifying logics, in which subversive technology and resistant youth are mutually recuperated and exploited' (Latham 2002: 194).

Some studies have speculated that the relative social disapproval facing lesbians and gay men in some areas resulted in 'online queer communities' and other forms of digital social participation that cut across geographic bounds (Nip 2004: 412, 424). Certainly isolation of sexual minority youth from each other is no longer clearly demarcated in terms of a rural/urban distinction nor along an axis of age. In the era of the Internet there is no clear rural/urban divide that can be mapped onto an isolation/access distinction, nor an idea that younger persons are necessarily *more* isolated from each other than, say, gay men in their fifties and sixties. Indeed, geography and location now have much less to do with access to opportunities for inter-youth communication or opportunities to be located in a non-heterosexist environment; rather access is more often determined by the economics and politics of the Internet. To give just one example from East Asia young homosexuals in Taiwan and South Korea made significant early use of the Internet to meet each other and to develop a certain semi-privatised form of community that could operate in a politically heterosexist country (Berry and Martin 1998). Where these facilitated not only one-on-one interaction that constituted new forms of relationships or sexual encounters but also new forms of community, it became therefore necessary to avoid the presumption that the ideal community forum for sexually-diverse youth was lesbian/gay venues, support groups and other institutions that depend on geographic mobility, physical presence and particular tastes in music, dance, alcohol and leisure activities.

Further, the development of online communities and the Internet's uptake by queer youth suggest a tendency by younger sexually-diverse persons not to be 'thrust' into face-to-face activity, sociality, support or other activities, but to undertake these at their own pace. What is necessary, then, for ongoing research is to consider the ways in which 'coping mechanisms' might not only be fostered through digital communication, but ways that permit those mechanisms to become available at a pace suitable to each individual person in need. From accounts drawn from Internet homepages, websites, livejournals, social networks and other digital communication, it is becoming very clear that the formation of sexually-diverse sociality not only cuts across physical distance but involves the overcoming of a sense of isolation at much earlier ages than it had in the past (prior to online communication). This is evidence of a shift from the dominance of the concept of isolation as distance-from-place to a more complex and multiple formation of isolation and integration through the framework of point-to-point narrowcasting across a network. For Manuel Castells (1997: 320–321), the concept of the network is constitutive of the contemporary media spectator as a communicative and interactive *node* on an unstable, shifting and expanding network rather than as a *passive recipient* on a broadcast vector. This provides a more productive way in which to understand shifting contemporary viewing patterns for, particularly, younger persons today.

No matter the disciplinary background or field, future research into queer youth suicide that seeks to explore the isolation claim needs to account for the fact that queer youth *now* are not the queer youth *of the past*, and the social, cultural and technological changes over recent decades have markedly changed the meaning of isolation in general, and the specificity of isolation for non-heterosexual younger persons. This is not, of course, to suggest that this assumption of youth isolation be replaced with one in which it is assumed that this previously-stated causal factor in youth suicide is overcome. Rather, it is important to consider what isolation means today, how it can take on new forms and open new questions, whether the online and network morphologies of communication overcome isolation or produce new forms of exclusion, and whether the technologies that allow one to discretely communicate with other queer youth or better access representations of non-heterosexuality really work to overcome a sense of remoteness or loneliness for *all* queer youth.

Assumption Three: Coming Out is Beneficial in Overcoming Suicide Risk

The idea of 'coming out' or revealing one's non-normative sexuality is in contemporary western culture an expectation from every lesbian, gay man or bisexual. Coming out is part of a narrative of queer selfhood governed by conventions and probabilities that have become widely incorporated into the mythos around non-heterosexual experience (Saxey 2008: 2, 41). The conventions of coming out emerge in the recent history of queer sexual cultures and were originally motivated conjointly within the political and the personal. The rise of the Gay Liberation movement during the early 1970s in the United States, United Kingdom and Europe, saw the coming out story become a communicative form operating within a political and communitarian framework. In his *Homosexual Oppression and Liberation* (1971), Dennis Altman suggests that to come out meant defying the most basic and deep-seated norms of a society that sees itself as based exclusively on the heterosexual family structure. He also described it as essential for those practising non-heteronormative sexualities to come out as 'gay' in order to facilitate the development of a sense of community (Altman 1971: 141), for the sake not only of the political benefits of ostensible numbers, but for the personal gains made by being a recognisable part of a community. As the rhetoric once suggested, 'out of the closets, into the streets' (Altman 1971: 237) – a motif which conceptually governed the development of 1970s queer community and political movement in Europe, the United Kingdom, the United States and Australia.

Subsequent to this historical juncture, we have witnessed the vast proliferation of coming out stories in fiction, GLBT community newspapers and verbal forms, most of which are marked by motifs of pride, overcoming shame, political numbers, activism and community belonging. The Gay Liberation movement and its related discourses of anti-establishment, radical activism and opposition to heteronormative institutions and models lost dominance within queer culture from the mid-1980s adoption of a lesbian/gay civil rights political model that refrained from seeking to critique or undo heterosexuality (Cover 2005a), yet the compulsion to unquestioningly 'come out' has remained within queer discourse as a particular formation for coherent selfhood, social participation and belonging. Academic, policy and public discussion on queer youth suicide has had a multiplicitous relationship with the ideas of both coming out and of passing, arguing at times both for and against coming out.

Coming out has been a major element in much research and writing on queer-specific suicide, with frequent discussion of either the benefits of coming out or the debilitating risks understood to be related to longer-term 'passing' or 'closetedness'. Rather problematically, it has often been assumed in such work that the distinction between passing and coming out is a discrete one (rather than the reality of blurredness and the need to repeat the coming out process to many others throughout the course of life). At the same time, and often following earlier queer writing that promotes outness, coming out is usually presented as wholly positive, with an implicit indication that passing is a failure. In Gibson's 1989 account of queer youth suicide, closetedness, passing or a failure to declare one's sexuality openly to peers and families was depicted as an added stressor that increased suicide risk:

> If closed about why they are, they may be able to 'pass' as 'straight' in their communities while facing a tremendous internal struggle to understand and accept themselves. Many gay youth choose to maintain a facade and hide their true feelings and identity, leading a double life, rather than confront situations too painful for them. They live in constant fear of being found out and recognized as gay (Gibson 1989: 112).

In this framework, passing or hiding one's identity can subject a younger person to homophobic attitudes and remarks by unknowing family members and peers, leading to emotional problems, withdrawal from sociality, chronic depression and despair (Gibson 1989: 113). Ultimately, Gibson described the identity development process of queer youth through a linear pattern of milestones and crises: beginning with a pre-pubertal self-awareness of difference from heterosexual norms, followed by an awareness of attraction to persons of the same sex, awareness of not fitting the 'social script' of heterosexuality, a period of crisis through self-denial or internalised homophobia, and finally coming out through public declarations. It was, however, implied that identity stability and overcoming of despair is achieved only through taking this final step (Gibson 1989: 115–122, 138). Although coming out was depicted here as involving its own risks, a tacit imperative to come out is given as the solution and resolution to that risk, as the eventual final step in overcoming the majority of obstacles facing queer youth as seen at the time Gibson was writing. The compulsion to come out and the early research which indicated that it has both political and personal benefits is derived from the idea that to name oneself as lesbian/gay publicly or openly produces the stabilisation of selfhood through acts of self-disclosure and self-labelling (Savin-Williams 1996: 155) often within a framework of overcoming of silence and shame (Rofes 1983: 28) and as an act of sociality through the attempt to articulate similitude and thus public membership of a queer community.

The emphasis on coming out draws at least partly on a North American identity discourse that posits integrity, honesty and openness, at times regardless of the risks that might be involved or claims to privacy (Cover 2000: 81–83). Contemporary political cultures of governance are willing to give a non-heterosexual person equal opportunity, but only as long as that person is (1) open about their sexuality if questioned, and (2) makes that sexuality invisible if so required (Bersani 1995: 67). This is a double-bind that, within the same logic of suicide research, leads to an ambivalent articulation as to how and where to find that middle-ground between outness and passing, between honesty and invisibility, the negotiation of which is a social requirement specific to queer persons. The notion of coming out has at times been depicted as a positive milestone, often a proxy for more complex understandings of identify formation or what has sometimes been referred to as 'gay-related development' (Friedman et al. 2008: 899). Where a declaration of non-heterosexuality as a milestone effectively 'works' for older adolescents and adults, this has frequently been translated as a positive event for *any* adolescent, thereby ignoring the fact that for younger teenagers and youth in particular circumstances or environments the push for coming out does not necessarily have a positive effect, nor does it necessarily and automatically produce resilience.

The benefits of coming out have, however, been debated to some degree in subsequent queer youth suicide literature. For one set of writers, remaining closeted or failing to come out or disclose one's non-heterosexuality is seen to be damaging, dangerous and exacerbates suicide risks. For example, McAndrew and Warne argue that "passing" can be detrimental to mental well-being' whereby an inability to integrate a sexual self with broader life compromises mental health, leads to inner conflict, internalisation of homophobia and a desire to 'destroy that part of themselves' (McAndrew and Warne 2010: 96). In that context, being out assumes not only honesty and openness, but a singular identity that is both public and private; by corollary, passing is that which is posited as a damaging and risky multiplicity of selfhood. Where passing is posited here as a risk, it is perceived as leading not only to (self-) isolation but also to an instability of mental health and wellbeing. Other writers have likewise argued that there is a risk of low self-esteem, anxiety and depression in being isolated through not being able to discuss sexuality with one's family, school, peers and friends, effectively hiding in 'multiple spheres of life' (Mishna et al. 2009: 1605). In some studies, coming out has been linked with positive self-esteem among queer youth, resulting in the sort of resilience and self-efficacy seen to operate as protective factors (Crisp and McCave 2007: 406).

However, there is an argument that while coming out might be highly beneficial for many youth – and studies of broad queer youth populations have generally shown this – the fact of being out can be an added risk factor, leading to either new or different forms of isolation, harassment or subsidiary risks such as family rejection and homelessness (Davis, Saltzburg and Locke 2009: 1031). In fact, this counter-argument was made very early on in the history of writings on queer suicide. Although he discussed some of the benefits of coming out, Rofes did point to the ways in which the idea of coming out had been mythically produced as a cure-all. Undoubtedly motivated by having witnessed the suicides of many adult gay men *after* publicly declaring a gay sexuality in line with the political motivation to do so in the 1970s, and writing for a targeted queer community audience, he found that the community push for coming out uncritically held too many expectations while disregarding the risks (Rofes 1983: 66). As he put it:

> Perhaps no myth is so dangerous to lesbians and gay men as the myth that claims that the act of 'coming out' as a gay person provides a person with a margin of insurance against self-hatred or self-destructiveness. This myth leads many lesbians and gay men to believe that, once able to be open about their homosexuality, their personal problems and anxieties will all fall by the wayside. Coming out is looked on as a miracle cure, a salvation from all shortcomings and malaise (Rofes 1983: 49).

Certainly maintaining closetedness into adulthood has been shown to be an unhealthy strategy adding to ongoing, permanent stressors as the performance of passing becomes more complex over time (Hegna and Wichstrøm 2007: 34), although among the relatively young the heightened risk of losing friends, being harassed or bullied is of much greater concern, particularly in terms of producing the conditions for suicidal behaviours (Mishna et al. 2009: 1607). The uncritical assumption that closetedness is a risk and coming out a solution in much suicide research has tended to lack age-specificity. Some recent work on youth suicide and isolation has pointed out that openly articulating non-heterosexual identity or behaviours at too early an age rather than delaying it 'to a safer time' may indeed be a significant factor in creating the social context in which suicide becomes thinkable (Zhao et al. 2010: 111).

As a coping strategy undertaken by queer youth, passing has in fact been investigated in older sociological studies of non-normative sexuality (Edwards 1996: 338). Warren referred to the necessity of character management and social presentation of one's self as a necessary coping strategy for marginalised youth and depicted this, in contrast to the idea that passing is dishonest, as 'avoidance without hiding' (Warren 1974: 94); that is, as a slightly more complex concept than can fit neatly in a paradigmatic in/out dichotomy. Troiden likewise referred to it as 'blending', suggesting that people in coping situations 'blend act in gender-appropriate ways and neither announce nor deny their homosexual identities to nonhomosexual others' (Troiden 1988: 56). As a strategy for coping with situations in which one would otherwise be *more vulnerable* if non-normative sexuality was revealed, there is certainly nothing unethical or dishonest about passing, nor is there a clear indication that remaining in this semi-closeted state is necessarily a greater risk factor than being otherwise open about non-normative sexual identity, desires or behaviours.

What is problematic, then, in some suicide research is the unquestioned assumption that coming out is necessary, that remaining closeted is an unnecessary stressor, or that for some younger persons obscuring a non-normative sexual identity, behaviours or experiences is not only necessary but might be beneficial. Additionally, the positing of outness and closetedness over-simplifies the ways in which young persons perceive and articulate identity and desire in public and private contexts. In other words, there is a need for the notion of coming out to be understood as beneficial *variably*, and for intervention, counselling and advice to ensure that there is a suitable counter to the social pressure that comes most often from media and queer community to out oneself. The compulsion to come out rather than to pass has been further problematised by some recent research which has indicated that coming out in the very early teen years is associated with significantly greater risk of suicidal behaviours (Suicide Prevention Resource Centre 2008: 20, Rosario Schrimshaw and Hunter 2008: 279), thought to be the result of having fewer coping strategies for dealing with stigma (Remafedi, Farrow and Deisher 1991: 874). Some writers have indicated that this may be related to 'pinning down your identity at a time when you are not certain of what you are' (Hegna 2007: 591), which is of course reinforced by the articulation of sexual identity to those who then go on to maintain surveillance over the veracity of that identity statement. Others have found that early identification and declaration of non-heterosexuality have led to increased experience of violence and harassment, thus increasing the risk of suicidal behaviours (Friedman et al. 2008: 892). Finally, there is also some evidence that the younger the adolescent at the time of identification and coming out, the less likely that person is to have access to supportive peers, thereby increasing the risk of suicide in the face of explicit or implicit harassment (Rutter and Soucar 2002: 294, Cloud 2005). The considerable shift in age of declaring a non-normative sexuality, with increasing evidence of younger persons coming out in the earlier teens rather than the early twenties (Cloud 2005), therefore has some considerable implications for how the notion of coming out is addressed in queer youth suicide literature, prevention techniques and early intervention.

Assumption Four: Hetero/Homo Sexual Identity is Innate

Although I address the issue of identity, fluidity and diversity of sexuality beyond the commonly-perceived dichotomy notion of hetero/homo sexual categories in later chapters, it is important here to acknowledge that a considerable amount of research and academic writing on queer youth suicide rests on a number of presumptions about sexuality itself. These might be explored further as a means of teasing out some of the difficulties and risks related to identity development and stabilisation around issues related to the fraught area of sex and sexuality. In suicide research, the categorisation of available sexualities is almost consistently as heterosexual and homosexual (with bisexual and transgender identities typically added to the latter term as a coalitional GLBTQ or 'queer'). What tends to be presumed in the vast majority of research is that these are the *only* ways in which sexuality can be categorised, and this is often the starting point for statistical data gathering and comparative research around different risk factors for heterosexual versus non-heterosexual youth (Walls, Freedenthal and Wisneski 2008: 21).

Yet, since the early 1990s, queer theory has taken to task the self-evident, common logic of the 'naturalness' of the binary opposition of heterosexuality and homosexuality and the idea that sexual and gender identities are innate, fixed and unproblematic. Eve Sedgwick critiqued the hetero/homo binary, pointing out that while it is the dominant means by which sexuality is categorised in contemporary western culture, there are alternative ways of framing sexualities, desires and erotics that do not fit neatly in the paradigm of same-sex or opposite-sex attraction and, in some cases, may not be about the gender of the persons involved at all (Sedgwick 1990: 35). The very idea of heterosexual identity or homosexual identity is, rather, historical, discursively-produced and has come to appear natural and timeless. Other queer theorists have furthered this critique, indicating that other ways of thinking about or categorising sexuality – including those which might be more sensible to a younger teenager than 'gay' or 'straight' – are suppressed and made silent by the monolithic nature of the hetero/homo binary (Hennessy 1994: 86–87). Where this produces risk for suicidality is for those who are unable to identify or perform identities which are in accord with either heterosexuality or homosexuality and, rather, experience an alternative form of erotics that remains unrepresentable or as an inarticulable residue figured socially as incoherent and unintelligible (Cover 2011).

At the same time, the idea of a sexual *identity* itself as an inner core self which directs and projects desire and sexual behaviour has been problematised (Butler 1990). Through the work of Judith Butler and others, queer theory has allowed us to de-naturalise the idea that sexual orientation or identity is innate, fixed and timeless for each individual and, further, that there might be better ways of thinking about sexuality and desire than through the notion of it emanating from an inner identity. For example, the theory of performativity that Butler introduced in *Gender Trouble* (1990) opened the possibility not only for thinking about gendered and sexual identities as the effect of culturally-signified acts, behaviours and performances, but also pointed to the ways in which the discursive governance of such acts leaves the identities constituted by those performances as contingent and available for resignification and subversion. None of that is to say that heterosexual and homosexual identities are not real or meaningful to the majority of sexual subjects today, only that (1) they are not natural or foundational but produced in contemporary culture through available discourses; (2) that there are other ways of categorising sexuality that are also culturally-produced and might have a better 'fit' for some vulnerable younger persons, although the discourses through which these alternatives are produces are often unavailable or marginal; (3) that heterosexuality and homosexuality as binary distinctions and as categories of sexual identity may not be meaningful to *all* youth.

Despite this twenty year-old critique, a broad range of research and writing on queer youth suicide has tended to leave the binary distinction of heterosexuality and homosexuality intact, as well as the expectation that youth who overcome risks in adolescence will or must stabilise an identity as either straight or queer (lesbian, gay or bisexual), which of course will not always be the case. Part of the reason for this continued reliance on the dominant binary understanding of sexuality is a failure of interdisciplinary communication between the humanities in which queer theory has developed its poststructuralist critique of sexuality and the social and health sciences approaches to youth studies and youth suicide. Of course, such failure to engage in interdisciplinary terms is not deliberate, but the result of the historical manner in which research disciplinarity with its primary assumptions, methods and exclusions has developed over time and continues to demarcate forms of knowledge and authorised approaches to understanding appointed objects of inquiry.

What can be found in the majority of suicide research throughout the 1990s and the early 2000s, then, is the assumption of the intrinsic 'truth' of (hetero/homo) sexual identity categorisation which assumes a simple and uniform process of identity development, as well as a classification of risks for queer youth that does not account for the broad diversity in how sexuality is thought, made meaningful or performed throughout different stages in adolescence. Much of this comes from the unproblematised and uncritical use of the notion of 'sexual orientation', which assumes that while there may be differences in how one produces an identity, there is a natural drive or inclination to direct sexual desire towards either one gender or the other. This assumption has some considerable impact on the ways in which studies of queer youth suicidality are constructed, including statistical sampling methods. Statistical measurement of rates has been a significant part of much suicide research, often regardless of whether a study is grounded in clinical, psychological or sociological approaches, and this has important implications for policy and funding of both research and preventative measures. However, queer youth suicide research statistics have been problematic from the beginning. Methodological problems such as comparing samples of queer youth taken from health and crisis centres with youth from general high school populations, in addition to differential definitions of suicide, ideation, intent and behaviour, have made cross-comparisons of heterosexual youth and homosexual youth problematic, particularly throughout the 1980s and 1990s (Rutter and Soucar 2002: 291). Hershberger and colleagues' reporting of survey response results, for example, made use of participants belonging to metropolitan lesbian/gay youth groups in a range of North American cities (Hershberger, Pilkington and D'Augelli 1997: 485–486). The authors acknowledged the recruitment as a shortcoming of the study, although what remained uninvestigated in their presentation of high suicide attempt rates (c. forty per cent of participants) was the probability that recruiting participants from those who attended youth groups is not necessarily representative of the broader queer youth population. The lack of rigour that marked, particularly, earlier foundational studies in queer youth suicide was once excusable as the work contributed to bringing the problem to light; today, a problem of methodology remains in much continuing work that fails to bring a more critical theorisation of sexuality to bear on the process of recruitment and sampling.

As importantly, such statistical research has tended to begin with the binary categorisation of sexuality as the primary form of categorisation and as the starting point of recruitment and often divorcing sexuality from other contextual factors,. By analysing those who have been categorised by survey or recruitment as homosexual/bisexual, or by comparing that group with heterosexual youth, problematically leaves out three possibilities for a more nuanced investigation of sexuality-related suicide. Firstly, this involves finding out what forms of resilience or vulnerability may exist for those who are *not* categorisable through the standardised and normalised dichotomy of sexual orientation. Secondly, by undertaking research that does not rely on single-dimensional inquiries into sexual orientation leaves little opportunity to account for differences between identity and sexual behaviour. HIV prevention research made such distinctions in the 1990s in order to target non-gay 'men who have sex with men', although as Igartua and colleagues (2009: 607) point out, because many adolescents are not yet sexually active, this particular distinction is not necessarily a useful one. Finally, avoiding the idea that hetero/homo sexual categorisation presents a timeless 'truth' of sexuality helps to overcome the problematic fact that some analyses of youth suicides have 'read' cases through the common framework of normative hetero/homo sexualities, and determined that suicide can be the result of a refusal to come-to-terms with *really* being lesbian or gay in a positive framework (e.g., McDaniel, Purcell and D'Augelli 2001: 96–97, Battin 1995: 12, Macdonald and Cooper 1998: 23–24, Dorais 2004: 24, King et al. 2008: 83). It is important here to avoiding dismissing the possibility that young queer persons might perceive sexuality in alternative ways, through multiplicities or in ways for which they do not necessarily have the full range of language to express intelligibly, including in research interviews.

Although Savin-Williams (2001: 5) made the point as early as 2001 that traditional empirical and theoretical paradigms that 'narrowly define sexual-minority adolescents in terms of those who adopt a culturally defined sexual identity label' need to be reconsidered, it has only been in the most recent literature that we see some critical examination of sexual categorisation and the role it might play in producing suicidal behaviours. For example, the Suicide Prevention Resource Centre's *Suicide Risk and Prevention for Lesbian, Gay, Bisexual, and Transgender Youth* (2008), notes most ethnographic and quantitative studies on queer youth suicide have required participants to self-categorise a sexual self-identity, occasionally adding the categories of 'questioning' or 'unsure' as descriptors. It is pointed out that these categories are not always meaningful in terms of the range of sexual expression among young persons, and that there is some value in asking about *behaviours* rather than orientation. I would add: not just of behaviours but, in addressing the very young and inexperienced, of desires and attractions. Zhao and colleagues have, more recently, presented a critical approach to queer youth suicide and vulnerability which expressly takes to task the assumptions of sexual identity as homogeneous, innate and dichotomous (Zhao et al. 2010: 110–111). By undoing identity from sexual attraction/behaviour, they found that adolescents who perceive themselves as heterosexual but engage in same-sex attraction or behaviour were *not* at greater risk of suicide than those who expressed both heterosexual identity and exclusive heterosexual attraction

(Zhao et al. 2010: 110). However, their participants who expressed GLB, queer and unsure sexual identities did indeed demonstrate increased suicide risk, suggesting that attraction and behaviour might not be the most significant factor in suicide ideation, but that risk and vulnerability might be better understood to be located in self-perception of having a non-normative identity (Zhao et al. 2010: 111). Most significantly, Zhao and colleagues have thereby concluded that the more simplistic dichotomisation of sexual orientation 'may not accurately capture the nature of risk related to GLB status' (Zhao et al. 2010: 111). This usefully points to the complexity of identity, the need to separate the performance of identity from the expression of non-heterosexuality, and the possibility that contemporary ways in which queer identity is constructed, constituted and performed may have the most significant part to play in enculturating vulnerability and suicide risk – a point I take up in more detail in Chapter 4.

Conclusion

None of this is to suggest that the research, studies, books and papers addressed here are anything but extremely valuable contributions to understanding and tackling the problem of queer youth suicide. Rather, it is to point to the ways in which the four assumptions that emerged in early studies continue to govern and sometimes constrain the available ways of thinking about queer youth suicide in academic research and, undoubtedly, in other areas of public deliberation. Ultimately, these four assumptions tend to cut a swathe across the field of research, whether studies are undertaken through sociological approaches, psychiatry, social psychology, epidemiology and paediatrics. Much of the reason for this is through citation of previous studies in a field in which the research has, for many years, been remarkably scant.

There is thus a continuing need to develop alternative thinking about suicide risk as a means by which to shed some light on the markedly complex social and cultural conditions through which youth sexual development and youth suicide risks are produced. What queer youth suicide research stands to gain from a critique that takes to task the common assumptions around sexuality and identity is an opportunity to expand our understanding of queer youth suicide by thinking in alternative or imaginative ways about sexuality and identity. This might mean incorporating approaches to queer youth suicide which begin with the idea that younger persons do not necessarily fit neatly into straight/queer distinctions and that a healthy young person might indeed be someone who fits more neatly into fluid, complex and changing self-perceptions of sexuality rather than a categorised identity. At the same time, examining the ways in which the imposition of monolithic heterosexual/homosexual norms in contemporary culture – rather than focusing on heteronormativity alone – might carry increased risks for vulnerable youth can be achieved through an approach which critically takes to task these four of those categorical assumptions.

Chapter 3

It Gets Better? Online Representations of Hope, Vulnerability and Resilience

A Google search on the phrase 'queer youth suicide' produces over 48,000 results; the phrase 'gay youth suicide' receives more than 60,000 and 'gay suicide' over 100,000. Compared with the relatively scarce references to sexuality-related suicide in popular film and television, news journalism and academic research, there has clearly been a massive surge in either the production or re-circulation of knowledge on this topic afforded by the Internet and digital media. Of course, not everything found on queer youth suicide online is positive, on-topic, provides resources or sympathises with the concerns of non-heterosexual youth, as there is some considerable anti-queer rhetoric to be found that either refutes the idea of queer youth suicide as a social problem, promotes it as the best outcome for sick individuals or discusses it in thoughtless, inappropriate and sometimes harmful ways. There are sites, however, that present original research, summarise existing research or link to many of the articles and books discussed in the previous chapters. The speedy availability of such a vast number of texts, writings, comments and ideas on the topic is likely to have an ongoing impact not only on how we understand and discuss queer youth suicide, but in terms of how resources for prevention and intervention are provided.

One thing that the advent of the Internet and, particularly, Web 2.0 participatory and co-creative online culture has produced is a significant shift in how knowledge on queer youth suicide is generated and disseminated. A number of sites, often broadly dealing with youth suicide in general, provide resources for counsellors, family and friends dealing with a potentially suicidal younger queer person, presenting links to credible organisations in different countries that host intervention programs. Many other sites online have allowed a new set of voices on the topic to be heard, including those of younger persons who have survived suicide and can thereby relate some of their experiences outside of the traditional mediated forms of news, documentary or ethnographic research. This is a change from the older models of media in which a range of factors such as newsworthiness, perceptions of public opinion, editorial approaches, ratings and other elements governing the dissemination of knowledge in broadcast and print now compete with narrowcast communication forms in which 'individuals and smaller groups have the potential to describe and publish their interpretations of the world' (Luders 2008: 697). Some sites such as, for example, *Darren's Boyfriend's Gay/Suicide Info Web Page* (http://darrenbf.tripod.com/index2.html) make use of this capacity by providing an account of the experience of losing a teenaged partner to suicide. More than a tribute page, it seeks to provide information for others who may stumble on it in a search:

> This page is written for the early teenager who has perhaps discovered he is gay, and doesn't feel too comfortable about it. It also has information for homophobes, suicidal people, and people who have had to deal with someone who has committed suicide. It is also a tribute to Darren.

Directed at queer youth, it crosses over between presenting homage and providing a set of resources.

The Trevor Project, related to the 1994 short film *Trevor* discussed in Chapter 1, is perhaps one of the more prominent online sites dealing with queer youth suicide. *The Trevor Project* delivers services to queer youth in the form of a United States telephone lifeline, an online question-and-answer forum and a confidential online instant messaging service for youth in crisis. It also provides a social networking community for queer youth and engages in research, policy development, advisory and liaison work. Founded at the time the film was first aired on HBO television in 1998, the organisation sought to fill a gap in resource and service provision by providing support to queer youth directly. Available through phone, online and chat services, it also provides online resources for educators, counsellors and parents as well as web seminars (webinars) and further reading resources. Significant in the constitution of queer youth suicide knowledges through the site is the focus on social and environmental factors that impact on non-heterosexual youth, making steps to ensure that sexual orientation or gender identity are themselves not viewed as risk factors contrary to popular assumptions (http://www.thetrevorproject.org/survivalkit).

Finally, there is the video blogging site *It Gets Better* (http://www.itgetsbetter.org) begun by columnist Dan Savage in response to the September/October 2010 spate of reported queer student suicides in the United States. This site is perhaps one of the more significant advances in how queer youth suicide knowledges have changed and developed as a result of digital participatory culture. The site hosts more than a thousand video contributions, many from queer adults who seek to provide hope for younger persons by showing that queer adulthood is markedly different from the experiences of harassment, bullying, loneliness or surveillance experienced by queer youth in school and family environments. This is among the first widely-available communicative media form to address directly queer youth on issues related to suicide, and the first to draw on lived experiences as a means by which to provide resources for queer youth resilience. The fact that these experiences are related through video-logs (vlogs) provides the texts with a sense of authenticity and a framework which often addresses youth directly on the topic of suicidality.

This chapter does not intend to undertake the mammoth task of untangling the hundreds of thousands of sites that mention or discuss queer youth suicide. Rather, it focuses solely on the *It Gets Better* site for two reasons. Firstly, as a response to the September and October 2010 suicides, this site comes from outside the fields of academic writing, preventative policies and interventional counselling, thereby presenting a new angle on queer suicidality. Secondly, by fostering the creation, distribution and accessibility of video comments from those who have reached adulthood and seek to provide information on what queer adulthood is like, it allows a significant number of new voices to contribute to preventative measures by demonstrating first-hand that there is reason for troubled, vulnerable and at-risk queer youth to maintain a sense of hope and thus not fall into despair or hopelessness that exacerbates suicide risk.

I will begin by giving some background on the *It Gets Better* project and showing the ways in which this fits with new thinking on the provision of resources online for at-risk younger persons. I then want to explore three of the ways in which the site and its aims operate to frame the issue of queer youth suicide and younger queer persons themselves. Firstly, the site aims to help younger persons overcome a sense of hopelessness – hope being a key concept in how we culturally perceive suicidality. By positioning queer youth as lacking in hope for the future, the site constructs the notion of youth within a linear pattern of development towards a sense of stability and normalcy as queer adult, which has important implications for how queerness is perceived in cultural and political terms. Secondly, the site operates to depict queer youth – somewhat generally, although certainly not intentionally – as vulnerable, at-risk and as victims, producing an overly-simplistic dual dichotomy of youth-vulnerability and adult-resilience. Queer youth are, of course, vulnerable to others in a continuingly heteronormative environment, and this is frequently exacerbated by the ways in which the culture of school and other institutions act to constitute queer as sometimes-legitimate and sometimes-invalid through intensive peer surveillance. However, how that vulnerability is represented, the extent to which *all* or *most* younger queer persons are shown to be victims has, again, significant implications for the ways in which subjects actively produce the resilience to 'get through' to the imagined 'better times' of adulthood. Finally, I will address some of the ways in which resilience is depicted as an attribute of selfhood that must be 'acquired', and how this has the effect of individualising the problem of queer youth suicide into a situation which, on the one hand, interprets the social problem of heterosexism as acts of individual bullying and, on the other, presents the building of qualities of resilience as the individual responsibility of queer youth.

The 'It Gets Better' Project

Columnist and author Dan Savage, with his partner, developed and uploaded a YouTube video in response to the spate of reported queer student suicides in September 2010. According to the *It Gets Better* website – which has subsequently encouraged and gathered together tens of thousands of similar videos – Savage's intention was to 'inspire hope for young people facing harassment' and to create 'a personal way for supporters everywhere to tell LGBT youth that ... it does indeed get better' (http://www.itgetsbetter.org/pages/ about-it-gets-better-project/). According to the site, there have been over thirty-five million video viewings, and the project has received video submissions from celebrities, activists, politicians, including U.S. President Barrack Obama and Secretary of State Hilary Clinton, as well as staff from a number of organisations such as Google and The Gap. *It Gets Better* is significant in the online provision of information about queer youth suicide in that this occurs not through older-models of digital text distribution and retrieval, but through a Web 2.0 environment; that is, digital media forms such as social networking sites, Wikis and YouTube that take advantage of networked interactivity to create participatory sites with a significant emphasis on audio-video production, sharing and collaborative discussion. In doing so, *It Gets Better* allows the discourses of queer youth suicide to be re-framed in terms more accessible to younger generations and for new voices to emerge and contribute to the broader knowledge framework on the topic.

In several ways, the site serves as a prevention and intervention resource for queer youth suicidality. Links on its opening page are categorised under the line 'I need help', providing a connection to the video list which can be searched by tagged keywords, as well as a resources page directing queer youth to external crisis services. The resources, however, are limited to *The Trevor Project* which has partnered with *It Gets Better*, giving phone numbers (for North America) and website links as well as a few inspirational phrases about the need not to feel ashamed of being different from others among one's school peers, family or community.

The use of the Internet for provision of help to at-risk groups is not new, as older Internet groups and, previously, newsgroups acted as communities of information, resource-sharing and mutual support. The effectiveness of such sites for the reduction of suicide is not without criticism, particularly from professionals who may feel that risks are heightened by the provision of inaccurate information or the amateur diagnoses by others of serious problems such as clinical depression. This has resulted in calls for considerably more work on how professionals can intervene with such groups and sites and engage users (Martin 2006: 3). Targeted sites such as the Kids Helpline have developed interfaces that will help to engage younger persons in the delivery of counselling services through real-time, text-based chat between individual counsellors and clients, freeing the provision of counselling and resource-sharing from geographical and temporal restrictions, although creating new barriers such as the inaccessibility of vocal, tone and facial cues in the counselling process (Beattie et al. 2006: 43–44). Such online service provision has been found to attract new clients who ordinarily would not seek professional help for suicide and self-harm risks, but make use of the sense of safety, anonymity and control provided through a networked communication environment (Beattie et al. 2006: 44).

Online, one-way information and resource provision is significantly different from online counselling and the use of forums, although there is little knowledge as to how younger persons make use of these sites and resources and if they assist in developing resilience. However, there has been considerable speculation that online resources provide new opportunities to reach queer youth who are at-risk and who might ordinarily not have an opportunity to access similar, non-digital resources. Silenzio and colleagues (2009: 469) have noted that a very high proportion of queer adolescents report that the Internet has been a significantly important resource and that this provides a highly useful platform for the targeted provision of prevention and intervention resources. The perceived anonymity of Internet searching and gathering of information (Caplan 2003: 629) for self-help activities of younger queer youth is, of course, safer and more readily accessible than older models of seeking out help and resources for queer youth issues through books and articles in libraries (Mehra and Braquet 2006: 19). This is not to say, of course, that there aren't new risks through this form of information-provision. In addition to the lack of professional oversight, forums, searches and sites can include malicious, negative commentary that might exacerbate risks of self-harm, as well as the fact that anonymity is perceived but not always actually the case, given the ways in which computer networks are easily capable of tracking Internet histories, potentially revealing such searches and site access in ways that could put a younger person in jeopardy in a home or school environment.

As resources, the *It Gets Better* videos are thus the production mostly of non-professionals. It is worth noting that not all the videos uploaded are by people who have been through the experiences of those they are addressing, and this includes a significant number of straight uploaders. Among them, of course, are politicians, many celebrities from film, television and Broadway as well as staff working in high-profile corporations in the United States and elsewhere. There are also a number of videos uploaded by younger straight persons who are not in positions that can generally yet effect policy – at least not individually. While such videos are obviously well-meaning and do demonstrate the widespread feeling among non-queer youth that bullying, victimisation, discrimination and ostracisation of queer persons are not acceptable, there is the risk of their being understood as patronising, reinforcing a sense of victimhood demarcated by queerness. This is particularly the case in which a young straight person, however well-intentioned, will comment 'knowingly' that life will get better for queer persons. For example, Jessi from Michigan provides a textual introduction to her video (http://www.itgetsbetter.org/video/entry/5jxq5kcxfxc/) which states:

> Hi! I'm a straight 16 year old high school student, and I've been wanting to upload one of these videos for such a long time … If you EVER feel like you need anyone, you can call the Trevor Project hotline at this number – 1-866-4-U-TREVOR 1-866-4-8-87386. Also, if you would ever like to talk to me, you can send me a message on facebook … I will be here to listen to your story. I would like to share this with you LGBT community to let you know that there is so much more to life out there!

In several ways, it is somewhat moving that this young person offers to reach out to unknown queer persons and, presumably for lack of politically-sound vocabulary, seeks to offer comfort to non-heterosexual youth. Importantly, there is a coalitional element explained in Jessi's video in that, as a Thai-American, she is able to articulate an empathetic connection with those who feel they do not fit in with the perceived majority or those who, like her, have been on the receiving-end of bullying. At the same time, however, there are problematic elements in such offers of availability which can masquerade as a form of counselling and which, in extreme cases of queer youth with clinical depression, requires the expertise to know when to refer to professional support. This is not, of course, to suggest that such uploads and offers of support were the major purpose of the site; in most cases these well-meaning videos were motivated by a desire to demonstrate care and concern for queer issues and persons in a manner that was readily-available and in the language of the *It Gets Better* project. Ultimately, the *It Gets Better* site provides one of the best resources for fostering resilience through first-hand accounts that are neither fictional nor mediated through counselling or other intervention or prevention discourses but through presenting actual to-camera faces and voices discussing experiences that will be both recognisable in some cases and unique in others.

Hope and Hopelessness

The primary motivation behind the *It Gets Better* project is to present the reality that no matter how unbearable or painful life is, a queer life will be – in the future – and as an adult – a liveable life. The tag-line of the site is: 'Many LGBT youth can't picture what their lives might be like as openly gay adults. They can't imagine a future for themselves. So let's show them what our lives are like, let's show them what the future may hold in store for them' (http://www.itgetsbetter.org/). The future is marked as that which a younger person should anticipate positively. Hope for the future is frequently presented as the anticipation of an end to school days. In the primary video of the site, Dan Savage's partner Terry describes his school experiences:

> My school was pretty miserable … I was picked on mercilessly in school. People were really cruel to me. I was bullied a lot. Beat up, thrown against walls and lockers and windows; stuffed into bathroom stalls. People shit on my car, people scratched my car, broke my windows. And my parents went in once to talk to the school administrators to talk about the harassment I was getting at school, and they basically said: 'If you look that way, talk that way, walk that way, act that way, then there's nothing we can do to help your son.'

But hope is immediately invoked:

> Honestly, things got better the day I left highschool. I didn't see the bullies every
> day, I didn't see the people who harassed me every day, I didn't have to see the
> school administrators who would do nothing about it every day. Life instantly
> got better (http://www.itgetsbetter.org/pages/about-it-gets-better-project/)

Similarly, a young woman who identifies as gay, in her late teens and currently
at school, made the following comments about the reasons why the experience
of being in school is painful and the temporal point at which one might expect
existence to get better:

> I'm here to say it will get better, especially when you're out of highschool …
> Because once you get out of highschool people really don't care who you like.
> When you're in highschool you have to deal – and in most schools, in elementary
> school – you have to deal with ignorant people who like to stab other people
> with their insecurities. You have a whole body of people who live off of the pain
> they can inflict on others. I'm gay, and I'm open, and I'm pretty sure just about
> everyone in my school knows I am gay, I have a girlfriend at school, we are both
> open, and we kiss and we hug, and people see, and they give us that stare like
> they're seeing an alien or something they've never seen before in their life. And
> we just laugh, and we think it's stupid to have such a reaction. We're human too,
> and you are human just like them … But I promise you it does get better, and you
> will be amazed at how great your life will turn out to be if you hang in there for
> a little while, and you walk through this rough patch with your head held high.
> Just keep your head up, don't let their stupid comments and opinions bring you
> down (http://www.itgetsbetter.org/video/entry/hd1kcgxzd_g/).

Such comments present a picture of school life, whereby the institutional
norms of secondary schools that depend so heavily on surveillance, discriminative
norms, economies of secrecy and disclosure permit bullying and ostracisation
to flourish and become, then, the site of hopelessness in what to many appears
at the time as a period of never-ending permanency. Indeed, teen-aged life has
often been figured in geographic terms as a kind of hopeless banishment from
the realities that are yet to come: Eve Sedgwick referred to this period as 'that
long Babylonian exile known as queer childhood' (Sedgwick 1993a: 4). The
emphatic focus on the institutional environment of highschool rather than family,
rural towns, closetedness, religious discourse or feelings of isolation is remarkably
important in changing the contemporary way in which the social situation of queer
youth suicide has been depicted. The discourse of the *It Gets Better* project and
contributions makes 'school' its object, and effectively separates the site of school
from other contextual and geographic factors such as rural and urban distinctions,
positing the institutional culture of schooling as predominantly similar from a
queer youth perspective.

One thing that has occurred in the public discourse on queer youth suicide
over the past two or three years is a new focus on bullying as that which makes a

young queer person's life miserable, lacking in hope and more likely to end early in suicide. Much of the discourse of bullying was produced in news articles in late 2010, particularly around the suicide of North American Rutgers University student, Tyler Clementi who jumped from the George Washington Bridge after his roommate remotely used a webcam to capture footage of Clementi during an intimate encounter with another man. The footage was digitally-distributed and caused humiliation (Foderaro 2010). News stories on other sexuality-related suicides at the time focused on taunting in school, bullying and humiliation as causal factors (McKinley 2010, Italie 2010, Tomazin 2010). A very large number of the *It Gets Better* videos refer to bullying as *the* social problem which establishes a desire to flee from intolerable pain through suicide. Bullying is, indeed, a problem related to youth suicide, defined usually as a subset of aggressive, unprovoked and repetitive behaviour intended to cause physical and/or psychological pain to the recipient (Kalliotis 2000: 50). While current research has noted that it is not yet possible 'to make causal inferences or conclusions that experiencing bullying increases suicide risks' (Kim and Leventhal 2008: 151), anti-queer bullying has known effects including psychological distress (Espelage and Swearer 2008: 157) and reduced social well-being (Hegna and Wichstrøm 2007: 35). Recent research has explored the relationship between homophobia and bullying, showing how homophobic epithets directed as abuse at any younger person are part of the standard media of bullying (Espelage and Swearer 2008: 155). Other researchers have suggested the opposite: that homophobia motivates bullying, conceptualising bullying as the mechanism for enacting aggressively heterosexist social attitudes (Mishna et al. 2009: 1599). Regardless of the causal relationship between the two, in depicting school as the site of anti-queer bullying, the *It Gets Better* project represents queer youth as losing hope of escape from the intolerable pain of bullying in its *persistence* and *repetition*.

However, the site's purpose is to show that escape from such environments is not only possible but should be expected. In what way, then, is this life that comes after school better, and how is that better-ness depicted by the contributors to the site? In the founding video, Savage and his partner describe a list of benefits of being out of school, including their relationship, the ways in which their families engage positively with the relationship, the adoption at birth of their son who is now thirteen years-old, their travels as a family to Europe, the pleasure taken in sociality with close friends. Finally, it is added that one element that is better is the absence of the bullies and tormenters from school: 'the people who were picking on me then are completely irrelevant, I don't know where they are now, I don't know if they're happy, I assume that they're miserable because miserable people like to make other people miserable – once I got out of highschool they couldn't touch me anymore.' In this way, the disciplinary regime of the bullying culture of highschool becomes that which one escapes in order to have a life that is better than being part of that environment as a young queer person. The inevitable, temporal moment of leaving school is depicted as the pivotal point at which 'it gets better' through the motif of escape, in addition to it being the moment of a shift into young adulthood. That is, escape from school and, simultaneously, escape from *being* a queer 'youth'.

Seven lesbian and gay professional staff working for the international firm Price Waterhouse Coopers compiled their stories into a video endorsed by the firm's senior partner and chair. Presenting short, one-or-two sentence bytes from each of the seven staff, experiences in school that mirror those described above were given, followed by commentary on how life was better afterwards:

> Things changed for me when I went to grad school really because a lot of people started joining our LGBT group, and then they changed again when I moved to New York City, I realised that really the world was different and New York City was a good example of that diversity … I really really did blast forward for the better once I came out: I now live in a great city, I have a great job and a great boyfriend … Doing well in school and not letting other things distract from my focus helped me to get a great career. And now I'll have the opportunity to transfer internationally for my career and get even more experiences out there. So I want to tell you it does get better and the best is yet to come, so be strong and take it day-by-day … So what's my life like now? It's amazing! There's not a thing I would change about it. I have an amazing partner, she is brilliant, she is selfless, she is compassionate, she is funny and she is exceedingly easy on the eyes. I work for an amazing firm that is a frontrunner and a leader in everything related to diversity and inclusion. Life does get better, it gets way better. Nothing in life lasts forever … I'm here to tell you from experience, it really does get better, hang in there … It really does get better, and I promise the bullying and the tormenting will fade away faster than you think (http://www.itgetsbetter.org/video/entry/vcdkiijcvue/)

Notably, the things about life that are better are described here in terms of geographic location (living in New York City), career (professional), domestic partnership (happily coupled). All of these are depicted as achievable subsequent to that pivotal moment of being able to move on from highschool and enter either working or university life. It should be noted, of course, that part of the aim of such corporate videos is to present a public relations textuality, requiring that the promotion of the firm is as much a part of the promotion of post-schooling life (Benn, Todd and Pendleton 2010). This might in certain cases skew the emphasis towards career success as the 'evidence' of queer happiness and the reason for hope.

While there might be good grounds for questioning the forms in which 'hope' is given, particularly when it centres on contemporary neoliberal representations of what accounts for achievement (career, domestic partnership, living in an expensive city), the provision of any kind of reason for hope is an important strategy in suicide prevention. Hopelessness is a key factor in much of the contemporary academic discussion of suicide risk in general and is often used as a predictor for recognising suicidal behaviour (Battin 1995: 13). This is also particularly associated with suicidality and queer teenagers. Hopelessness is usually understood as despair or desperateness, the lack of expectation of a situation or goal one desires or feels one should desire. For Holden and colleagues, hopelessness is counter to social desirability, which is understood as the capacity to describe oneself in terms by which society judges a person as legitimate or desirable (Holden, Mendonca and Serin 1989: 500). Psychological and psychiatric measurement techniques frequently rely on Aaron T. Beck's Hopelessness Scale, which utilises a twenty-question true/false survey designed to measure feelings about the future, expectation and self-motivation in adults over the age of seventeen years as a predictor of suicidal behaviour. Beck and colleagues attempted to provide an objective measurement for hopelessness rather than leave it treated as a diffuse and vague state of feeling in patients with depression. The tool asks a series of questions, most about the future, presenting a score on whether or not the answers given were true or false. Questions include: 'I might as well give up because I can't make things better for myself'; 'I can't imagine what my life would be like in ten years'; 'My future seems dark to me'; and 'All I can see ahead of me is unpleasantness rather than pleasantness'. Responding true to these indicates hopelessness. Responding false to some of the following also indicates hopelessness: 'I can look forward to more good times than bad times' and 'When things are going badly, I am helped by knowing they can't stay that way forever' (Beck 1974). While these questions and the scale are not used uncritically, the relationship between the discursive construction through the questions of what constitutes hopelessness and the aims of the *It Gets Better* videos are notably comparable. The objective, then, of the videos is to provide evidence and, perhaps, instil hope that would allow such questions to be answered differently, particularly to be able to give a true response to the last question above. Hallway Allies liaison support group, which operates across university campuses and high schools to prevent bullying, stated in this representative way in the introduction to their video contribution: 'Remember to keep your head up, highschool doesn't last forever' (http://www.itgetsbetter.org/video /entry/5wwozgwyruy/) . Or, as Rebecca in the introductory statement of another video contribution put it:

> You may be feeling like this pain will last forever, like you have no control, it's
> dark, oppressive and feels like there is no end. I know – I get it. but I promise …
> hang in there and you'll find it … Wait – you'll see – it gets better! (http://www.
> itgetsbetter.org/video/entry/wxymqzw3oqy/).

As can be seen, such video examples respond to a discourse of hopelessness aligned with the framework exemplified by Beck's scale, prompting queer youth audiences of these videos to imagine a future for themselves, to understand hope in the temporal terms of future wellbeing, and to know that the future does not necessarily hold the same kinds of unpleasantness as experienced in the everyday high school environment.

For those whose work focuses on the causal relationship between depression and suicide, hope and hopelessness are sometimes given as the mediating factor, in which the extent of hope or hopelessness plays a significant role in the likelihood of depression transforming into suicidal intent or behaviour (Chapman, Specht and Cellucci 2005: 559–560). Findings suggest that the extent of hopelessness about the future impacts on protective factors such as adaptive coping: 'Perhaps, in the presence of hopelessness, it is difficult to generate meaningful reasons for living, or for employing adaptive coping strategies; consequently, individuals contemplate suicide as a way to achieve emotional relief or to escape stressors altogether' (Chapman, Specht and Cellucci 2005: 566). Combined with a stronger focus on hopelessness caused by social factors specific to non-heterosexuals, much writing on queer youth suicide has utilised this motif in the framing of suicide risk factors. Grounded in the tacit assumption that a sense of difference from norms is often identified by others in such a way that results in insult or hurt (Eribon 2004: 97–98), some writers have found that hopelessness in combination with depression underpins the risks factors for sexual minority youth more so than for other youth (Walls, Freedenthal and Wisneski 2008: 21). The notion of hopelessness and the attempts to understand risk factors through it are relatively recent in contemporary research on queer youth suicide, shifting towards the relationship between suicidal subjects' sense of the future and its relationship with depression (McDaniel, Purcell and D'Augelli 2001: 85). Kulkin and colleagues utilised a youth suicide attempter list, the first eight entries of which were 'Feeling hopeless about the future; feeling I can't be helped; having thoughts about harming myself; feelings others are to blame for my problems; feeling unsure of my own self-worth; being unable to express my feelings well; having a negative attitude toward life; being fearful' (Kulkin, Chauvin and Percle 2000: 14). As predictors for queer youth suicide intent, these again focus on the sense of hopelessness specific to non-heterosexuals. In contrast, Remafedi and colleagues found low levels of hopelessness and acute depression among suicide attempters, although they did note that the sense of hopelessness during the period of the attempt may have lifted by the stage of participation in the study through either treatment or the passage of time (Remafedi, Farrow and Deisher 1994: 134). Interestingly, Hegna and Wichstrøm present hopelessness in a slightly different form, suggesting that the comparatively high levels of hopelessness experienced by queer youth growing up in a heteronormative context may be the result of the absence of role models, social structures and sexual scripts for the future of which most heterosexual youth have significant access (Hegna and Wichstrøm 2007: 23). The association between feelings of hopelessness and at-risk queer youth thus forms part of the knowledge framework through which queer youth suicide is understood, and this is further underscored through the *It Gets Better* project in terms both of its overall aims and much of the content of its videos.

Dorais linked hopelessness with exhaustion (from persistent torment) as a major element in the unliveability of queer youth lives, finding that depression was not necessarily a significant factor despite the common approach by professionals to associate depression with suicide attempt uncritically (Dorais 2004: 81). He noted that the hopelessness risk factor was exacerbated for those who were unable to find others 'with whom they could discuss their distressing problems' to find the 'support and encouragement they needed to develop any hope for a future less bleak than the one they anticipated' (Dorais 2004: 74). This moves the question of hopelessness in research and writing on queer youth suicide towards the desired outcome articulated by the *It Gets Better* project: the engagement with others that supports and encourages the development of hope for a less-bleak future than is currently felt. Whether that engagement operates in an online capacity as effectively as Dorais suggests it shall in a face-to-face discussion is as yet unknown, although recent thinking on the capacity of online communication and resources to provide a supportive environment would indicate some considerable optimism that this will be an effective strategy.

Vulnerability and Resilience

Through the manner by which queer youth are addressed and positioned in the *It Gets Better* videos, non-heterosexual younger persons tend to be depicted and positioned as always vulnerable. In several ways, the content of select videos works to *confirm* the vulnerability of the queer youth they seek to address, often by acknowledging one's own vulnerability in youth. For example, in a video by Adam, vulnerability is invoked through being positioned to feel affectively as worthless:

> You probably feel like nothing because of the stuff people say to you. I felt like nothing when I was a kid. But if you take your own life, that's when you let what they say to you become true. That's when you become nothing. And I came very close to that (http://www.itgetsbetter.org/video/entry/x93qvrwo3rm/).

In a video compilation from staff and students at Clayton State University, one contributor makes the following statement which again uses the mode of addressing queer youth to indicate the commonality of feeling hurt and vulnerable and how these can lead to suicide ideation:

> It hurts deep down to have those feelings, to have the feelings that it seems like you are in a complete, deep dark hole, and it feels like you're the only one that's there, and most of the time you just feel like giving up (http://www.itgetsbetter.org/video/entry/sho0u49iuyi/).

The address, to the queer youth as intended viewer, interpellates a representation of a queer youth population for whom vulnerability is endemic. Such vulnerability comes to be discussed simultaneously through victimhood as the following extract from PriceCooperWaterhouse's queer staff indicates:

I remember what it was like in highschool. My hair was cut short and a lot of people made assumptions about me and said things ... being pushed into a locker, called a fag, getting your books knocked out of your hands, laughed at ... being bullied, pushed down when I was walking home from the bus stop ... enduring the name-calling, the finger-pointing, the whispering ... When I was in high school I wasn't out, and there was no group, there was no support group, so I was definitely in the closet ... I was miserable during this time because I wasn't being my true self, I wasn't interacting with people on a genuine basis, and I was holding my personality and myself back (http://www.itgetsbetter.org/video/entry/vcdkiijcvue/).

Other videos, particularly those presented by well-meaning straight persons giving their support, have a tendency to reinforce the association of all queer youth with vulnerability and risk through the form of direct address. Queer-addressing-queer invokes community while straight-person-addressing-queer-youth constructs minority status and thereby emphasises vulnerability. For example, a video uploaded by Melissa states the following:

This will get better every day of your life. As you grow, you're going to become more comfortable with yourself ... You are somebody who has dealt with hardship, you're somebody who has an honest assessment of yourself, you're somebody who's willing to be brave and strong and stand for what you believe in, you're true to yourself and the world needs a lot more people like that (http://www.itgetsbetter.org/video/entry/eylymwlhpik/).

In addressing queer youth as people who will in time become comfortable, strong, brave and active, queer youth not individually but as a group are thereby represented as uncomfortable, living with hardship, not-yet-strong, vulnerable. What occurs here is different from the videos which are uploaded by queer adults and other older queer youth. When those address queer youth as vulnerable or as victims, it is through articulating a notion of similitude – my experience is the same as yours (but it will get better, as it did for me). When it is a straight person, usually announcing heterosexuality early in the video, vulnerability is invoked through heterosexual authority directed towards minority youth – you are vulnerable because you are not one of us (although your life will get better). In terms of the discursive positioning of queer youth, then, the distinction between straight author and queer audience in the address transforms the perceived vulnerability of queer youth into victimhood.

The depiction of queer youth as always already vulnerable in the videos mirrors some older problems that were encountered in earlier research on queer youth suicide. Inherent in such thinking was that non-heterosexual identity as minority, stigmatised and as *the* central factor in young queer person's sense of selfhood is at the core of the array of psychological and social elements that put a younger queer person at risk (Hegna and Wichstrøm 2007: 23). At times, the vulnerability of queer youth is nuanced so as to be depicted as the result of being non-heterosexual in a heterosexist society, although there is a tendency then to depict heterosexism as the natural outcome of heterosexual majority, with vulnerability and victimhood therefore the result of being in a queer minority. The majority/minority binary is thereby presented not only as natural and logical in terms of population numbers but as timeless and – most importantly – as impacting on *all* queer youth. As Fenaughty and Harré put it:

> *All* L/B/G youth grow up in heterosexist societies, thus one could argue that *all*
> L/B/G youth are 'at risk.' Resiliency enables the identification of L/B/G youth
> can be helped to survive a heterosexist world (Fenaughty and Harré 2003: 18).

What the authors here are suggesting is that suicide risk is endemic to being queer, albeit to being queer in an unchangingly heterosexist world – that appears to be international and universal by virtue of the term 'societies'. Heterosexism and heteronormativity are, of course, not only pervasive but problematic for any younger person who feels that he or she may not necessarily 'fit' within that framework of legitimated sexuality, desire and behaviour. Different from the ostensible reinforcement of heterosexuality through homophobia, heterosexism is more than the positing of different-gendered sexual desire, identity and behaviour as normal or allowable, it continues to operate as a key source of social reward, particularly for the young (Flowers and Buston 2001: 51). In this framework, queer youth become not only automatically vulnerable, but the vulnerability is figured as *internal* to their non-normative identity, whereas resilience is *external* and to be developed through support and sociality and internal*ised*. However, what is needed in this respect is an understanding that heterosexism and other social conditions are not risk factors which are imposed on a minority group, but comprise the social, cultural and discursive contexts in which persons classifiable as minorities form identities and a sense of subjecthood.

There are two issues for how queer youth suicide is understood that emerge from this particular formation which posits non-heterosexuality as the problematic source of suicidality. Firstly, there is the assumption that the vulnerability to suicidal behaviours for queer youth is the result singularly of sexuality, rather than looking to the fact that sexuality is one facet of identity – an important and sometimes fraught one for adolescents in general – located within a complex of other formations of identity and selfhood. This is part of what Diana Fuss has identified as the 'synecdochical tendency to see only one part of a subject's identity (usually the most visible part) and to make that part stand for the whole' (Fuss 1989: 116). This ignores the opportunity to think through the conditions of queer youth in terms of the interaction between different facets of identity (such as gender and ethnicity, but also personal experience), different contexts in which identity is performed and different institutional settings that vary in response and valuation of non-normative aspects of subjectivity, thereby allowing a vulnerability not to be an attribute of being a queer youth, but to be understood as produced across a nuanced and complex array of factors.

The second and perhaps more important issue is that the presentation of queer youth as being at risk of suicidal behaviour *per se,* and without regard to other factors both environmental and psychological that can be altered, reinforces the notion that queer youth are vulnerable *because* they are queer – or at least queer in a heterosexist society. Positing a sub-population as vulnerable because they are in a minority has the tendency to remove any sense of agency from that group as a whole (Meyer 1996: 102), leaving the subjects at-hand as knowable only through victimhood. Neither vulnerability to suicidal behaviours nor resilience that prevents them are built-in factors of a person or group, whether categorisable as part of a minority or not. As Jennifer White recently put it,

> we might want to ask ourselves, what are the consequences of locating risk within persons or races (e.g. 'Aboriginal suicide')? More importantly, what fresh possibilities might be opened up by thinking about risks for youth suicide in other ways? For example, what difference does it make, if any, to understand and locate risks for suicide within oppressive social practices, like racism … colonization … heterosexism … and limiting definitions of masculinity…? (White 2009: 3–4).

Significantly, White's call to re-think minority suicides in terms of social formations and the means by which 'minority' is constituted argues for the need to complexify how we understand suicide by shifting the responsibility from the minority subject to the broader field in which that subject experiences a minority status or categorisation.

Ritch Savin-Williams has taken issue with some of the ways in which queer youth generally are depicted as vulnerable, as victims and as suicidal. He argues that to propose that queer youth are automatically vulnerable to suicide obscures the truth that there are many more resilient, non-suicidal queer youth and that instead it is important to determine what makes *some* queer youth more vulnerable than others; by corollary, what therefore makes some queer youth more resilient than others (Savin-Williams 2001: 7). Indeed, the primary objective of *It Gets Better* is to instil resilience through hope, although how the notion of resilience against vulnerability or victimhood is framed tends to be dichotomous. Queer youth are presented here in precisely the manner in which Savin-Williams argues against, as automatically vulnerable and at-risk as a result of being non-heterosexual in a heteronormative culture. At the same time, strength and resistance to vulnerability are associated with queer adulthood. That is, not only does it get better when one has broken away from the institutions that cause queer youth pain, but one is apparently no longer vulnerable to insult, discrimination and bullying. Both vulnerability and resilience are, then, presented as mutually-exclusive through a double association: queer youth-vulnerability and queer adult-strength. Resilience, then, is figured as the capacity to wait patiently for adulthood rather than attempt to escape intolerable pain through suicide; that is, to wait until one is in a position to cross the dichotomy not only from queer-youth-to-queer-adulthood, but from vulnerability, risk and victimhood to strength, resistance and inviolability.

In her more recent work, Judith Butler (2004) has shown how a common, corporeal vulnerability is not only what makes possible an ethics of non-violence but that, through the precarity of life, vulnerability to violence is a trait shared by all human subjects. Underlying her argument is the point that vulnerability is not the same for all subjects, and that some subjects' lives are perceived as more vulnerable than others (Butler 2009: 22–23). However, in stating that we are *all* vulnerable to violence, language, demarcations and the acts of others through the very precarity of life does not mean that acts of declaring a subject or a group as vulnerable is not an act of violence in and of itself. What can be understood here is that not all queer youth are (1) vulnerable to suicide as an outcome of queerness, and (2) vulnerable *because* they are queer. Rather, the identification of queer youth with vulnerability is problematic in that it establishes stereotypes which themselves can produce ways of being, thereby actively *making vulnerable* or producing queer youth as vulnerable in ways which – of course, unwittingly – enact a violence against queer youth themselves.

Resilience and the Individualisation of Suicide Factors

A notably problematic element in the discourse around the *It Gets Better* project involves the fact that much of the rhetoric of overcoming hopelessness and vulnerability and developing resilience *individualises* the problem of queer youth suicide. Rather than calling for research, preventative change or interventional resources, it suggests that queer youth must tackle suicidality or suicide risk through waiting with some patience for adulthood and thereby for separation from the environments of bullying, harassment, ostracisation or stigmatisation. By operating within a contemporary neoliberal conceptualisation of risk, selfhood and sociality (Terranova 2009), the rhetoric presents the responsibility for developing resilience to queer youth as individual acts – such as the act of being strong in the face of bullying, or the act of seeking help when required – rather than through cultural change or intervention in the norms of school institutional culture. For Foucault, a neoliberal governance framework requires that risk and vulnerability are managed and mitigated by individuals – a contemporary social formulation that is in contrast to that which neoliberalism rejects, being the socialisation of welfare and the collective approach to risk (Foucault 2008: 143–144). This neoliberalism is reflected in many of the *It Gets Better* videos. As Savage stated in his initial upload:

> If there are fourteen and fifteen and sixteen year-olds, thirteen year olds, twelve
> year-olds watching this video, what I'd love you to take away from it is, really,
> *it gets better*. However bad it is now, it gets better. And it can get great, and it

can get awesome, your life can be amazing. But you have to tough this period of
it out, and you have to live your life so you're around for it to get amazing, and
it can and it will (http://www.itgetsbetter.org/pages/about-it-gets-better-project/)

In other words, the onus is on the queer youth addressed to be tough, to
endure this painful period, to develop on one's own an inviolability in order
to get beyond school and into queer adult life. Fenaughty and Harré (2003)
concentrated their study of the risk and resiliency factors related to young gay
men in New Zealand on the relationship between these and positive stereotypes
and representations, positive family acceptance, school and peer support of
non-heterosexual youth, participation in support networks, personal self-esteem
and other coping mechanisms. While the analysis of the 'seesaw' balance between
resilience and risk in terms of each of these has been an important step forward in
understanding the context in which queer youth suicide is made possible and/or
mitigated (Fenaughty and Harré 2003: 4), the meaning of resilience is produced
as an individual quality of those who, individually, succeed to overcome the
seemingly-permanent obstacles facing queer youth, such as bullying, shame and
ostracisation. Tremblay and Ramsay identified a number of problems with the
reification of resilience in the study of suicide, indicating that coping tends to
be celebrated whereas blame is placed on those who fail to cope (Tremblay and
Ramsay 2004). This is effectively a double-bind for queer youth who, on the
one hand, are depicted as endemically vulnerable and, at the same time, as being
accountable for their own lack of resilience.

The focus on bullying as a suicide causal factor, as found in the *It Gets Better*
videos and in much of the news reporting of queer youth suicide in late 2010,
also becomes individualised. This shifts the focus of suicide cause from the
broad social and cultural problems of heteronormativity and identity formation in
heteronormative contexts to 'a few bad apples' who inflict pain through harassing
queer youth. That is, bullying comes to exceed but also erase its own implication
in being the enactment or ostensible performance of heteronormativity. Two
elements are expunged in a discourse which posits suicide as a rational response
to bullying within a cause-and-effect linearity. Firstly, the broader cultural
framework of heteronormativity which authorises the bullying of those expressing
or suspected of non-heterosexual behaviours or attractions is made invisible.
Secondly, mental health issues, depression, anxiety and the complexity of factors
that place non-heterosexual youth at risk are removed from the depiction of the
suicidal queer youth, again reinforcing the individualised idea that queer youth are
responsible for developing their own manner of coping. Depicting bullying as a
preventable but individual act in such a way that both represents and erases from
view the context of heteronormativity problematically calls for a struggle against
the act rather than that which authorises it. At the same time, the representation of
bullying as that which will, in the future, be avoided in adult life obscures the ways
in which bullying's effects are ongoing over a longer period and can continue to

lead to suicide as the means of escaping earlier bullying's persistent repetition as trauma.

Conclusion

The *It Gets Better* phenomenon presents wholly new ways in which queer youth suicide is addressed and discussed while, simultaneously, providing a new resource in the form of videos by queer persons (and others) that aim to establish a sense of hope and a realisation that the painfulness, vulnerability, bullying and discrimination endemic to the queer youth experience are overcome later in adulthood. Although the depiction of queer adulthood is sometimes given in narrow terms, the capacity of the site to aid in the increase of resilience among queer youth is likely to be quite significant, particularly given it shifts the discourse of queer youth suicide from that of the 'expert' addressing the vulnerable to, in many cases, genuine voices of others who have shared similar experiences. At the same time, it problematically depicts *all* queer youth as automatically vulnerable as well as presenting the onus of developing resilience against bullying on individuals rather than critiquing institutional cultures that legitimate heteronormativity or surreptitiously authorise that bullying and calling for institutional change.

In ensuring that queer youth suicide does not slip wholesale into a discourse in which all solutions to overcome hopelessness and vulnerability are individualised – even if through support in a service-client interventionist framework (Battin 1995: 15) – it is important perhaps to move away from the specificity of queer youth experiences and locate these within the broader context of the experiences of hopelessness and vulnerability that are risks for *all* younger people. One way in which to counter the positioning of queer youth as vulnerable and lacking hope as we see in the *It Gets Better* videos is to think about queer youth suicide from the perspective not of 'queer' but of 'youth'. That is, to focus on the 'teenaged' element of identity rather than sexuality, given the fact that many adolescents have difficulty grasping the gravity of suicide and the impact of succeeding in a suicide attempt, while simultaneously addressing the pressures on younger persons to balance a relatively broad range of demands in a number of contextual environments: school, family, peers, media and other 'measures' of normality (Tefft 2000: 67–69). This is not to suggest that there is a homogeneous group that we can consider 'youth' which would result only in framing younger queer persons through a western cultural practice of 'generationalism' which has often been deployed in such a way as to prevent younger persons from holding speaking-positions in cultural, political or critical terms (Davis 1997: 1–20). While there are some cultural similarities between youth at any one particular time, it might in fact be more appropriate not to attempt to imagine a distinction between queer youth and straight youth but to focus on how certain subcultural elements of a broader young generation – such as vulnerability – might be exacerbated among younger queer persons rather than being seen as a particular trait. Where gay/straight alliances worked well to draw together a broader range of youth in their similitude *as youth*, the minoritarian discourse at play here unhelpfully reinforces the separation into specificities of hetero and homo. While this is not in any way to suggest that the *It Gets Better* project is not one of the most valuable undertakings for addressing contemporary queer youth suicide, it is to point out that unwittingly its discourse can produce a situation in which politically and culturally the mechanisms are in place to refuse to act ethically towards queer youth in seeking change to the social situations that place them in the ostensibly vulnerable position in the first place.

Chapter 4
Reconstitutions: Identity, Subjectivity and the Dominant Discourses of Sexuality

The first three chapters of this book have explored some of the ways in which the concept of queer youth suicide is constructed in a range of media, discourses and cultural formations, as well as the mechanisms that tend to produce an ongoing perception of a link between youth non-heterosexuality, vulnerability and suicide. I would like to turn in the remaining three chapters to a critique of queer youth suicide research from the perspective of poststructuralist theories of subjectivity and embodiment, affect including shame, and identity in the context of queer community and the ways in which it includes and excludes particular subjects. Poststructuralist accounts of identity and sexuality that have emerged through cultural studies and the more canonical strands of queer theory have remained relatively absent from queer youth suicide research and particularly that research which emerges from the health sciences and within some parts of sociology. The broad argument put forward in this second half of the book is that by looking at some of the contingent, complex ways in which identities are produced through discourses of adolescence and development, through sexual categorisations, through psyche and shame, community belonging and exclusion, stereotypes and coherence present powerful ways in which to understand the phenomenon of queer youth suicide and why queer youth are more vulnerable to suicidality. This is not, of course, to overturn or disavow the important contribution to understanding queer youth suicide that comes from analyses that focus on depression, incidents such as bullying or other cultural factors but to see how these can all be related to the complexity that is sexual identity itself.

Broadly speaking, analyses of sexuality-related youth suicide tend to 'read' suicide cases as being about a refusal to come-to-terms with *really* being lesbian or gay in a positive framework (McDaniel, Purcell and D'Augelli 2001: 96–97, Battin 1995: 12, Macdonald and Cooper 1998: 23–24, Dorais 2004: 24) or, alternatively, leaves unquestioned the assumption that sexual identity is innate (Savin-Williams 2001: 5, King et al. 2008: 83). This is an area in which queer theory – the application of poststructuralist critique to the fields of gender and sexuality – can make a contribution to furthering the knowledge on why younger non-heterosexual persons have a higher level of vulnerability and risk of suicide and self-harm. After two decades of queer theory, we have a powerful set of tools for the investigation and understanding of the complexity, multiplicity and cultural constitution of sexual identity. These tools, however, are rarely used in contemporary discussions, academic literature, intervention strategies, policy and service provision for youth at-risk of suicide and self-harm. Whether suicide is best understood through mental health frameworks or through the relationship between the individual and sociality, it is never disconnected from the ways in which identity is constructed and performed in cultural contexts; this connection is even more pertinent in the case of sexuality which, unlike other axes of identity, involves particularly trajectories of *becoming* in a normalising framework, whether those be heteronormative or homonormative 'expectations'. Queer theory provides an apparatus for the examination and critique of identity formation and makes powerful, albeit complex, arguments for the ways in which identity in not an attribute of selfhood but a *process* constructed in language, discourse, cultural norms and (often implicit) practices of regulation and regimentation. The utility of queer theory for the study of sexuality-related youth suicide and self-harm is found in its capacity for providing a fresh look at a number of alternative ways of conceiving of sexual identity, development, desire, attraction, awareness and disclosure. Given the ways in which much literature on sexuality-related youth suicide assumes the innateness rather than constructedness of identity (Cover 2005b), as well as the fact that advocacy and policy concerns have tended to determine the ways in which youth suicide has been studied (Savin-Williams 2001: 5), examining how identity formation from a queer theory perspective might be related to queer youth suicide has benefits for the field and, ultimately, for furthering prevention and intervention.

I discuss in this chapter some of the ways in which the suicidal behaviour of non-heterosexual younger persons can be investigated from the perspective of a critical interrogation of identity and subject formation. 'Becoming queer' (or lesbian or gay or bisexual) involves a process that often is not well-understood for the most part because very young persons in the early process of 'sexual becoming' are rarely interviewed, interrogated or have their stories captured during this tenuous period of the early teenaged years (Goggin 1993: 120). Becoming a sexual subject – or gaining a sexual identity – is a process not just of discovery of sex and sexuality at an appropriate, culturally-legitimated age, nor is it a shift into adulthood or a loss of 'innocence'. Rather, from a queer theoretical perspective, it involves the re-configuration or re-organisation of a sense of identity from that which is understood through all the demarcations that are known from childhood (race, gender, ethnicity), and all the personal and experiential traits, to one which must include a sexual categorisation as heterosexual or homosexual. For those whose sexual becoming takes the path of non-heterosexuality, sexual identity formation is a more complex process, not least because it involves negotiating and stabilising an identity which is marginal and non-normative (Talburt, Rofes and Rasmussen 2004: 8).

With a view to extending further the utility of critical/queer theory into the fields of youth studies, suicidality and the cultural representation of sex and sexual information, this chapter investigates two elements of the constructedness and performativity of non-heterosexual sexual identity that shed light on the ways in which vulnerability is constituted in the processes of identity formation that, in extreme cases, can make a life unliveable: firstly, through understanding that sexual identities are not innate but involve a process of becoming, I discuss how non-normative identity formation can produce heightened risk despite increasing social tolerance for queer sexualities. It is in the specificity not merely of non-heteronormativity but of a shift or 're-constitution' from selfhood to sexual selfhood in early adolescence that is a primary site of the 'making vulnerable' of those who are not well-resourced to engage with that process fluently. Secondly, as all sexual identities are developed within a framework of encountering the legitimate, culturally-acceptable discourses of sexuality that demand a coherent and intelligible (hetero or homo) sexual identity, the performance of a recognisable sexual subjectivity involves specific forms of normativisation, surveillance, self-surveillance, policing, regulation and regimentation. By drawing on Durkheim's sociological approach to suicide and social regulation, I want to show here that expectations and demands for coherent and intelligible non-heterosexual identities enact an over-regulation or regimentation into recognisable (hetero or homo) sexual norms of the self that can be related to the risk of suicidal behaviours. This is, then, a means by which to show how and why identity formation in non-normative contexts around the sensitive areas of sex, desire, attraction and sexuality contribute to the complex spectrum of youth issues – both social and psychological – known to result in increased suicide risk. I will begin with a brief overview of the strands of queer theory that emerged from the Foucauldian post-structuralist writings of Judith Butler and Eve Kosofsky Sedgwick and the ways in which sexual identity development and youth vulnerability can be understood through contingency and constructedness before addressing these alternative ways of approaching queer youth suicide from the perspective of identity formation and sexual becoming.

Queer Theory, Sexual Identity and the Hetero/Homo Dichotomy

As a field of critical, literary and social inquiry, the form of queer theory utilised here and in the following chapters is built predominantly on Foucault's work on the construction of knowledge through power and discursive arrangements, as well as the feminist and post-structuralist challenge to the notion that gendered and sexual selves are essential. Using discursive analysis, critique and deconstruction, queer theory argues that there is no natural sexual identity, rather that all meaning is socially constructed through discourse and this includes the meaning both of sexuality and of identity. All sexual identity is thus constituted in language, culture, relationality and other sign-systems and queer theory allows an approach that radically critiques the normalising processes of discourse, the dominance of dichotomous approaches to categorisation such as the hetero/homo binary and, in doing so, actively seeks to subvert normativity by showing that sexualities can be conceived alternatively, and that they are contingent, fluid, changeable over time. Disputing the hegemonic status of identity politics as a means by which to understand non-normative and minority sexualities and argue for inclusion, rights or policy initiatives (including those around youth suicide), queer theory presents the counter-argument that the reification of identity creates norms that support the majority and produce oppressive representations of homogeneity by articulating an over-simplified and ultimately unsupportable idea that sexualities are fixed and biologically-determined. Although there are strands of queer theory that are grounded in psychoanalysis as well as under-theorised versions which actively celebrate essentialist notions of identity, the form of queer theory that has the greatest benefit for producing new ways of thinking and critiquing the social situation of queer youth suicide has its foundation in post-structuralism and in the argument that sexualities only become knowable and meaningful through the discursive deployment of power.

Queer theory developed in the late 1980s and early 1990s with theorists examining in critical detail the ways in which sexuality, gender and subjectivity are socially-constructed. Drawing on Michel Foucault's *History of Sexuality* (1990), Eve Kosofsky Sedgwick pointed to the ways in which the commonly-known categories of sexuality – 'heterosexual' and 'homosexual' – are presented through a binary that is historical, mythical and without 'natural' or 'essentialist' foundation (Sedgwick 1990). Sedgwick's analysis of the binary has been a significant cornerstone of much queer theory work which has often sought to deploy deconstructionist analyses to re-think sexuality along lines alternative to the dominant classification of sexual desire and identity in hetero and homo terms. By starting with the notion that sexual identities only emerge in the nineteenth century (there were always heterosexual and homosexual acts, but no identities or personages built on these acts) when particular western medical and psychiatric discourses began to dominate and describe sexuality through these two identity categories (Foucault 1990), queer theory opened a number of questions: (1) what other ways of categorising or depicting sex, sexualities and sexual behaviours were there historically, before the dominance of contemporary discourses of sexuality; (2) what alternative or subversive ways of thinking about sexuality might be developed in the future; (3) who is excluded from the contemporary discourses of sexuality and the hetero and homo classifications; (4) in what ways do these categorisations constrain and/or regiment subjects in their sexual behaviour, preference or identity?

For Sedgwick and many other queer theorists, the hetero/homo binary categorises all subjects as sexual species; as *either* heterosexual *or* homosexual (or, as bisexual, representing both sides in the dualism as a form of hybridity), which means that the basic way in which sexuality is classified *always* involves viewing desire as desire towards a *gendered* other (opposite-sex desire; same-sex desire). That is, contemporary western sexual regimes make desire the primary category of classification and other tastes, practices or attractions subsidiary. That is, for a queer person same-sex desire is given as the common denominator and then other means of categorisation or constitution such as desire for a particular look, age or ethnicity, or a particular way of engaging sexually with another are built on top as 'optional extras'). The hetero/homo distinction does not mean, however, that there are two equal ways of desiring gender that are both acceptable or that involve a choice. Rather, the binary is deployed in the name of heterosexual normality (Sedgwick 1990: 1), meaning that, as with all dichotomous language formations, the former term is dominant, normal and natural, while the latter term is minority, non-normative and sometimes unnatural or improper. As a way of conceptually organising sexuality and identity, the binary relies on stereotypes in order to communicate and culturally 'recognise' the non-normative (Cover 2004); simultaneously it masquerades as timeless and ahistorical, although what we learn from queer theory is that this particular way of thinking through sexuality only emerged in the last century-and-a-half and was developed through the use of particular languages, concepts, symbols and institutions. That is to say, the dominant contemporary framework through which sexuality is depicted and disseminated is contingent, temporary, culturally-specific and not necessarily any better a way to think about sexuality than any other, even if it is popular, dominant and deeply-felt, even if the mechanisms of that discourse give many of us a sense of deep attachment to our stated and self-declared sexualities as prescribed by the hetero/homo binary.

What queer theory points to is that there is no foundational, logical, biological or ethical reason why sexuality should be shackled to gendered objects-of-attraction, that there are ways to think about, critique and perform erotic-desire that are different from the contemporary cultural imperative of sexual-beings dichotomised as heterosexual and homosexual. Eve Sedgwick suggests that certain

> dimensions of sexuality, however, distinguish object-choice quite differently (e.g., human/animal, adult/child, singular/plural, autoerotic/alloerotic) or are not even about object choice (e.g., orgasmic/nonorgasmic, noncommercial/ commercial, using bodies only/using manufactured objects, in private/in public, spontaneous/scripted) (Sedgwick 1990: 35).

There are also discernible trajectories of desire or attraction generally not encompassed in dialogue on sexuality. Gender – *any* concept of gender – might be discharged entirely from sexual attraction or practice. Time, space, place, the disunified body, or, as Elizabeth Grosz hints, body-parts that are not usually constituted as libidinal or gendered zones (Grosz 1994: 139), may just as logically be the codes or factors which constitute the intelligibility and naming of a sexual act. In other words, there are a range of possible logics that can organise sexual thinking, and *gender* is only *commonly* considered the primary factor in classifying sexual attraction because it is the result of deployments of disciplinary and biopolitical power. Forms of sexual fluidity and configurations of sexual subjecthood that are not dependent on gender-based trajectories of desire arise at the margins of contemporary culture, but they depend for cultural intelligibility, stability and identity on the sociality of a recognisable logic. It is true that some people might be positioned to cite a discourse or discursive platform that permits the coherent construction of a fluid, non-gender-trajected sexuality, and are subsequently able to make sense of it to themselves and to others such that there will be little problem functioning as a subject, engaging in sociality and social participation and forms of belonging.

For the advancement of knowledge on sexuality-related youth suicide, queer theory's critique of the 'naturalness' of the hetero/homo binary has a number of implications. A relatively broad range of investigative studies into youth suicidality have relied on the assumption of two, discrete sexual orientations, rather than exploring the ways in which (1) there can be a broader and more complex set of understandings of sexuality, sexual desire and sexual behaviour that may not fit within the gender-trajected binary 'options'; and (2) that for younger persons, desire, behaviour and sexual awareness may not necessarily be related unproblematically to gender or to the available cultural categories. A small number of researchers discussing youth suicide have pointed to the need to address the complexities of defining sexuality (King et al. 2008: 83), the fact that many youth populations may have same-sex desire but might not necessarily identify as homosexual/ bisexual (Savin-Williams 2001: 5) and that identity conflicts around not fitting within the binary definitions of sexuality may be factors contributing to negative psychological well-being of non-heterosexual youth (Hegna and Wichstrøm 2007: 23). These important contributions, however, remain in the minority and there is significant scope for the field of suicidology to consider sexuality from the more complex angles presented by critical queer theoretical approaches – indeed, for many younger persons sexuality is very complex yet is not often described openly as such given the limitations of the languages available through which to think sexuality and sexual identity. Queer theory's contribution to the complexification and production of non-foundationalist understandings of sexuality could, I am arguing, be reflected more strongly in research on youth suicide by acknowledging and investigating the role of the contingency of the contemporary sexual order.

Within queer theory and cultural studies, Judith Butler projects one of the most useful post-structuralist articulations of how identity is constructed and constituted in language, culture and discourse and the means by which many of us have such a deep attachment to our identities despite their contingency (and the fact that linguistically they tend to undo themselves). Butler demonstrates that identities are constituted through performances which are 'in accord' with pre-existing culturally-given categories of identity. For example, a queer male performs homosexuality through acts, desires, attractions, behaviours and tastes that are recognisably 'homosexual' as learned in discourse. In performing an identity – which is never a conscious or voluntary act – one cites and repeats the category and the information given culturally that makes that category intelligible and recognisable to oneself and to others. Such performances are repetitive and come to stabilise over time, retroactively producing the *illusion* that the performances manifest from a fixed, inner identity core (Butler 1990: 143). That is, our actions and performances do not stem from an inner essence but constitute it. Following Nietzsche, she points out that there is no 'doer behind the deed', that is, no static sexual subject (being) revealed through sexual behaviour or desire (doing). Rather, we perform our sexual identities *over time* in accord with discursive expectations and cultural demands for coherence, intelligibility and recognisability. Identity is the compulsion to reiterate 'a norm or set of norms' which 'conceals or dissimulates the conventions of which it is a repetition' (Butler 1993: 12). The performative expression of same-sex desire, attractions and behaviours that occur in line with recognisable and discursively-given norms constitute the queer subject much as the articulation of opposite-sex desire forms the heterosexual subject. For Butler, identity is thus manufactured in the languages, concepts and ideas available to a culture at a specific point in time, meaning that, following Foucault, the division of sexuality into heterosexual and homosexual identities is not only something relatively new, but may not be the only or best way in which to think about sexual desire, orientations, preferences or tastes. That is, all identities are constituted within ambiguities, incoherences and inconsistencies, but for the sake of coherence we are required to disavow, suppress or reinscribe in order to perform as an intelligible and coherent self (Butler 1990: 31–32, Butler 1997: 27). The cultural demand to articulate sexual identity as constant, fixed, coherent and intelligible means such disavowal of any alternative are produced through cultural regimentation and regulation.

In Chapter 2 I made a number of points regarding the ways in which a critique of the over-simplified view of identity as always fixed within the idea of a natural hetero/homo dichotomy has generally been absent in the theorisation of sexuality-related youth suicide; that is, accounting for the processes, contingencies and constructedness of sexual identity formation is rarely addressed in much suicide literature. Only in very recent work has the notion of the complexity of sexual identity and identity formation been tackled. For example, following the separation of definable same-sex sexual behaviour from gay or bisexual identity that occurred in HIV prevention strategies, Zhao and colleagues (2010) have recently noted that many adolescents with same-sex attraction identify as heterosexual, many younger persons report being unsure about sexual identity, and that very little is known about how those who do not fit a clear heterosexual or homosexual identity are at risk of mental health problems, self-harm and suicidality (Zhao et al. 2010: 105: 110). Broadly speaking, the study of sexuality-related youth suicide can benefit from taking on-board queer theory's more complex understanding of identity formation and contingency, an understanding that identity does not stabilise for everyone quickly, that behaviours and performances constitute identities but may do so in contingent and temporary ways, and that in the specific case of youth sexuality, instability and uncertainty as well as the pressures to perform sexuality in accord with cultural demands for coherence may contribute to risk factors and overall vulnerability. That is, rather than assuming the innateness and fixity of hetero and homo sexual identities, the contingency and instability of sexuality can be put to the forefront of questions, theorisations and critiques about what makes a queer young person vulnerable and at heightened suicide risk. What can be argued, then, is that the cultural imperative that we classify ourselves as heterosexual or homosexual, regardless of whether we may or may not individually be able or willing to perform that blank, binarised act of category assignment (Sedgwick 1993b: 117), puts younger persons at greater risk if they are (1) in the difficult process of shifting towards being a sexual subject in a period in which gendered-definitions of hetero/ homo desire do not necessarily 'fit' with childhood's polymorphous erotics; or (2) are wholly unable to be categorised in terms of the hetero/homo binary due to a deeply-felt attachment to some other way of categorising sexuality for which they may not necessarily have the language or the critical skills, such as through queer theory, to articulate and understand radical, subversive and non-normative sexual possibilities. Risks, then, include the possibility of being classified a non-subject or incoherent, or suffering identity breakdown or mental stresses from the pressure to undergo that transition from subject to sexual subject and to do so in a way which narrows down the possibilities of sexual performance into a discrete, possibly unworkable category of sexual identity.

Becoming Sexual and the Pressures of Cultural Coherence

If we are to think about queer youth suicide from the perspective of the discursive constitution of identity as understood through queer theory, then we need to acknowledge that in the specific case of non-heterosexual subjectivity, there are particularly culturally-constructed moments and processes of becoming a sexual being involving a shift from child to young adult, an encounter with discourses of sexuality and a realisation of non-normativity. The process of becoming a sexual person and of gaining a sexual identity as an element of one's subjectivity at the appropriate, sanctioned age (Fraser 1999: 101–110, Hargrave 1992: 59) involves an initial encounter with the discourses of sexuality and a re-organisation or re-constitution of how one behaves, desires and performs selfhood in the context of sexuality, for sexual desire has new significations once the discourses of sexuality are applied. Any polymorphous, non-gendered erotics that belong properly to childhood are to be re-organised in a manner that regiments and contains sexual articulation within the given discourses, the hetero/homo binary and the demand for sexual identity coherence and intelligibility. Under queer theory's conceptualisation of sexual identity, both heterosexual and queer subjectivity are specific performances of categorical subjectivities that are *inaugurated* at particular temporal moments for each subject in a life-span, unlike other demarcations of identity such as gender and ethnicity which are expected performances from a much earlier age. This inauguration occurs through a socially-legitimated injunction to be a *sexual* being which in contemporary folklore is (symbolically) begun by the parental 'birds and the bees' speech. When the culturally-appropriate age is reached, the injunction is *to be (coherently sexual)*; to submit to discourse and articulate or perform intelligible and recognisable behaviours, attitudes and desires of either heterosexuality or homosexuality. The move from 'I' to a 'gay' or 'lesbian' or 'straight' 'I' is not simply a further step in a linear process of 'becoming', but involves the re-constitution of the subject *in accord* with the laws of the hetero/homo binary and all its possible significations (Butler 1991: 18).

The reason that sexual identity is inaugurated somewhat differently from other elements of identity/subjectivity is due to the ways in which sexuality is imagined in regard to children before that particular, legitimated age of sexual becoming. Children are expected in our culture not to *have a sexuality* until puberty (at the earliest) and to have it explained to them by parents, teachers, through sex education classes, sex education manuals, by gossip among their peers or through other encounters with discourses of sexuality. This is despite the psychoanalytic and ego-psychological belief that the foundation of sexuality is in childhood, despite the current era's obsessive surveillance of childhood sexuality (Foucault 2004a: 257), and the fearful belief by parents and teachers that 'tomboy' girls will become lesbians and effeminate boys will become gay (Probyn 1996: 110). As Sedgwick has put it, 'this society wants its children to know nothing' (Sedgwick 1993b: 3), by which she means that discourses of sexuality are ostensibly denied those under certain ages until the sanctioned, appropriate, culturally-legitimated ages. While these ideas endure, there remains a particular cultural revulsion for discussing sexuality and childhood together or for assuming that children express erotics in any form. As Foucault (2004a: 270) pointed out, in the mid-nineteenth century there arose a simultaneous process of close surveillance of children's sexuality and a distancing from it or 'forgetting' that children do behave in sexual ways, and this continues to frame the field of youth sexual becoming today.

The idea of sexual becoming is thus located in a cultural concept of temporality, linearity, lifecycle and milestones such as beginning school, puberty, graduation. *Becoming* sexual and being inaugurated into the knowledge of sex and sexuality is one of those culturally-anticipated milestones, closely linked with the requirement to go on to articulate a clear and recognisable sexual identity. With this in mind, we can say that there is an expected (if not necessarily universal) *encounter* with the discourses of sexuality followed by a demand we perform a recognisable sexual identity through intelligible behaviour, fixed desires and unified patterns of selfhood that stabilise over time. Today, it is the case that most western children will first encounter discourses of sexuality in their very early teen years through media (Greenburg, Brown and Buerkel-Rothfuss 1993: 209, Ashcraft 2003, Cover 2000, Cover 2002) and that this will be a discourse which demands the construction of a sexual identity as either heterosexuality or heterosexuality's other (homosexual). Thus, all sexual subjectivities are formed in the *re-constitution* of subjectivity under a regime of expectations around sexuality subsequent to that encounter with sexual discourses. Discussing lesbian identity, Butler suggests that: 'It is through the repeated play of this sexuality that the 'I' is insistently reconstituted as a lesbian "I" ...' (Butler 1991: 18). This is key to that moment of becoming: in the encounter with discourses of sexuality, the subject is culturally-expected to reconstitute himself or herself as a *sexual* subject in accord with the recognisable categories of hetero and homo.

For Butler, to be 'constituted' means 'to be compelled to cite or repeat or mime' the signifier itself (Butler 1990: 220) – there is thus an assumed subject, usually teenaged, who 'encounters' that compulsive discourse and in the moment of the encounter is required to adopt or add new codes of performance, re-constituting subjectivity and self-awareness as a *straight* or *queer* subject. This of course leaves open the possibility that one may be re-constituted differently at different times: the avowed heterosexual who in her fifty-third year suddenly becomes a lesbian and comes to stabilise as one with the retrospective 'sense' that she always already was lesbian, for example. It is important to acknowledge that the moment of encounter with discourses of sexuality does not result in a re-constitution that is immediate and permanent, but stabilises like all identities over a longer period (Butler 1993: 9). The process of identity stabilisation is, particularly among the young, a period coterminous with that commonly articulated through concepts of anxiety, stress and crisis; these have often been thought to set the stage for suicide ideation in cases of extreme vulnerability and risk (Drummond 1997: 929). There is a period of adolescent instability that Dorais describes as an 'anxiety-ridden and anguished period of self-questioning' (Dorais 2004: 75). It is at this stimulated moment in which the self and self-identity as it had been *previously* performed is thrown into disarray that suicide becomes the option by which one can find a solution to the potentially unbearable destabilatory effects brought about by the encounter and the compulsion to align oneself or one's non-normativity with the latter term of the hetero/homo binary. That is, identity disarray through the question 'what after all am I, sexually, if I do not fit hetero, homo or bi?' can in extreme cases produce unliveability, whereby destabilisation of coherent selfhood leads to a detachment from living, because there is no clear self to perform such attachment to life. Of course, this does not occur in all cases and that period can be one in which any person – straight, queer or otherwise – not only works through but thrives. Of course, we know little about the factors that make, say, a young queer person going through the process of identity stabilisation in early teen years capable and resilient. But we do know that for those less-resilient, the sense of anxiety can be exacerbated by the interpellative effects of bullying, harassment, shaming and exclusion, even at a time before one is really sure what sexual identity one will be performing. A number of studies have, indeed, already shown that the early teenaged years are the 'high risk' period for suicide attempt and ideation: Remafedi and colleagues (1991) studied 137 males who identified themselves as gay and bisexual ranging from fourteen to twenty-one years, reporting that about a third of the suicide attempts occurred during the year that they had been identified as gay or bisexual. More recent work has continued to suggest a link between the time just following the 'revelation' of one's non-heteronormative sexuality and the high risk period for suicide attempt (Dorais 2004: 13). Orlando (2000) affirms that of those who were identifying as lesbian/gay or bisexual at the time of a suicide attempt, that attempt was made in the first year of identifying or understanding themselves as lesbian, gay or bisexual. In other words, the period of risk identified in these studies can be understood as risky not only because the subjects were young, but because this is a culturally-sanctioned life period of sexual instability and unknowingness.

The moments of encounter, change, and non-heteronormative identity development have been discussed variously in theories of homosexual identity formation (Nungesser 1983: 77–8). Vivienne Cass (1979), for example, identified six stages of identity construction, leading from 'identity confusion' through a move toward a homosexual self-image as 'identity tolerance' toward 'identity pride' and the synthesis of a homosexual identity as an integral element of a personal 'self'. More recently in their work on queer youth and health, Mark Friedman and colleagues utilised four milestones in what they call 'gay-related development'. These are: '(a) age of initial awareness of same-sex sexual attraction, (b) age of first same-sex sexual activity, (c) age of deciding that one is gay, and (d) age of first disclosure that one is gay' (Friedman et al. 2008: 893). While such theories of identity formation usefully point to the ways in which sexual identity development is a process undertaken over time, this pattern of development is given in a linear fashion, normalising the process with an anticipated outcome whereby those who struggle through this period in non-normative ways are marked as failing, vulnerable or at risk. Much of the problem with developmental work on adolescent identity is that such 'studies generally pay little attention to the nuanced and often-contradictory identity constructions of young people themselves, ignoring the diverse facets of self performed in everyday life and popular culture' (Maira and Soep 2004: 250). What this developmental framework lacks, then, is an understanding of the contingency and tenuousness by which non-normative sexual identities develop, depriving us unfortunately of the opportunity to investigate how that very contingency and tenuousness might be related to vulnerability of all youth in the develop of sexual subjecthood. At the same time, such theorisation has had a tendency to produce an idea that there is a pre-identity (homosexual) that is unknown to the subject as a child but that the young person will come to 'realise' this subjectivity before stabilising and then disclosing this 'always having had been' selfhood to others. The revelation that occurs in the encounter actually constitutes the prior or pre-identity meaning for the queer subject the process involves significant retrospection and reinscription of the past a 'queer past'. Given that this is a more specific form of memorial reinscription for a queer youth than a straight youth, the increased 'work' of producing linear coherence of the past and future sexuality is more destabilitory and therefore more risky.

Ultimately, no one knows what makes a person desire in a particular way (same-sex or opposite-sex or both or fluidly or otherwise), but to assume that this is inherent, pre-determined and innate in the subject, and to assume that at a particular age it comes into being and kick-starts a process of identity development is to ignore the ways in which culture, language and discourse govern the demands for coherent identity – and that means to ignore the opportunity for cultural change to the ways in which we perceive sexuality itself as a means of intervening in a process that, clearly, carries risks for some. If processes of identification are central to becoming sexual and to becoming either heterosexual or homosexual, then there are concerns for younger persons in the latter group given the less-available resources and the continued exclusions – not for the identity itself but for how that process plays out in early adolescence through culturally-constituted norms. These concerns can be approached and understood as pivotal in the formation of conditions for sexuality-related suicide. This is particularly important when noting that the younger the age in facing a non-normative process of sexual identity formation, the less support, experience and resilience that person will have to cope with that process of non-normative sexual becoming.

The multiple ways in which the relationship between becoming a sexual being and vulnerability can be figured are outlined in a recent example in Dorais' study of suicide among young gay men in Canada which theorised, investigated and identified a series of teenaged suicidal 'types', including two that relate to stages of identification, development and outness: (1) The Perfect Boy who has always been expected to present himself in the most 'normative' of capacities and is perceived as a traitor should he come out as gay; and (2) The Chameleon who is aware of his homosexual desires and identity but masquerades as heterosexual in public (Dorais 2004: 37). Both of these figures represent suicidal forms located in the junctural 'encounter' with sexual discourses, and in the expectant period of 'becoming' between awareness and disclosure. The Perfect Boy's risk period is at the very early stages of 'awareness' of non-heteronormative orientation – that is, unlike his peers who may have been re-constituted as heterosexual subjects, he has recognised or re-constituted himself as queer. Such a process is not, of course, as stable as lesbian/gay coming out narratives often put it. From a queer theory perspective, then, what has to be asked of course is what is it about the process of identifying with the discourses that make queer sexualities intelligible that puts the Perfect Boy at risk? And how, for the Chameleon, does the instability of an inside/outside dichotomy and an awareness/disclosure couplet operate to make that young person vulnerable? In both cases, what queer theory contributes to answering these questions is the fact that the process of becoming a queer youth through the encounter with discourses that make sexualities intelligible is one which places particular stresses and strains on a young person. Where the self is required to be re-constituted as a (minority) sexual self, that process of re-constitution from encounter to articulation involves pressures, then, that are specific to those who go on to articulate non-normative sexualities – that is, any sexuality that is not considered heteronormative. In the context of queer youth suicide, then, turning attention to the ways in which identity is formulated in the narrow terms of linear development is a necessary task in understanding why queer youth are more vulnerable to identity breakdown and detachment from living, including particularly those who find themselves living in liberal, tolerating and non-homophobic environments.

Sexuality and Identity Regulation as a Suicide Factor

One of the ways in which we can find an approach to queer youth suicide from the perspective of identity occurs if we begin by recognising that not all youth undergoing the process of encountering discourses of sexuality and being re-constituted as having a sexual identity are made vulnerable – rather it is only a small number. In other words, to understand the specificity of the process requires looking at identify formation from the perspective of Butler's queer theories of identity in a way which incorporates Durkheim's models of suicidality and regulation. By turning to Durkheim and the older sociological models of suicide, this is not to suggest that what we know from psychological accounts about depression, mental health and interventionist practice are not relevant; rather it is to provide a particular framework in which queer youth vulnerability to suicide, depression and mental health concerns occurs through particular processes and practices of sexual regimentation. The point of juncture between Durkheim's approach to suicidality and Butler's understanding of identity formation is that of regulation, whereby suicide can occur in the context of an over-determined regulation of the self, but where identity is formed according to queer theory within regulatory practices. As Butler has put it, regulation impacts significantly on the liveability of the subject: 'subjection is the paradoxical effect of a regime of power in which the very "conditions of existence," the possibility of continuing as a recognizable social being, requires the formation and maintenance of the subject in subordination' (Butler 1997: 27).

While liberal discourses often celebrate the possibility today of both heterosexual and queer sexualities as freedoms, both in fact are produced through normalisation, regimentation and strictly-surveillanced regularisation. For Butler, and by extension for queer theory, the performative self is produced as an effect not just of language, discourse and cultural significations but of regulatory ideals. Regulatory ideals are truth regimes (Butler 2005: 30) which establish norms, exclusions, categories and identities. Through processes of subjection and regulation, subjects are produced and required to perform, behave and desire by maintaining and exploiting the cultural demand for 'continuity, visibility, and place' (Butler 1997: 29). That is, it requires the subject to respond and 'fit' within regulatory norms in order to fulfil the condition of existence through performing as a 'recognizable social being' (Butler 1997: 27). In the case of sexuality, it is what Butler refers to as the heterosexual matrix or the cultural expectation of a mutual relationship between gender, sex and desire which operates as 'a norm and a fiction that disguises itself as a developmental law regulating the sexual field that it purports to describe' (Butler 1990: 136). The demand that non-heteronormative desire and behaviour be encapsulated into the latter term of the hetero/homo binary as an identity that is intelligible and recognisable to others and to society more broadly is the *truth regime* which regulates sexuality, sexual behaviour and desire into a coherent identity – an identity which works for some but which, for others, may be an unliveable, inarticulable form of selfhood. Importantly – and from a Foucauldian perspective – regulation is not repression acting on a natural 'field of pleasure and desire' (Butler 1997: 58); rather, it is part of a cultural, discursive and knowledge-based apparatus which constitutes subjects under the rubric of regulation and formation. Thus, it is not to say that the regulation of sexuality into recognisable heterosexual and homosexual subjects represses some kind of natural, broad or fluid sexual desires or that we can throw off the shackles of regulation of sexuality in favour of the pre-nineteenth century greater pleasures and behaviours that did not transform into categories or attributes of individual subjects (Butler 1999). Rather, regulation is the *condition* of identity, including sexual identities as they are inaugurated in early adolescence and as regimentary developmental processes re-constitute the subject into a sexual subject.

However, for some the experience of becoming sexual and thus being 'regulated' will be different from others. For those who will – for whatever reason – not 'fit' or be able to perform coherently within the dominant (hetero/homo) sexual regime, there is the consequential risk that imperils

> the very possibility of being recognized by others, since to question the norms of recognition that govern what I might be, to ask what they leave out, what they might be compelled to accommodate, is, in relation to the present regime, to risk unrecognizability as a subject or at least to become an occasion for posing the questions of who one is (or can be) and whether or not one is recognizable (Butler 2005: 23).

In other words, to risk not being a coherent and recognisable sexual subject by questioning, critiquing or resisting the violence of social regulation or over-regulation is to risk access to subjectivity, social participation and belonging, to risk exclusion from intelligibility and selfhood. It is when such regulatory power is perceived as an *unbearable* over-regulation that suicidality becomes the thinkable path of flight from unliveable pain; the logical outcome of seeking to stop 'stopping the unbearable flow of consciousness' (Shneidman 1985: 36). In the case of sexuality, this is exacerbated by the social anxieties related to sexual norms. In the process of re-constituting the subject as a (non-hetero)sexual subject which produces identity 'by supplying and enforcing a regulatory principle which thoroughly invades, totalizes, and renders coherent the individual' (Butler 1997: 85–86), the over-regulatory demand for coherence and recognisability is also that which produces vulnerability for those who are struggling with that re-constitutive moment of regulation.

In the context of theories of suicidality, Durkheim's sociological approach presented two possible classes of suicide that relate not to how individuals are *integrated* into a society (such as his egoistic and altruistic models), but how society *regulates* individuals (Durkheim 1952: 258). He concentrated on anomic suicide, which he understood to result from a lack of regulation of the individual, such as might occur when an individual gains sudden wealth and no longer has his or her life ordered and organised by a particular economic standard (Durkheim 1952:

243). That is, vulnerability to suicidal ideation and behaviours resulting from a sudden and unexpected under-regulation produces a breakdown in the attachment to living that is constituted in self-coherence and self-identity. He also pointed to the possibility of over-regulation, whereby an individual is overwhelmed by the regimentation of life. Writing in the nineteenth century, Durkheim considered this a rare form of suicide and he did not elaborate on either causes nor why it was not worthy of more discussion (Thompson 1982: 113). What can be argued here, however, is that theories of suicidality in which regulation is adjusted, changed or altered suddenly provides a lens for understanding how the specific constitution of non-normative sexual identity produces a subject who is vulnerable and at risk.

In the normative, culturally-driven process of sexual becoming, childhood sexuality is always less-regimented and often does not signify as sexual (to the subject at least). But in encountering the contemporary discourses of sexual identity, the subject is imposed not only with sexual information and the requirement to articulate a clear and coherent sexual identity, but a requirement to be more regimented; to performatively align childhood erotics within the newly-acquired constitutive social codes and norms. In other words, the child-becoming-adult is required to reign in the multiplicity and polymorphous nature of desire, behaviour and erotics into forms which are recognisable through the hetero/homo binary, producing not just an over-determined regulation of sexual selfhood in that process of becoming, but a loss of that which came before. A subject's overall identity is never complete, it is always in process of becoming and is built from a range of discursive identity categories or what might be thought of as 'coordinates' of identity. Each individual self is an expression of a series of coordinates that are performed 'in accord' with culturally-given norms, even if they are sometimes performed in opposition to those norms. It is in the addition of sexuality as a *required* and *regimentary* coordinate of selfhood in early adolescence that re-constitutes that range of coordinates in ways which, for some, is an over-regulation of selfhood that may prove unliveable.

In Chapter 1, I discussed the queer youth suicide film *Trevor*, pointing out that as thirteen year-old Trevor underwent sexual awakening and a growing development of same-sex desire or attraction, he found himself under increasing pressure to regulate his behaviours, his walk, his tastes and ultimately his desires – or face ostracisation and marginalisation. This was represented not by his object of desire's rejection of him but, more strongly, by his friends who pointed out the problems in the 'obviousness' of his queer behaviour. Where those activities, tastes, and attitudes were once considered spurious and disconnected, they are regimented by being re-signified as code for non-normative sexuality. That is, sexuality comes to regulate dispersed and multiply-constituted elements of selfhood in order to fulfil the cultural demand for subjective coherence and intelligibility, forcing a narrow identity category not only on the subject but on the diffuse performances of taste. In that sense, not only is it a regulation but it is also a loss of prior significatory practices – a loss which must be mourned. If these tastes must be done away with in order to conform to a recognisably heteronormative performance, or if they are to be re-signified from simply being tastes and behaviours and stances to being the stigmatised markers of non-normative sexuality, then whether they are excised or re-signified, they must be *mourned*. As Butler indicates, mourning involves the agreement 'to undergo a transformation (perhaps one should say *submitting* to a transformation) the full result of which one cannot know in advance' (Butler 2003: 11). Yet, in reverse, submitting to a transformation through the re-constitution of the self also requires mourning the loss of the tastes or their prior, and relatively harmless, significations. The demand that one mourn their loss, disguise their existence or exist under the stigma of re-signified tastes is the evidence to the self of the way in which a new and particularly narrow regulatory regime comes into play when one is asked to shift from being a subject to being a sexual subject at the culturally-sanctioned age.

Thus it is in the (usually) early-adolescent moment of the re-constituting of the self as a sexual self within the truth regime of the dominant discourses of sexuality that *over-regulation* of the subject can make a life that once was lived an unliveable life. Again, it is worth stating that this is exacerbated for those who are younger and have fewer resources for managing not only the process of sexual becoming, but the impact of social regimentation and regulation of sexual selfhood as well as the re-signification of the past as a queer past. Considerable research to date has concluded that queer individuals who have begun their sexual journeys in the very early adolescent years are often most at risk of suicide (e.g., Fenaughty and Harré 2003: 4, Zhao et al. 2010: 111). What this suggests is that the lack of experience and the lack of access to the tools that can help make self-identity and sexual-identity coherent and recognisable leaves the subject vulnerable to suicidality (Durkheim 1952: 247–248). What occurs, then, in the re-constitution of the subject as a queer subject is the developmental incompatibility of a simplified and unified childhood identity by the acquisition of an identity 'coordinate' that is incompatible with the subjectivity that has been playing out with stability. The over-determined regulation of the self as a sexual self requiring new forms of self-surveillance ('am I too effeminate?'), and behaviour ('is this normal enough?') and identity ('am I gay?'). Perhaps the most vulnerable moment occurs not just for the young and less-experienced but in the *suddenness* of the re-constitution of subjectivity as sexual subjectivity and the re-regulation of the self through sexual knowledge regimes. In questioning the options and strategies available to negotiate 'a sudden and unprecedented vulnerability', Butler finds that the possibility of wishing for death as a vain attempt to deflect vulnerability is among the possible reactions (Butler 2004: 42).

An article in the *Akron Beacon Journal* of January 4 1998 gave a lengthy description of the suicide (a year earlier) of fourteen-year-old Robbie Kirkland. Although an isolated case, it follows the pattern of many accounts of sexuality-related youth suicide which, on an initial reading, indicates identity confusion and difficulties in developing a positive attitude to lesbian/gay sociality leading to depression and the unbearability of living (Dorais 2004: 44). However, the case also demonstrates the argument that suicide attempts are available to be read differently in terms of the available knowledges around sexuality and identity. Prior to his suicide, Kirkland had made at least one attempt, and had absconded from home. As the news story describes, in addressing his earlier depression, a therapist confirmed 'that Robbie was gay', a fact accepted by his family: 'His father, John Kirkland; his stepfather, Dr Peter Sadasivan; and his sisters Danielle, Claudia and Alexandria tried desperately to make Robbie feel normal.' The support from his family appears to be considerable and is discussed in a gay-affirmative tone of liberal positivity. 'But Robbie refused to attend local gay support meetings with his mother, and refused to speak to gay friends she wanted to bring home for him to meet. His depression grew worse' (Kinz 1998). One reading of this article depicts Kirkland's suicide as the result of being a young homosexual male who, despite a supportive environment, has refused to accept positively his non-heterosexuality, become depressed and taken the terrible path towards suicide.

However, within a queer-theoretical approach that takes into account becoming and regulatory constitution, it is possible to read the news story otherwise (which is not necessarily to assert an alternative truth here): Kirkland's suicide might well have had nothing to do with overwhelming homophobia or an inability to act on his desires; nor a depression brought upon by a sense of intolerance or shame. It is unknown why he committed suicide – the reasons belong to Kirkland alone. But this tragic act can be read through queer theory as being the response to an inability to form an attachment to regulation under the narrow categories of sexuality as hetero or homo; the unbearability of being assigned a category within the dominant discourses of sexuality. As the article suggests, his parents attempted to 'affirm' he was 'gay'. His refusal to participate in articulating a gay identity through sociality and support groups can be read alternatively as an incompatibility with the authorised, homo-positive discourses and the hetero/ homo binary depiction of sexual subjectivity. While therapists and parents read his non-normativity as 'gay', his desires indeed may have been incoherent to himself, unknowable in terms of the dominant hetero/homo logic presented to him as *the* logic of sexuality and unrecognisable by the expert and the family. They may have been 'broader' than the intelligible and regulatory categories of sexuality permit discursively, or they may have reflected the polymorphous erotics of childhood. The gay identity was *conferred* on him, by 'expert' therapists, by caring parents, and by a discursive framework which demands the performativity of sexual identity in narrow, legitimate and regulatory terms. But that interpellation may not have been compatible with his felt erotics, placing him in a vulnerable position in which sociality through identity coherence becomes impossible.

In this reading, Kirkland's suicide may thus have been brought on by his resistance to self-categorisation of this unintelligible desire as compatible with hetero/homo regimentation. His *refusal* of the 'hail' of discourse to subjectivity – while possibly having no other 'available discourse' or framework through which to articulate these desires – points to an inability of discourse to synthesise wholly or capture the full complexity and multiplicity of erotics. This suicide formation stems, effectively, from the shame-causing failure to meet expectations of normativity (Fullager 2003: 297), but we are no longer talking about normativity as heteronormativity. Rather, it is in the failure to present identity coherence *at all* that suicide becomes the logical means by which to cease the pain of dislocation from normative sociality. Resistance, in some formations, is failure, and this is where the celebration of subversive refusals to accept conferred identities need be wary of the ways in which such dislocations due to unintelligibility can be debilitating and dangerous. That is not to say there should be no subversion of sexual norms, only that within the normative developmental framework of adolescence such unconscious, involuntary or unintelligible subversion may make a subject vulnerable; encouraging younger persons to view sexuality through a wider lens than is typically presented in contemporary regimentary sexual discourses is thus a necessary means by which to reduce such risks.

For a subject such as Kirkland (at least in terms of a queer theory reading of this news article), the available platform for the expression of sexuality, identity and desire was limited to 'gay', regardless of his actual experiences and any notion he might have had to desire otherwise, whether conscious or unconscious (Ahmed 2004: 149). In not having access to alternative, radical or competing discourses of sexuality, a coherent social identity becomes impossible, resulting in marginalisation and unintelligibility. If we can read his sexuality as being neither compatibly nor coherently heterosexual or homosexual, nor even the 'catch all' category of the bisexual or the 'bi-curious' (Farquhar 2000: 231), then we need to utilise queer theory's interrogation of sexual subjectivity to understand how the multiply-constituted, complex subject is made vulnerable and placed at risk by the 'unavailability' of a broader, competing range of sexual discourses.

Conclusion

The discovery of sex, the discovery of genitals that do new things, the discovery of attractions and desires, the occasional clarity over how a life-pattern can be traced from puberty to sex to relationships – all of these are things that as human beings we are expected to enjoy, although we do usually acknowledge that this process of sexual becoming is anxiety-ridden and worrisome for most due to the problematic treatment of 'sex' and 'sexuality' in contemporary culture. But the process of sexual becoming compels the need to enjoy these on the one hand, and face a potentially difficult encounter with discourses that code one as desiring the 'wrong way' or that re-constitute a sense of self awkwardly and regulate sexual selfhood in unbearably pressuring ways that lead to suicide as the attempt to escape that unbearability of regimentation. A solution to youth suicide is, in much literature, focussed on cultural change in order to eradicate the idea of same-sex desire as wrongness (e.g., Rofes 1983: 115–124). But, from a queer theory perspective, what it leaves intact is the question of the risks that are brought about not from being queer, but from being part of that process of becoming, re-constitution and regulation for a queer person. Michael Warner made the salient point that 'People know more about the messiness and variety of sex than they allow themselves to admit in public' (Warner 1999: 18). This is certainly true for many, but perhaps not so much for younger persons who, as a result of their relative lack of experience, knowledge, choice – indeed, as a result of the lack of encounter with multifarious and diverse discourses – have potentially very little understanding that sex is messy, varied and disparate, and that sexual identities are complex, tangled and wonderfully multifaceted, and that stereotypes are multiple, and that there are many different ways to be a particular subject under a particular category, banner or label.

In order to consider how a queer-theoretical approach to sexuality-related youth suicide can contribute to intervention and risk reduction by looking at the regulatory processes of (non-normative) identity formation, it needs to said that youth and the very young require educational and informational resources not merely to learn to live comfortably in the existing sexual categories of hetero and homo, but in order early on to be prepared for the stressors of being re-constituted from a child to a sexual subject; that is, to be aware that the stabilisation of desires, behaviours and selfhood can, after all, be conditioned and constituted by multiplicity and ongoing uncertainty and thereby to have an available framework through which to subvert the over-determination of regulation in the constitution of sexuality. This is not to disavow any agency younger persons might have, nor to suggest that younger persons in the process of sexual becoming are either naïve or blank slates. Rather, it is to acknowledge that a lack of coherent information alongside the narrowness of dominant discourses of sexuality and the heterosexual/homosexual binary are responsible for the risks to which some people are subjected in that process of sexual becoming.

Chapter 5

Tensions: Suicide, Sexual Identity and Shame

Both historically and epidemiologically, queer youth suicide has frequently been framed through a concept of shame. According to Eric Rofes, the two subjects of homosexuality and suicide 'share a parallel history of shame' (Rofes 1983: 1). In its more simplistic depictions, shame is understood as a reaction to the cultural representation of non-heterosexuality as wrongful, sinful, criminal, pathological or disturbed – a conception combining religious perspectives on sexual diversity (sin) and older medical and psychiatric understandings of non-heterosexuality (deviance) within the figure of the homosexual personage (Foucault 1990). Under this view, it is said to peak at a moment of insult (Eribon 2004: 15), ridicule (Saulnier 1998: 53), physical violence (Hunter 1994: 103), blackmail (Rofes 1983: 29), rejection (Schneider, Farberow and Kruks 1994: 119–120), or to be produced through the pressures of closetedness (Rofes 1983: 66) or self-repression of desire (Scheff and Retzinger 1991: xix). Often it is connected to a long-term loss of self-esteem and the production of an internalised self-hatred (Fullager 2003: 299) and longer-term psychological consequences leading to self-destructive behaviours (McDermott, Roen and Scourfield 2008: 817).

At the same time, shame has long been figured as a cause of suicide more generally. Within psychological, medical and mental health models, shame can lead to depression, intense anxiety and other serious mental health disorders, hence the circumstances which make suicide a possible outcome (Mokros 1995: 1092). The experience of shame leads to suicidality in that suicide is perceived as the logical solution to 'intolerable self-ridicule (pathological shame) and to the impossibility of reclaiming or achieving a sense of social place' (Mokros 1995: 1096). It has been argued that shame is one of the basic components of a suicide syndrome, in which it results from failure in a major social role and the anticipation of negative reactions from others, often where one perceives oneself as being unable to restore one's position in a social group (Lester 1997: 353). Edwin Shneidman suggested that *all* suicide is an attempt at flight or escape from an intolerable situation, and predicates shame as a possible cause of unbearable psychic pain (Shneidman 1985: 26–27). Other writers have discussed the ways in which shame, along with feelings of isolation and other manifestations of stigmatisation, are causes of mental distress leading to self-harm (Erwin 1993: 444). Scheff and Retzinger identified it as the basic engine of repression, the sort that can lead to emotional violence that finds a physical outlet in self-harm (Scheff and Retzinger 1991: xix). For Durkheim, shame was an element in obligatory altruistic suicide (Durkheim 1952: 221) whereby one is expected to suicide for the sake of a society which deems that subject shameful and thereby unacceptable. Thus, suicide is frequently represented as a result of, or an escape from, shame.

Over the past few years, a number of queer theorists have begun to interrogate the notion of shame, particularly doing so from a Foucauldian perspective that allows shame to be understood not through psychological and psychoanalytical frameworks, but as that which is productive, culturally-specific, contextual and circulates through relationality (Probyn 2004, 2005, Ahmed 2004, Munt 2007, Halperin and Traub 2009). Much of this important work has looked to the ways in which shame operates differently for different persons and, significantly, for different groups, in addition to developing ways in which shame can play a role in an ethical human society. For example, exploring the ways in which feeling shame over poor behaviour to another might transform not only the situation of relationality between subject and other but also transform the perpetrating subject himself or herself. In looking to shift shame from the therapeutic and individualistic perspective (Halperin and Traub 2009: 23), shame becomes characterised as that which, in some contexts, can generate abasement, abjection, despair, inward destructiveness or extroverted contempt of others (Munt 2007: 216, 203), but in other contexts is creative and restorative, capable of mobilising 'the self and communities into acts of defiant presence, in cycles of disattachment and reconnection' (Munt 2007: 216). Thus shame can be both individuating but affectively uniting marginalised persons who share that shame and can recognise it in each other or in shared experiences (Moon 2009: 359). In other words, the unknowability and unpredictability of shame as a culturally-produced and relational affect rather than a universalised human emotion allows several new ways of thinking about it beyond the narrow framework in which it is seen to be purely a debilitating effect that must be worked through or overcome. Much of this recent work, however, has not addressed the ways in which this re-configured approach to shame fits within concepts and theories of suicidality. Given the relationships between, on the one hand, queerness and shame and, on the other, suicide and shame, it is thus valuable to consider how these new approaches shed light on queer youth suicidality as well as thinking through some of the shortcomings of these new approaches for advancing knowledge in understanding queer youth suicide.

What, then, is shame in the context of queer youth vulnerability? In much writing, policy, theorisation and public discourse on queer youth suicide, shame is usually articulated as a causal factor of sexuality-related suicidality (McDermott, Roen and Scourfield 2008, Hillier and Harrison 2004: 80–81); and is frequently understood to be produced through specific acts of homophobia designed to cause feelings of shame (McDermott, Roen and Scourfield 2008: 819), bullying that makes use of homophobic remarks to engender shame (Espelage and Swearer 2008: 155) and anti-gay behaviour that manifests in bullying (Mishna et al. 2009: 1599). That is, there is a tendency to figure shame through performatives, actions and behaviours such as insult, abuse and acts of isolation and alienation. Ridicule, as an interpellation of shame, is common in discussions of queer youth suicide, particularly given the extent to which bullying utilises persistent ridicule as a tool of disempowerment. Shame in this view is presented as the *effect* of behavioural traits which either utilise or are motivated by homophobia. While these are important points contributing to an overall perspective on the past and continuing environment for younger queer persons, the conception of shame in these accounts is problematic by its articulation as a negative effect of 'homophobia' which, it has been argued, individualises the ways in which queer youth are made vulnerable or ashamed (Walton 2006: 14) or views the production of debilitating shame as the result of individualised and conscious acts which can be prevented.

The concept of shame continues to be under-theorised in terms of the ways in which it operates to produce non-heterosexual vulnerability and risk. Given the fact that explicit media representations of non-heterosexual behaviour or personages as indelibly shameful have become increasingly rare, as well as the fact that the environment in which uninhibited homophobia is the ostensible mechanism for shaming has lessened considerably while high suicide risk for young queer males continues (Hegna and Wichstrøm 2007), it is important to ask in what ways shame continues to play a role in creating the circumstances that make suicide thinkable. That is, to ask what are the cultural factors which allow shame to be felt as an affective emotion, and what opportunities and barriers there are for reducing the effect of shame in suicide risk for non-heterosexual younger persons. As Michael Warner argued, despite discourses of GLBT pride, queer sexuality is 'marked by a primal encounter with shame' (Warner 1999: 8). Following recent cultural theorisation of shame, the concept can be better analysed through understanding the ways in which shame is implicated in the constitution of identity to the extent that it ought be treated as more than 'a peculiarly painful feeling of being in a situation that incurs the scorn or contempt of others' (Lloyd 1958: 23–24). Rather, shame has such centrality to subjectivity that, as Elspeth Probyn has pointed out, it not only makes us human, but 'remakes us human', radically inflecting the ways in which selfhood, the sexual self and the sexualised body operate in the context of relationality (Probyn 2000: 25, Probyn 2005). From both theoretical and interventionist perspectives, there are significant opportunities to re-examine how queer youth and suicide are conceptually linked within a framework of shame.

This chapter explores some of the ways we can re-think queer youth suicide through the relationship between shame and identity. The aim here is to draw on some of the new and recent theorisation of shame, but to do so in a context that relates it back to its known role in suicidality. That means, in part, being somewhat cautious about celebrating the utility of shame: when it persists as a debilitating form that makes life too unbearable to be liveable, then we need to consider ways in which it operates differently for the more vulnerable, the isolated and those who might live young queer lives away from the collectivity of communities that better make use of shame for positive outcomes. Through analysing a small handful of accounts of sexuality-related suicide and suicidal behaviour, I will take shame to task by coming at it from four different angles. Firstly, it is important to look at it from the perspective of imitation and identification. An ongoing debate in suicidology over the idea that suicides can be the result of imitating others (significant others or media depictions of suicide) has been relatively inconclusive, for the most part because the proponents of the idea tend to draw on a somewhat over-simplified understanding of how audiencehood and meaning-making works. By looking, however, to the ways in which queer youth identity is formed through group affiliation, identification and stereotyping, there is an argument that a sensibility of shame is infused into the production of marginal sexualities. Secondly, understanding shame through the concept of tension allows us to begin to understand some of the ways in which social, cultural and familial expectations on a younger person to be heterosexual can induce a sense of shame through a failure to live up to the standards of significant others in one's life. This helps to provide a lens for making sense of inner tension between sexual selfhood/desire and the cultural and social expectations of others. Extending on this form of conflict, I will thirdly discuss shame from the perspective of the distinction between a self-identity that is formed and performed 'privately' and the problematic way in which surveillance over sexual identity occurs among, particularly, young school-aged men. In this perspective, shame is the product of anxieties formed in the face of persistent surveillance, measurement and policing of heteronormativity by one's peers. Finally, I will address the ways in which shame is constituted through non-normativity and, simultaneously, constitutive of the non-normative subject. No matter the extent to which queer sexualities are deemed tolerable, to be positioned as uncommon, legitimate-but-not-as-legitimate-as-heterosexuality, or even exotic and a spectacle does not eradicate the role of shame in subject formation. Being categorised as non-normative – even in positive and pride-inducing ways – extends to how belonging operates as a basic but not universally-available requirement for subjectivity.

The latter three approaches, in particular, shed light on how shame can be understood through tensions between self and expectation, private and public and identity and normativity, thus indicating some of the ways in which it is implicated in sexuality-related suicide by creating unbearable conflict and anxiety from which the most vulnerable are positioned to seek escape. This is to understand shame not as an extra-cultural or universal human constant but as 'social knowledge' that occurs within relationality and reciprocity (Warner 2009: 289–290); not as an act of humiliation that is internalised but as an 'attitude demanded of the inferiorized' (Adam 2009: 304). It is cultural knowledge that separates the 'queer' from the 'norm', adhering to positions of nonconformity in the gaze of the other (Moon 2009: 359). In that sense, shame need not be understood merely as an effect of stigmatising attitudes and behaviours, but as a highly complex aspect of sexual subjectivity, requiring perhaps that we re-think how contemporary culture produces sexualities and identities. The texts analysed here are drawn from an eclectic range of sources (news articles, fictional and biographical accounts), but what unites them is the centrality of a link – sometimes given as a causal relationship – between queer youth suicidality and shame; in all cases sponsoring

readings which launch the possibility for rethinking sexuality-related suicide from
different angles.

Copycats, Stereotypes, Group Identity and the Imitation of Shame

Among the spate of sexuality-related youth suicides that received high-level media
coverage in late 2010 was that of Oakland University student Corey Jackson,
aged nineteen. According to Oakland County's *Daily Tribune*, Jackson was not
known to be the subject of bullying or harassment, contrary to the trend in reports
during September and October 2010 which fixated on bullying as a causal factor.
His suicide occurred just prior to a nationally-designated day to wear purple to
honour the recent suicides of gay teenagers in the United States (Hopkins 2010).
Comments from a close friend of Jackson stated that he had 'discussed the recent
string of gay teen suicides nationwide and knew of today's event to recognize those
who died. "He was aware of all that," said Chico, questioning whether publicity
surrounding the suicides may tell others facing difficulties that "this is the thing to
do"' (Vanasco 2010). At first glance, this would suggest that Jackson's death falls
into the category of an imitation or copycat suicide, and this does warrant some
investigation given the quick succession of queer youth suicides in late 2010.

Imitative or copycat suicides have a checkered history in suicide literature, with
Durkheim exploring how the suicides of others in close geographic proximity can
impact on one's consciousness and imagination re-figuring the self in a collective
state that is neither a copy nor a model but a *giving over* of individuality to the
imagined collectivity of a suicidal group (Durkheim 1952: 125–126). Durkheim's
analysis, of course, pre-dates the media-saturation of contemporary sociality which
has been the central theme of more recent research into suicide imitation. The
New Zealand Ministry of Health, as an example, views the research as providing
evidence that there is an increased risk of 'copycat' suicides or suicide 'contagion'
resulting from media and public communication that may influence a vulnerable
person 'struggling with apparently insurmountable personal, interpersonal, or
family problems' (New Zealand Ministry of Health 2000). Blood and Pirkis (2001)
investigated some of the reasons why a heightened rate of suicides might occur
after media depiction, arguing that in general terms there is some evidence of a
causal link between depictions of non-fictional suicides and subsequent attempts,
limited evidence in the case of fictional depictions of suicide, but that there are
several questions for further research and a need to develop a more complex
theoretical framework for understanding how imitation suicides can be discussed
and recognised.

The idea that media depictions of suicide are likely to lead to a spate of further
suicides has traditionally relied on a simplistic 'media effects' approach that is
now very much outdated within media reception theories and audience studies.
Based on an over-simplified linear understanding of communication, media
effects theories include various ways of understanding the media process from the

perspective that changes in belief and behaviour occur through subjection to mass media forms (Shannon and Weaver 1949). While media stories can indeed influence the behaviour of others, the ways in which that influence occurs is complex and always contingent (Curran 2002: 158). Media recipients make meanings based on existing knowledge, environment and available discourses (Bennett 1983). In the case of suicide imitation, then, it is important not to assume that media depictions or news stories about queer youth suicide directly cause subsequent suicides by vulnerable younger gay men and lesbians; rather, if there is any relationship – as Blood and Pirkis have argued – it is more complex than a linear effects model can show. Indeed, if the media effects model and the deterministic argument for suicide imitation were the case, there obviously would be many more lesbian/gay youth suicides than currently attempted.

Yet if we are to make sense of Corey Jackson's seemingly imitative suicide, we need to find a means by which to explore the possibility of some form of imitation without assuming an overly-simplistic media effects or contagion model. Rather, we can complexify the cultural context in which queer suicide is depicted by thinking through the ways in which the commonality of queer shame is brought into the picture. Shame, in Jackson's case, emerges as a figure in the narrative around his suicide with the phrase of one of his fellow students who was asked about causal factors: 'It could be like self-imposed feelings because you have been told since birth you should be one way' (Hopkins 2010). What the phrase points to is a formation of shame that operates to police the interface between the normal and the abnormal (Moon 2009: 359). If shame is to be understood as the product not just of individuals who have been explicitly and deliberately shamed but, as Warner points out (1999: 8), a culturally-produced core element in non-heterosexual identity, then the above account of Jackson's suicide can be understood to involve the ways in which he is emplaced within the 'collective identity' and 'collective shame' of non-heteronormativity. This is not, therefore, a copycat in which the suicide of another, similar person with whom Jackson might have identified fosters his own suicidality. Rather, it is imitative of the perceived causal factors of the queer suicides around him, one of those being the production of selfhood in similitude of shame, which then becomes a factor in his own suicidality.

If, in poststructuralist accounts of identity and subjectivity, an identity is formed by the citation, repetition and stabilisation of a set of discursively-given or culturally-understood norms and categories, then a significant element of that production occurs through identification with a perceived group, in this case a perception of queer community, category and recognisable behaviours that present a cultural sense of coherence. Indeed, belonging is a central motivator for the intelligible and recognisable construction of identities, for without recognition as a subject, social participation is disallowed (Butler 1997: 27). For Sally Munt, shame is never individual but always intrapsychic, which means it operates at times at the crossing point between the individual subject and the group. Such groups, she argues, 'contain individuals who internalise the stigma of shame into the tapestry of their lives, each reproduce discrete, shamed subjectivities ... patterns can be detected as shared shame scripts' (Munt 2007: 3). That is to say, rather than suicide being imitative, a particular scripting of the group as *shamed* can become a function or element of an individual subjectivity, enough so to lead to suicidality in the face of the unbearability of the sensibility of shame. One, of course, does not simply *belong* to any group, even by virtue of an identity attribute that can be considered the same as that of others in the group; rather, one *produces* belonging through an element of the performativity of the self which 'cites' the norms that constitute or make present a community or group (Bell 1999: 3). Thus, forging a sense of belonging is an integral part of the development of non-heteronormative sexual identities – a belonging that is at once built on difference from a broader norm (heterosexuality) and similarity among a community (homosexuality). For many non-heterosexual youth, this may not necessarily be the collective production of self-identity through routes that involve face-to-face interaction in geographically-bound spaces, but through media representation, digital communication and other forms of textuality, reception and engagement. Such a position is to suggest that the self is constituted within the *collective* identity of audiencehood rather than through a one-on-one identification with a character, representation or depiction. Rumour, innuendo, graffiti and other communicative forms – which are often more ostensibly conveying connotations of shame – are just as implicated in the collective formation of self-identity from this perspective.

While there are enormous variances in how one performs an identity in order to belong to a minority group, one path through which that is achieved is through the citation and performance of a stereotype – not because one has been duped into thinking that the stereotype is truthful or real, but because by the very nature of stereotypes, it is the easiest and most coherent path. Stereotypes link an identity category – usually a minority representation – with a set of behaviours, attitudes, desires and norms (Rosello 1998). Easily recognised because they are built on repetition and difficult to eradicate, stereotypes work as a 'package' or 'byte' conveying a significant amount of (not necessarily accurate or truthful) information about an identity or identity-group. In that sense, stereotypes are consensual, communicative and operate at a collective level within ongoing social processes (Karasawa, Asai and Tanabe 2007: 516), thereby implicated in the ways in which minority sexual identities are performed towards collectivity, coherence and belonging. In the case of queer stereotypes, this has at various times been the linkage of male homosexual identity with effeminacy, rampant consumerism, over-stylisation, dishonest disposition or hypermasculinity (Cover 2004: 86), and lesbian identity with mannish imposter, fanged vampire, prim professor, frustrated nun, or man-eating monster (Creed 1995: 87). But core to many of these early stereotyped depictions of sexual non-normativity is the notion of failure, inadequacy, exclusion and shame, as seen in particular in the stereotype of the 'sad young man' identified by Richard Dyer (1993: 87–88), which links homosexuality with attributes and dispositions of tragedy, loneliness, marginalisation or unhappiness revolving around shame.

In identity terms, it is the stereotype that is cited and performed, and in order to do that in a coherent, intelligible and totalised way it requires not just the performance of the identity category through a declaration or self-naming, but the performance of the ideas, behaviours, norms, attitudes and attributes – including shame – that are conveyed within the stereotype as a unit of speech. That is, performing the attributes and behaviours constitutes the identity. As Butler writes, 'performativity must be understood not as a singular or deliberate 'act,' but, rather, as the reiterative and citational practice by which discourse produces the effects that it names' (Butler 1993: 2). To extend this from the idea of an individual performance to the collective, stereotypes are an effective way in which to forge an identity that bonds with the group through ease of recognisability. In order to belong (which may be trajected towards a future belonging), one performs and stabilises an identity that one *assumes* (1) has similitude with others in the perceived group or community; and (2) is perceived to be recognisable to others in that group. In both cases, this is regardless of whether stereotyped behaviour, attitudes, ideas or performances have been 'tried and tested' within a group context.

Although there are many representations which operate to disavow and counter older stereotypes of homosexuals in contemporary media, popular culture, public policy, education and self-help rhetoric, the persistence of shame at the 'core' of older stereotypes remains; it is not a considerable stretch to assume that for many younger persons without the age, experience and cultural literacy to explore alternatives, such older stereotypes are believable, recognisable and seen as the means by which belonging to a minority community is made through intelligible performance. That is, the stereotype of the shamed queer person interpellates a young subject as one who, in performing oneself within perceived norms in a trajectory towards community belonging, is imbued with shame as a core element of that performativity. Effectively, there are two stereotypes at play in the case of queer youth suicidality here: the one which links the collective identity of homosexuality with the behaviour and attributes of shame; and the one which links the identity of the shamed self with suicide as the logical outcome (Kral 1994). The queer youth, then, risks approximating or repeating the cultural knowledge of the two stereotypes asserting these links that bridge non-heterosexual identities and suicidality through the production of the self in shame. Rather than imitation of the suicide of other queer youth, an unbearability of living is produced by identification with the notion that others commit suicide *because* shame is the integral part of the non-heteronormative self; the self is performed as unliveable in collective shame.

For Jackson, then, one possible understanding of his suicide is that in recognising the stereotype of the shamed-and-thereby-suicidal queer youth in the media depictions fostered or furthered his own shame, leading then to his own suicidality. This is not, of course, to suggest for certain that his suicide was produced through the process of group identification and the performance of stereotyped queer shame and suicidality. Rather, his ultimately unknowable suicide prompts us to consider the ongoing risks and vulnerabilities that occur when non-normative sexual identities are produced by means of forging necessary coherence and intelligibility through ineradicable stereotypes of queer shame, queer vulnerability and queer suicidality. Once again, it is through opening up the field of possibilities for identity and sexuality to occur otherwise and by the sharing of a broader, less-stereotyped and less-narrow set of depictions of non-heterosexuality that the risks of a self produced in the context of shame can be at least partly mitigated.

Expectations of the Self: The Ego and the Ideal

Although it does not present a complete story on queer youth suicide, a psychoanalytic framework usefully points to some of the ways in which shame is produced as an effect of tensions between selfhood and expectation. A simple definition of shame within psychoanalysis begins with what it is not: according to Gerhart Piers and Milton Singer (1971: 28), shame is not a set of 'inferiority feelings' nor is it a re-direction of some primal sense of sexual shame. For them, shame is 'a distinctly differentiated form of inner tension which as such is a normal concomitant of ego development and superego formation, at least in our culture' (Piers and Singer 1971: 17–18). The psychoanalytic view of shame follows Freud in indicating that it operates as a form of 'psychic strain' originating from a conflict with the superego, loosely understood as the internalisation of socio-cultural norms playing a 'civilising' role over the ego and id. Operating alongside the super-ego which has a normative role, the 'ego ideal' is formed in the process of overcoming childhood narcissism through identification with the central figures of parents, teachers and significant others. It forms a set of expectations or goals for the self which are governed by the moral super-ego component, and establishes an internal demand that the subject change in order to achieve the ideal.

In that sense, it can be understood as a set of cultural expectations effectively required of the self at a local level – that to which one's ego must aspire. For Piers and Singer, the ego ideal represents the sum of positive identifications with the (representative) figure of the parent 'who explicitly and implicitly gives the permission to become like him, and the narcissistically expecting parent and the parent who imposes his own unobtainable ideals on the child' (Piers and Singer 1971: 26). It contains layers of later identifications which the authors understand to be more superficial but of social importance, and these include the social role that an individual assumes in different social situations. In this psychoanalytic framework, shame is constituted in the difference between the ego and all the cultural and experiential forms from which the ego ideal is made up. The tension between the two when expectations are not met initiates the sense, feeling or affect of shame not as an unwillingness to conform to an expectation but an inability to do so even when one might indeed be willing. Such shame might be produced in the queer person who wishes to be straight, or the young person who feels that his or her parents, friends or significant others will be – or have been – disappointed in a discovery of non-heterosexuality, no matter how tolerant they will be of the difference.

From a queer theory perspective, it is useful to look at this framework as a particular and specific cultural formation of shame through which certain identities are produced in vulnerability through tensions between the expectations of significant others (parents, siblings, peers) and the queer self. That is, to work with the tension between the self and the expectations of significant others, but to de-universalise the process and shift it from one which occurs within the psyche to one which is governed by subjectivity in its relationality and sociality. Significant others in the life of a young queer person often unwittingly utilise the field of heteronormativity or compulsory heterosexuality in order to structure or re-structure the subject. Such re-structuring is not, of course, an attempt to transform a subject from a homosexual to heterosexual, nor is it ostensible pressure to change. Rather, it operates to draw attention to that which is characterised as non-normative, thereby not 'ideal' and thereby producing shame through the failure or inability to become that ideal under the gaze of the other. The parent who is initially disappointed in his or her child but comes to accept the child's different sexuality – in a situation in which homosexuality is articulated as legitimate but not the *most* legitimate – is an example of the tacit ways in which the expectations of significant others operate. The story is common: for example, Australian PFLAG national spokesperson Shelley Argent has related that subsequent to learning her son is gay, she 'cried for months' over what was a 'terrible time', with 'tension in the house' as the family 'all had to get used to the knowledge that James was gay' (Argent 2010). All of these reactions are part of a common cultural narrative, the result of which is usually a tolerant parent overcoming the difficult revelation that a child falls outside of heteronormativity. But what effect does this familiar scenario of initial disappointment, shock or dismay have in reinforcing expectations that cannot be met and inducing shame in a young person at a crucially vulnerable and difficult step in the articulation of a non-normative sexual identity? More importantly, how does this initial 'disappointment' performatively produce and reinforce social expectations that are presented as the ideal and thereby re-structure the subject as shamed?

In Leroy Aarons' account of Bobby Griffith, who killed himself in 1983 aged 20, we see an example of the shame that results from tension caused by the inability of the self to meet the specific, local and cultural expectations of others. As a child and within the clichéd description of the sissy boy (Sedgwick 1993b: 154), Bobby asked for a doll. As Aarons tells us, his mother was concerned about the embarrassment and the possibility he might be teased at school. But more importantly, the mother denied him because of a 'sense of threat to her carefully ordered existence' (Aarons 1995: 46). She was, he points out, the 'architect of her own religious universe' (Aarons 1995: 50) which suggests that the strictures of Bobby's upbringing were not about religious doctrine but order and conformity. As Fullager has aptly put it, 'metaphors of order and chaos figure in the shamed subject's quest for transcendence, mortification or redemption' (Fullagar 2003:

298). The persistent surveillance and social ordering by his mother worked to structure Bobby's desires through the mutual interpellation of his sexual selfhood and a set of normative ideals and expectations, whereby shame was produced in the failure to live up to those standards or ideals; this is the shame that comes through risking 'the withdrawal of the approving gaze of loving acceptance' (Munt 2007: 224), which can be as much an imagined possibility of withdrawal as a real experience of it. No homophobic slur nor insult need be made, nor an ostensible heterosexism or demeaning of non-normative sexualities; indeed, Mrs Griffith appeared to be sensitive, kind and well-meaning towards her son.

The story of Bobby is not the account, then, of an isolated young man who kills himself in the face of overwhelming homophobia, bullying, self-hatred or shaming humiliation and ridicule. Rather, he was a socially-active, sexually-active young man living in the early AIDS-era of the contemporary gay community of San Francisco. But what is demonstrated in his story is the way in which shame is produced through the tension between self (how Bobby understood and performed his desires, attractions and sexual behaviours) and the normative ideals (how those significant in his life sought, albeit unwittingly, to present and inculcate a set of measures of the normative). When ongoing tension and anxiety over the *discrepancy* between the self as it desires and the ostensible expectations of significant others becomes not only apparent to the subject but a source of anxiety or unbearability, shame is exacerbated to the extent that suicide develops as the seemingly logical solution – a flight from the intolerable pain of the persistent feeling of shame and its attendant subsidiary emotions (Shneidman 1985: 26–27). In order to overcome that shame produced in that tension, Bobby longed, as Aarons put it, 'to be liberated from the tyranny of external approval' (Aarons 1995: 128). Where the desire for the normality of expectations and ideals cannot overcome 'the affective intensity attached to stigma' (Carter 2009: 588), this liberation, of course, comes in the form of the finality of suicide.

Private Sexualities and Public Surveillance

Another site of tension through which shame is produced can be found in the interface between the public and the private. This is particularly notable in regard to the ways in which queer youth sexuality is often considered in terms of that distinction in relation to secrecy – the secret desires one keeps to oneself, the attractions that will for now remain private and unrevealed to peers, the elements of identity that one may act upon but only without the broad knowledge of others. This is the framework of queer youth privacy which occurs at times when one feels those desires and attractions will draw stigma if revealed. Within a culturalist perspective, shame here is produced in the possibility of public exposure which, for some, is neither a problem nor has negative connotations. For others, it turns on, as Siebers has put it, 'the movement between private and public realms' where the closet is marked as the site of shame only because of the possibility of revelation (Siebers 2009: 205). The idea of exposure or revelation that floods the self with shame is, in Warner's terms, about being witnessed as a non-normative individual, even if that witnessing is imaginary or supposed (Warner 2009: 293). Thus, shame in this framework operates within yet another set of tensions, this time between the self and sociality that is overdetermined by the possibility of an unwanted revelation.

The private/public distinction, reductive as it is (Gal 2002), can also be a useful concept for thinking through the idea of (non-hetero) sexual identity and its relationship with shame, since non-heterosexual sexualities – and particularly lesbian/gay sexualities – have a very specific sort of relationship with the concept of 'public', by which there are at times the requirement that one be closeted rubbing up against the social syndrome in which *honesty* about one's sexuality requires that one 'out' oneself publicly (Cover 2000: 79–83). There has been significant discussion of both the benefits and detriments of younger queer persons being public about one's sexual non-normativity, with some writers feeling that maintaining secrecy is debilitating and viewing public declaration among one's peers and family through 'coming out' as producing necessary self-esteem (Crisp and McCave 2007: 406, McAndrew and Warne 2010: 96, Smalley, Scourfield and Greenland 2005: 144). Others have argued that coming out at too young an age can lead to greater anxieties, potential victimisation and social, family and economic problems (Mishna et al. 2009: 1607, Hegna and Wichstrøm 2007: 34, Ryan et al. 2009: 350). The complex arrangements of passing and/or coming out frame the ways in which we tend to think about queer youth and vulnerability in terms of the distinction between the private and the public.

In the case of non-heterosexual youth, part of the production of shame is in the *risk* of discovery of that sexual self-knowledge which one has – often by necessity or to avoid victimisation – kept hidden. This is not to consider shame as an individualised and internalised fear of discovery, but to show precisely how it is produced in relationality (Munt 2007: 220–221). Being closeted, hiding or passing requires a self-conscious and theatrical performance, typically through policing one's own gender behaviour, vocal articulations, quality and tone of voice, walk, stance, clothing, attitudes, desires, likes, dislikes and tastes. A not-yet-disclosed non-heterosexuality is thus already a pseudo-public sexuality because it requires a capacity to sense the ways in which one's own body and one's own self are viewed by others. That is to say, the articulation of subjectivity through the private knowledge of one's sexual self within the context of passing as otherwise in public involves conscious 'performance work', which is comprised of managing the possibility of being shamed by facing the imagination of that shame on a regular basis. One of the ways in which this sense of a public surveillance produce shame for the not-yet-disclosed private subject is elucidated in a Melbourne newspaper story about a queer youth who had attempted suicide:

> Travis Macfarlane was 13 when he realised he was gay. He was 14 when he first tried to kill himself: 'I played football and did all the things guys are supposed

to do. I was so good at being 'straight'. Every day I would think, 'am I walking straight, am I doing what straight guys do, is my hair too gay looking?' ... But boys, he says, are like hawks, waiting for the first sign of difference ... 'I was so angry with them, I was thinking, "I'm trying to be straight, give me a chance."' (Curtis 1999: T1)

For Macfarlane, the public ideal of selfhood is a normative and masculine set of codes of behaviour or performance fixating on what young men 'are supposed to do'. His articulation of the intensity of surveillance here is significant, regardless of whether that is a heightened perception of being policed by his peers due to the knowledge of a discrepancy between private self and a more public image; ultimately it increases his level of anxiety, anger, stress and shame at the potential risk of failure to maintain the necessary public image by which he passes in an institutional environment which seeks to identify any breach in heteronormativity.

That moment of feeling that one might be or has been 'discovered' produces shame at a level that can be debilitating and prompt suicide as the logical escape. It locates one within a sense of a dominated and shamed group (Warner 2009: 288), but it is also about the concern that such membership with be discovered. In an emotional speech following the spate of queer suicide reports in the United States in September and October 2010, Fort Worth City Councilman Joel Burns used his announcement time to tell the story of his own youth suicidality. He points to the normality of his upbringing, the occasional teasing that all kids face, and his general confidence in his early teenaged years until the tension between emerging private feelings of difference and public expectation is marked by the fear of discovery and subsequent shame:

> One day when I was in the ninth grade, just starting Crawley High School, I was cornered after school by some older kids who roughed me up. They said that I was a 'faggot' and that I should die and go to hell where I belonged. That erupted the fear that I had kept pushed down: that what I was beginning to feel on the inside must somehow be showing on the outside. Ashamed, humiliated and confused I went home – there must be something very wrong with me, I thought. Something I could never let my family or anyone else know (http://www.youtube.com/watch?v=ax96cghOnY4).

What Burns' story articulates is that shame as a complex set of tensions emerges in the realisation of a distinction between public expectation and private sexual self, described here through the metaphor of the inside and the outside. The shame-risk here is produced by the tension-stressors of feeling affectively a need to work harder to prevent others from discovering his secret, a need to work harder to keep desire from becoming apparent externally under the gaze of others, to prevent a collapsing of that carefully-forged inner-outer distinction. The extent to which such work to maintain passing, work to avoid shame and work to maintain privacy becomes unbearable – particularly when others comparatively do not have to self-surveil to the same extent – is something which needs much further exploration.

The public/private distinction is, of course, a highly unstable one although this instability fruitfully shows up the way in which tensions over private sexuality and public selfhood can be problematised. Indeed, patterns of public/private knowledge, awareness, disclosure and behaviour are blurred at both an experiential level and within the discursive framework that produces the concepts of a public and a private self (Gal 2002: 81). The relationship between private and public marks the specificity of a queer identity, teenaged vulnerability, the propensity for the experience of shame, and the ways in which a non-heterosexual subjecthood can have a peculiar relationship with concepts of commonality. Contrary to some of the recent approaches that seek to constitute shame in its productivity, Warner points out that to be shamed by the sense of one's sexual desires figured as 'innermost privacy' does not lead to subjects being drawn into commonality by witnessing each other's shame (Warner 2009: 294). Rather, it exacerbates the distinction between the public and the private, whereby privacy, secrecy and the closet become the greater retreat or, for some, the unliveable space.

Heteronormativity and Non-normativity in the Face of the Other

A further way in which the connection between shame and queer youth suicide can be figured involves acknowledging that shame is produces through being considered or depicted as *other* in the face of a group, community or social institution that is grounded on normativity. This differs from the above approach on the normality predicated on surveillance, for that is about the *risk of disclosure* of sexual non-normativity. Beyond the inside/outside and passing/out dichotomies, the shame that is predicated on the body in normative space is a formation which infuses all elements in the constitution of self-identity through being socially positioned as other, regardless of the actual reactions or behaviours of others. Normativity is, as Foucault argued, an effect of power. He pointed to the power of normalisation which established itself after the eighteenth century not through any singular institution but through the interactions between different institutions (Foucault 2004a: 26) from medical and legal opinion (Foucault 2004a: 42) to education and the family (Foucault 1994: 53–54): 'The norm consequently lays claim to power. The norm is not simply and not even a principle of intelligibility; it is an element on the basis of which a certain exercise of power is founded and legitimized' (Foucault 2004a: 45). A critical approach to shame can help us to see that it is something which is produced in identity in the context of contemporary regulations of sex and sexuality, rather than in the more specific acts of homophobia, discrimination, heterosexism and bullying.

This is not, however, to suggest that heterosexuality is presented as the norm while non-heterosexuality is its inverse, the abnormal, for today it is more complex than that. While lesbian/gay sexualities might be tolerated, celebrated, made spectacle or increasingly experienced as 'common', they remain a construct built on *differentiation* from a norm by virtue of being marginal, less-common, the so-called 'ten per cent', external to expectation or spectacle. Michael Warner has recently put this in the framework of the contemporary cultural imagination of statistical and demographic social organisation, whereby subjectivities are revealed in 'their lawfulness by standard distribution; the norms and averages of population' whereby one experiences shame in the degree of *deviance* from this imagined 'distributional norm' (Warner 2009: 291). This is to suggest that queer sexuality no longer operates in contemporary culture within the disciplinary and institutional separation of the normal from the abnormal, the dichotomies that align normal and heterosexual and legitimate against abnormal, queer and sinful/criminal/other. Rather, it draws attention to the importance of contemporary biopolitics as a technology of power that makes populations and multitudes its object through statistical measurements of ratios, rates, forecasts and estimates (Foucault 2004b: 242–243, 246). For Foucault (2004b: 253), norms circulate between the disciplinary mechanisms of power that, through institutions surveil and normalise individual bodies, and through biopolitical mechanisms which seek to regularise larger bodies or groups of people by the regularisation of processes of life and living. Where disciplinary power mechanisms, of the sort that have been much discussed in queer theory and cultural studies distinguish between the normal and the abnormal, the regulatory functions of biopolitical power technologies *plot* the normal and the abnormal along 'different curves of normality' whereby certain distributions are considered to be 'more normal than the others, or at any rate more favorable than the others' (Foucault 2007: 63). What this means for sexuality is that in some contexts, including the contemporary neoliberal formations of governance and society, the strictures of the hetero/homo binary *do not* map to a normal/abnormal set of mutually-exclusive categories. Rather, it is a matter of distribution and distance from the norm. Heterosexuality is discursively performed as normative, and the non-normative sexual identities such as queerness are non-normative by nature not of opposition but of distance from the normative along a curve. This is why it is possible to state today that in legislative and certain social formulations, non-heterosexuality is not only tolerable but is also considered a legitimate sexual identity, *but* heterosexuality remains the '*most* legitimate sexual orientation' (McDermott, Roen and Scourfield 2008: 827, *emphasis added*).

Two elements for understanding sexuality-related suicide and shame emerge through the capacity to think sexuality in terms of contemporary biopolitical governance arrangements that exceed categorisations and dichotomous oppositions. The first is that shame is produced not through the stigma of being the 'wrong' category (shamed homosexuality) but in terms of the *relative distance* from that which is considered the normative. Hence a legal and (contextually) socially-acceptable sexual identity such as 'lesbian' or 'gay' can still be produced within and through shame, but this is shame based on its distance from the normative. Secondly, that shame is mutually about the 'place' one might find oneself on the imaginary social curve of normativity. To be out of the norm is to be out of place, but at the same time the shame of being out of place is that which simultaneously occurs through the place of the body in spatial and geographic terms with regard to the construction of normativity. This occurs when attention is drawn to non-normative identity, making the subject feel the shame experienced, as Probyn has put it, 'when a body knows it does not belong within a certain space' (Probyn 2004: 334). To be 'out of place' through being unable to articulate oneself and one's bodily desires within the norm is – for those without the cultural skills or resilience to produce a new form of subjective citizenship that mitigates against marginalisation – a debilitating shame.

I want, finally, to give a brief reading of the much-reported suicide of Tyler Clementi that occurred in October 2010. Clementi's death comes closest to the articulation of a suicide resulting from the shame caused by specific, homophobic acts as proffered by a number of writers on the topic of shame and suicide (McDermott, Roen and Scourfield 2008, Espelage and Swearer 2008). However, through a close examination of the reports and public knowledge on the tragic Rutgers University case, it is possible to understand shame as a particular formation that is produced in being declared, revealed and ultimately interpellated not as gay but as *non-normative* in a manner by which the self becomes publicly *totalised* as non-normative (marginal; other) in contrast to the self-perceived knowledge of the complexity of one's self-identity. In the much-publicised case, Clementi killed himself by jumping off the George Washington Bridge subsequent to being publicly shamed by his roommate who used a remote camera to capture and broadcast footage of Clementi in an intimate encounter with another male. While the act of humiliation was – whether intended or not – an act of shaming, it also made broadly public Clementi's sexuality (or assumed homosexuality) to a much wider circle than, according to reports, had been aware. That is, regardless of whether or not Clementi was struggling with the difficulty of same-sex desires or articulated his sexuality with pride, his non-(hetero)normativity was made known to others in a way that was beyond his control, invoking what must surely have been a severely debilitating formation of shame through exposure and loss of ostensible control of knowledge about himself.

To be 'outed' as non-normative produces a different form of shame from that which involves personal and deliberate choices, however culturally-conditioned, around closetedness and passing. The act of outing is something which may not be designed or undertaken deliberately to cause shame but which, by the nature of revealing one's non-normativity in some form or another among a group or community through which that person might normally pass without having to feel he or she is outside of the range of the normal, induces shame not as inferiority but as outsider, marginal and other – not belonging. As one *New York Times* report explained, 'he was not well known by others in his dorm' as his 'college career had only just begun' (Belkin 2010); a not-unfamiliar scenario in which a quiet young person slowly and gradually gains social confidence and increases familiarity with a wider circle over time. Because he was not well known, his capacity to move through social and educational life without having to face even the risk of stigmatisation through non-normativity was considerable, but that control was taken away by the act which publicly shamed him by drawing attention to his non-normative sexuality (regardless of the fact most of his fellow students would probably not have found it reprehensible in any way; that is beside the point). As an option for flight from the intolerable sensation of the inward-looking destructiveness of shame (Munt 2007: 203), suicide becomes again the logical alternative for someone who may not have had the resilience or detachment to live, at that time, a life that is at-a-distance from the normative with a sense of self-esteem.

The act of outing others has been controversial in the past, as it has at times been used as a political weapon and the topic underwent some queer community debate over whether outing would ethically constitute a breach of privacy or an unwritten community 'rule' of shared secrecy (Mohr 1992). Certainly, when revelations of one's homosexuality are not about drawing attention to a person who has spoken publicly against homosexuals or are not about the transfer of power from a protected official to the public (Gauthier 2002) – and Clementi was neither of these – then the act of outing is a disempowerment because it reduces the capabilities of an individual either (1) to develop the necessary resilience to be out *over time*, or (2) to maintain protection from harm, or (3) to avoid being totalised as non-normative and queer where totalisation occurs when the onlooker sees a part of one's identity standing for the whole (Fuss 1989: 116). As an example of how younger persons feel about the act of outing, the following statement from a twenty-two year-old graduate student appeared in a video contribution to the *It Gets Better* website (http://www.itgetsbetter.org), and indicates some contemporary attitudes to the importance of controlling information about one's non-normativity while young:

> Please know, you have the *choice* of when to come out. It's not my decision for you to come out. It's not your friends' decision for you to come out, it's not even your parents' decision for you to come out. Ultimately, coming out is a personal choice, and if you are ready to come out, then come out. If you're not ready, then it's okay. It's going to be okay. I feel that sometimes even though that we encourage people to come out of the closet, we ultimately deny them their choice. As in the Rutgers case, Tyler Clementi was not given a choice. Regardless if he was out or not, his roommate had no business in doing what he did. He had no business of taking away his ultimate choice (http://www. itgetsbetter.org/video/entry/tunr4ghbv2k/).

Although this advice couches the decision around the extent to which one declares or discusses sexual non-normativity with others in the liberal-humanist terms of *choice*, it does point to the veracity with which controlling information about one's non- normativity is sometimes a necessary protection against the effects of shame.

Within the framework of looking at sexuality-related suicide linked with shame over being identified or declared among a group of others as non-normative, it is useful to consider how shame manifests in the positioning of the affective body in (heteronormative) space. Following Silvan Tomkins (1962), several writers on queer theory have examined the formation of shame as an embodied affect. For queer theorist Eve Sedgwick, shame undertakes a double movement 'toward painful individuation [and] toward uncontrollable relationality' (Sedgwick 2003: 37). This is to locate shame within a concept of embodied subjectivity constituted within sociality and belonging; the body which moves amongst other bodies and through bodily crowds. The location of shame here is the body, and that is important when we are thinking about queer youth suicide, since both sexuality and suicide are indelibly tied to concepts of the body, embodiment and bodily affect. Indeed, there is some semantic similarity between the terms shame and reference to the body. For example, Freud's use of the term shame – in the German, *Scham* – has been linked with the traditional reference to the naked body or the genitals, the genital region being referred to as *die Scham* (Piers and Singer 1971: 18–19), seen in the more archaic English phrase to 'cover your shame'. While not merely about genitalia or nakedness or sexuality, the experience of shame as affect is bodily: the blush, the lowering of the head and eyes. The affect of non-normative sexual shame is thus produced by the body being or feeling out-of-place (Halperin and Traub 2009: 9). As Sara Ahmed argues, affective shame produces a desire for concealment, turning away the body and attempting in some manner to hide: 'An ashamed person can hardly endure to meet the gaze of those present' (Ahmed 2004: 103). The intensification of the bodily surface results from the perception of being out-of-place as both a familial outsider and a person of sexually non-normative identity that infuses his subjectivity with shame.

In that sense, we can think about the shame Clementi must have experienced in exposure of his non-heteronormativity not as a response to homophobia or ridicule, but as being rendered visible or exposed (Fullagar 2003: 299, Siebers 2009: 205) as non-normative through an act which was disempowering – that is, experiencing the pain and sometimes humiliation of having one's entire bodily selfhood infused with the knowledge of one's non-normativity under the relational gaze of others. For Clementi, this is in the sense of not belonging among the broader Rutgers University students among whom he previously had moved without the feeling of being out of place in what he might have read as exclusively heteronormative space (Oswin 2008: 90). As Foucault points out, the norm's function is not to exclude or reject; rather it is a 'technique of intervention and transformation' (Foucault 2004a: 50) which exceeds any single institution or goal (Foucault 2004a: 26). An act which unwittingly draws attention to the non-normativity of another is one which discursively seeks to transform the subject: not from homosexual to heterosexual, but a disempowerment by removal of the protections of secrecy.

It is important to bear in mind here that tolerance of non-heterosexuality, supportive environments, anti-discriminatory rules, statutes or laws and so on may – for an individual subject – be meaningless. Although there are certain norms which govern the depiction and performance of lesbian, gay and bisexual sexualities, queer persons remain non-normative in contemporary culture by the very simple fact of being rendered on the biopolitical social scale of normativity as *less common* and, broadly speaking, not expected or anticipated by significant others, whether parents, family, friends, fellow students or those whom one is yet to meet. It is not that Clementi's non-heterosexuality was revealed by the distribution of the footage, but that the distribution interpellated him as non-normative. When the norm that is the law which prescribes sexual normativity and non-normativity by distance from the normative on the curve of normality is at stake, the disempowering interpellation of a subject as a non-normative subject becomes cause for shame which is experienced as affect – the embodied nature of this shame being exacerbated in Clementi's case by the fact that it is not only an accusatory 'he is gay' but evidence distributed of his body engaged in the non-normative act which 'proves' it.

A corollary of this approach to shame is that one does not, indeed, need to be non-heterosexual to be positioned as non-normative, to affectively feel out-of-place, or to be made vulnerable to suicide as the escape from the intolerability of being persistently rendered distant from the recognisable norm. This is clear in the case of two eleven year-old boys in the United States who killed themselves within a fortnight of each other. Carl Walker-Hoover of Massachusetts committed suicide by hanging himself with an extension cord subsequent to enduring ongoing homophobic taunts at school. Ten days later in Georgia, Jaheem Herrera hanged himself with a belt, likewise after enduring relentless homophobic taunts (Blow 2009). While constant bullying undoubtedly played a significant role in creating an environment in which these two eleven year-olds could not bear to continue living, it is also likely that the shame which made suicide both thinkable and the logical pathway to escape was produced in the context of being located or placed as non-normative. It is unknown, of course, if these two boys would have eventually had a queer sexuality (had they lived), and it is uncertain if either was old enough or had the experience to have a clear sense of sexual desire or sexual identity. But what is known is that by being subjected to such taunts on what was probably a school-wide basis induced shame at *not belonging*, not being perceived as 'normal' and requiring them to endure that pain under the relational gaze of others as they moved about their schools or neighbourhoods in their everyday lives.

Conclusion

Shame in its multifarious forms has significant vigour and intensity in the ways in which it produces, inflects and conceptually-organises (1) tensions between self and expectation, (2) between public and private desires, and (3) the valency of different and complex placement of bodies in regard to relations of non-normativity and place. In order to combat the debilitating impact of shame and the ways in which for some of the most vulnerable it leads to suicidality, there is a continuing need for political and cultural activism in two fields. Firstly, further work is needed to overcome the social ways in which non-heteronormative desires, behaviours and identities are target for shaming practices. This is a struggle that needs to happen at a number of levels. Preventing or mitigating individual acts of shaming is part of that; but so too is working for continued cultural change and transformation to re-figure non-heterosexuality from being not only non-normative or at-a-distance from the norm but often as about the worst non-normativity possible. Despite the pragmatism of discourses of pride (McDermott, Roen and Scourfield 2008: 826), which has shifted from a community political articulation to a neoliberal set of private declarations bolstering the individual or coupled self (Oswin 2008: 92), pride discourses have never been able to be fully separated from concepts of shame (Halperin and Traub 2009: 3–4) and often, in turn, produce new elements of shame that thereby produce new non-normativities.

Secondly, there is a need for queer communities, social workers, teachers, parents and youth themselves to turn the experience of shame into a less debilitating scenario and protect against it resulting in escape through suicide. This is not to suggest that affective shame invoked by one's non-normativity is right or good, nor that shame should be considered something that is, in neoliberal terms of self-help discourse, a barrier to be overcome on a journey towards self-pride and self-sufficiency. As Thomas Scheff (1994) has pointed out, shame in contemporary culture tends to remain unacknowledged and denied. Where shame can be considered both positive and productive (Probyn 2000: 23), it is thinking about shame – rather than avoiding thinking about it – that can result in positive outcomes for vulnerable youth. By encouraging younger persons to accept and acknowledge shame as an affect which prompts self-reflection, resilience can be developed. Indeed, in some formulations of suicidality and shame, it is thought that those who respond to shame by anger may be less likely to attack the self through a suicidal act (Lester 1997: 354). The fact that shame will be experienced by different queer youth in different ways and to varying degrees (Adam 2009: 304) likewise means that the ways in which to reduce risk of suicide in regard to shame will be always different and varying. At the same time, this is where shame becomes productive, although such productivity is most often thought of in terms of collective responses and social transformation.

Chapter 6
Community: Homonormativity, Exclusion and Relative Misery

An element that has not been well explored in research and literature on queer youth suicide is the extent to which contemporary GLBT community norms, practices, cultures and representations might unwittingly be implicated in some of the difficulties experienced by younger queer persons, particularly in reproducing forms of isolation and exclusion. A significant strand of research that goes back to writings on queer youth vulnerability from the 1980s focuses on the effects on young queer persons of being isolated from access to other queer persons, queer communities, institutions, support groups and social activities. Queer youth isolation was first identified by Eric Rofes who suggested that 'estrangement from the traditional support systems within our culture' was one of the major factors contributing to lesbian/gay suicides (Rofes 1983: 47). The resulting logical argument is therefore that greater access to lesbian/gay-specific social institutions, venues, support groups and cultural practices provides means for developing resilience against queer youth vulnerability and suicide risk. Paul Gibson's 1989 report viewed isolation experienced by non-heterosexual youth as one of the most critical factors in suicidality (Gibson 1989: 128). For Gibson, causal factors for queer youth suicide include the difficulties encountered by younger persons in dealing with a sense of isolation from queer community:

> First they must come to understand and accept themselves in a society that provides them with little positive information about who they are and negative reactions to their inquiries. Second, they must find support among significant others who frequently reject them. Finally, they must make a social adaptation to their gay or lesbian identity. They must find where they belong and how they fit in with a social structure that either offers no guidelines for doing so or tells them that they have no place (Gibson, 1989: 112).

He pointed out that 'Gay youth frequently do not have contact with other gay adolescents or adults for support' (Gibson 1989: 128). Kulkin and colleagues (2000: 11), similarly, suggested that there are not enough role models or media representation, leading to isolation with many other studies arguing that queer youth are at risk as a result of a perceived sense of isolation (Nicholas and Howard 1998, Emslie 1996, Gross 1991, Kendall and Walker 1998, Macdonald and Cooper 1998, Morrison and L'Heureux 2001). The psychological distress caused by isolation has similarly been identified by a number of other writers on queer youth suicide (Saulnier 1998, Kulkin, Chauvin and Percle 2000: 11, Dorais 2004: 6).

Problematically, much of this approach has relied on the idea that once a younger queer person is able to access queer life in the form of institutions, recreational venues, nightclubs, bars, support groups or other forms of community, the risk of suicide resulting from a sense of isolation is mitigated. Such queer sites, organisations, spaces and media representations are presented as the 'saving refuges' which provide a stability for lesbian and gay youth 'who have reason to feel that they are living in enemy territory' (Gross 1998: 98); access to GLBT community as a young adult is seen as both a source of hope and aspiration for overcoming a feeling of aloneness. In some ways, this access risks being understood as a kind of magic solution, such that the 'problem' of queer youth suicide is one which is located only within the context of younger persons who are not *yet* in a position to become part of the sociality of queer culture, but will be 'safe' and no longer vulnerable once they do so (disregarding the possibility of a distinction between same-sex behaviours and desires and queer identity, or even the possibility that some queer persons may not wish to participate in GLBT culture as part of a queer identity). This has led to something of a vacuum in understanding the ways in which transitioning into sociality in a minority community has its own risks, as well as the ways in which all minority communities depend on exclusions – both symbolic and actual – in order to maintain a sense of community and cultural bounds. Furthermore, it ignores the fact that suicides occur among young men who are indeed already accessing community institutions or social life and, in some cases, are fully entrenched in it. In 1993, popular Sydney gay scene party-boy, Todd Macbeth, hanged himself. The local Sydney lesbian/gay newspaper *Sydney Star Observer* gave his death headline status. Another article on Macbeth's 'queer youth suicide' followed in 1997 in *OutRage Magazine* (Widdicombe 1997). Macbeth inhabited the Sydney scene and Darlinghurst ghetto of the 1990s, yet his suicide came as a shock to the community. Public disbelief occurred because this was not the suicide of a melancholic, sad, lonely and isolated person or a teenager who had not begun to socialise on the queer scene. While, as with all suicides, the causes, reasons and thinking behind his actions are unknowable, it serves as a reminder not to neglect the fact that there are those who find access to the supposed 'saving refuge' of queer community, are no longer isolated from other queer people or stuck in homophobic environments, yet are still vulnerable and at risk of suicidal behaviours.

In this chapter, I explore a number of ways in which we can re-think the possibility of queer community and queer social life as a 'saving refuge' and ask whether its current formation might contribute to suicide risks by exacerbating the experience of vulnerability, isolation and exclusion. That is not to criticise queer community nor to suggest that overcoming a sense of isolation – whether through physical access to queer recreational venues or through engaging with media and informational resources and representations – is not centrally important in reducing the risks of youth suicide. Rather, it is to ask if some of the mechanisms by which community formation, membership and identity operate might not have their own or additional risks. Two factors are important here: Firstly, that contemporary western GLBT communities are *homonormative*. The term homonormativity was first coined by transgender activists to indicate the ways in which gender-nonconformity tended to be excluded from being seen as an issue for queer community politics and inclusivity (Bryant 2008: 456), although it was later used by Lisa Duggan (2002) to refer to the ways in which GLBT community politics had adopted a more conservative and assimiliationist political strategy aiming for recognition of rights as a discrete cultural grouping (Epstein 1990: 290). This is a different method of political activity from the earlier Gay Liberationist anti-establishmentarian stance (Altman 1971), with the newer rights politics relying heavily on 'safe' community representations deemed acceptable to broader society. Representing queerness through affluence, fitness, aesthetically-competent, whiteness and other narrow depictions ultimately required the promotion of queerness through consumption while excluding all that which is deemed undesirable or politically unpalatable. This critique opens up the possibility of asking what such exclusions – whether actually experienced or perceived from afar – might do for vulnerable queer youth. Secondly, I would like to look at the ways in which such homonormative community boundary-policing can, for some, be seen to establish and reinforce particular stereotypes for the performance a queer identity. Stereotypes present the idea that in order to perform a coherent queer selfhood, there is some considerable pressure to adapt one's sense of identity in order to participate in – or belong to – a minority community. In many cases, such homonormative stereotypes that centre on taste, aesthetics, affluence and career choices are produced and reinforced in media which may be accessed by much younger queer persons, long before the possibility of physical social activity in community is possible – that is, long before the opportunity to realise just how diverse and complex most queer people really are. The perception that one is required to perform and, indeed, conform to a set of narrow stereotypes in order to be coherently queer is, again, an added pressure that increases vulnerability.

In order to tease out some of the ways in which contemporary homonormativity presents risks, the aim here is to examine queer homonormativity in terms of its impact on vulnerable or excluded youth through the framework of 'relative misery', which is an important notion in suicide theory relating to how perception of the self in comparison with peers in one's sociality can create greater suicide risks than the 'absolute misery' among a shared group. As Margot Weiss put it, the use of homonormativity as a key term in critique

> asks us to think through the ways that sexuality structures relationships among individuals, groups and the state. Tropes such as exclusion, erasure, pathology, recognition, or visibility point to shifting understandings of equality, freedom, and difference, and these refigured landscapes must be addressed in our activism and our scholarship (Weiss 2008: 97).

That is, narratives that assume *all* queer persons are made vulnerable through heteronormativity can be put in question by interrogating the ways in which structures that operate to produce a normalised queer sexuality likewise produce exclusions and erasures. By deploying that call for critique within the context of queer youth suicidality, this final chapter examines some of the ways at which we can come at the conditions that make queer youth suicide possible and thinkable from a queer culturalist angle rarely discussed in the social and health sciences. It allows us to consider how suicide risks are produced – or contributed to – not only through the forms of marginalisation experienced in heteronormative contexts but by the 'mainstreaming' of queer culture itself.

From Heteronormativity to Homonorms

Heteronormativity – the presumption that the most legitimate form of sexual identity, desire and behaviour is heterosexuality – is a continuing pressure on younger persons who may not conform to that sexuality or desire in that particular way (or perceive themselves to desire as such). Most children are raised in the presumption of heterosexuality and most attitudes about gay men, lesbians and other non-heterosexual persons and behaviours are developed in the context of heteronormativity (Becker 2006: 202). Heteronormativity does more, of course, than exclude queer persons from being seen as expressing a normative sexuality; it excludes the vast array of sexualities, desires, behaviours and possibilities that one might experience in the process of sexual development and that which might not be as easily-categorised and knowable under heterosexuality (Meyer 1996: 96). It excludes, but in the neoliberalist and biopolitical framework of contemporary western culture, such exclusion is neither complete nor wholesale. Rather, it excludes non-heterosexuality by placing it on a distribution curve, whereby non-heterosexual desires, behaviours and identities deviate from a norm or average or commonality, but are valued differentially in terms of the distance from the norm (Warner 2009: 291).

Heteronormativity is not, however, the only form of normativity around sexuality, desire, behaviour and identity. Rather, sexuality is fraught with persistent dialogue and debate on what constitutes norms and values (Attwood 2006: 78–79). While such debate does not result in a set of definitions as to what constitutes 'normal', it does produce different valuations of legitimacy. That is, the discursive imposition of norms has a tendency to produce definitional foreclosure on alternatives (Butler 1990: 15–16). What that means is that within the context of heteronormativity, all other alternatives are not invisibilised but spoken about, although such speaking can often produce them as non-normative or less-legitimate rather than included among the range of socially-acceptable sexualities that Gayle Rubin referred to as the 'charmed circle' (Murphy, Ruiz and Surlin 2008, Oswin 2008).

The continuing existence of heteronormativity and the ways in which it produces heterosexuality as being at the pinnacle of acceptable and legitimate forms of sexual expression is thus a causal factor in the making-vulnerable of younger persons who are unable or unwilling to perform sexual desire within that context or framework of sexual subjectivity, and this is due to the distance or exclusion from normativity, the correlative shame or the inability to form and perform a coherent sexual identity, both recognisable and intelligible, for the sake of social participation and belonging. However, normativities persist in other realms, including those which are discursively established as heterosexuality's oppositional other. The argument here is that such norms that circulate and produce queer community cultures, identities and formations of acceptability are just as normative and disciplinary as those found in heteronormative environments and contexts. Thus the disciplinarity of a minority community tends to involve the hiding of inequalities (Anderson 1983: 7) and the production of identities through discipline, surveillance, and border policing. The disciplinary measures and indicators of belonging and production through queer community occur, today, through homonormativity. The point of distinction here rests on the difference between biopolitical forms of governance which produce the curve of normativities, and disciplinary governance which operates at the local, institutional and community levels which more rigorously applies categorisation, exclusion and policing of the non-normative on a different scale (Foucault 2004b: 242). That is to say, while these two forms or technologies of power produce (hetero and homo) sexual identities, the biopolitical tolerates at least some variance in making whole, broad groups and populations its object of measurement and regulation, while the disciplinary polices at the level of the individual and the body through surveillance and normalisation (Foucault 2004b: 245–246). As a mechanism of power, the latter is deployed at the level of the community with a who-is-in and who-is-out categorisation of norms, which includes the deployment of homonormativity as a narrow 'in' category of normalisation. Homonormativity is thus a concept by which one can launch a critique of contemporary queer culture and politics, its complicity with broader social frameworks and the exclusions that, however unintentional, are produced and which can be damaging for those vulnerable persons who would benefit most from an inclusive, communitarian and welcoming culture.

Homonormativity, Neoliberalism and Queer Community Representation

When theorist Lisa Duggan identified homonormativity as the contemporary framework for queer community and political organising that effectively reduces the 'gay public sphere' to consumption spaces and gentrified neighbourhoods, she was criticising not the ways in which queer community has developed as a minority culture, but how the politics of queer culture had begun to operate within neoliberal norms. She found that homonormativity produces:

> A politics that does not contest dominant heteronormative assumptions and
> institutions but upholds and sustains them while promising the possibility of
> a demobilized gay constituency and a privatized, depoliticized gay culture
> anchored in domesticity and consumption (Duggan 2002: 179).

That is, the contemporary assimilationist politics which seeks legislative protections
and inclusion in conservative institutions such as marriage and military service
invisibilises, for Duggan, the radical political potential of a queerness that actively
critiques the dominance of heterosexuality and heteronormative assumptions.
This effectively sustains those assumptions that serve only a small minority of
queer people who benefit from a politics that upholds neoliberal norms (Murphy,
Ruiz and Surlin 2008: 1). Lesbian/gay politics arose out of Gay Liberationist
revolutionary rhetoric based on the Freudian-Marxian stance of Herbert Marcuse
and was expected to lead to an 'end of the homosexual' via social transformation
to a new society 'based on a "new human" who is able to accept the multifaceted
and varied nature of his or her sexual identity' (Altman 1971: 241). In his later
analysis of lesbian/gay politics Altman bemoaned the fact that '[t]he expectation
that the growth of gay self-assertion would lead to a much greater degree of
androgyny and blurring of sex roles seems, at least for the moment, to have been
an illusion' (Altman 1982: 14). The gay assimilationist lobby politics, operating
on the 'default model' of the Civil Rights approach in the United States (Sinfield
1996: 271), became the dominant cultural mode of lesbian/gay politics since the
early 1980s. It is a politics not of change or resignification of power-relations
themselves, but a bourgeois politics that seeks through legislative change,
lobbying and policy protections for the inclusion of queer sexuality as a cultural
category of rights (Epstein 1990: 290). That is, alternative sexualities are not to
question heterosexual dominance, but to exist as a GLBT or queer culture that sits
as a category within a 'safe' multiculturalism in which all difference is categorised
around labelled subjectivities, based on the idea of fixed and discrete identities that
do not question each other or the dominance of one particular category or norm.

While some writers have suggested this came about through the proliferation
of neo-conservative opinion in queer political institutions during the 1980s and
1990s (Vaid 1995: 37–38, Doyle 2008: 213), for Duggan the current political
culture of lesbian/gay communities is the result of encroaching neoliberalism
as the means by which minority politics, culture and identity are thought,
organised and framed. Neoliberalism applies an economic model and technique
of analysis to all non-market domains of social existence, and that includes
sexuality, community, identity and belonging. For Foucault, neoliberalism is a
governmentality framework through which power mechanisms, subjectivities and
ways of thinking are produced in contemporary culture. Reaching its fruition in
policy in the late 1970s and 1980s in western nations, it did not suddenly come into
being, but is the result of a historical set of developments emerging over time since
the eighteenth century and ultimately supporting and providing a rationale for the
contemporary neoliberal state, its politics, governmentality and policies towards

economic management and culture (Foucault 2007: 348). Neoliberalism produces the subject as an 'economic subject' through freedom from state 'interference' in all areas related to the acquisition of wealth, the role of labour and the market (Terranova 2009: 243). Interwoven with the juridico-legal structures and institutional disciplinary mechanisms (Foucault 2007: 7–8), neoliberalism's power technologies govern the production and constitution of identity and selfhood that is prompted towards behaviour driven by self-interest not only in economic terms but within the economic rationalisation of the social and behavioural (Toscano 2007: 74). That is, self-interest not merely in seeing the self as a participant in the market, but selfhood itself as an *entrepreneurial* activity in which one is responsible for investing in producing one's identity through consumption. In that sense, what occurs for sexuality is that the discursive production of sexual selves, expectations, normativities and minority communities is increasingly undertaken through an economic rationalism that expects government intervention only in the conditions of the market and not the mechanisms of the market (Foucault 2008: 138). It thereby rationalises identities, minorities and difference in terms of economic advantage, and in which individuals are free to become the *homo oeconomicus* or economic man whose responsibility is to work and to look after his or her own interests (Foucault 2008: 143–144) – not a businessman in the traditional sense but an entrepreneur of the self, building identity through consumption. As a consumer, the *homo oeconomicus* is actually a producer of one's own satisfaction (Foucault 2008: 226), which includes responsibility for the satisfactory production of one's identity, safety and happiness through economic consumption rather than the expectation that this will be provided by any social, governmental or communitarian activity (even though sometimes it is). It results in the loss of the radical critique of the heteronormativity of neoliberalism and its institutions and the loss of a queer community of care and responsibility that saw mutual supportive and collective behaviour in political activity and in the responsibility towards the newcomer, the vulnerable, the unwell and the young not only through the nascent years of 1970s Gay Liberation but also during the crisis of HIV/AIDS.

Because neoliberalism makes use of the power mechanisms Foucault identified as security and the biopolitical rather than the more institutionally-based disciplinarity that maintain norms at more local levels, neoliberalism has, in fact, benefited lesbians and gay men in several ways. Disciplinarity produces the idea of norms and thereby a set of references by which the normal can be distinguished from the abnormal (Foucault 2007: 63). However, biopolitics and security – which deal not with individuals or institutions but work as technologies of power that makes whole populations their object while supporting the neoliberal freedom of market exchange – plots normality by establishing an interplay of normativities; that is:

> different distributions of normality … acting to bring the most unfavorable in
> line with the more favorable. So we have here something that starts from the

normal and makes use of certain distributions considered to be, if you like, more
normal than the others, or at any rate more favorable than the others. These
distributions will serve as the norm. The norm is an interplay of differential
normalities ... (Foucault 2007: 63).

What that has meant for sexuality and for homosexuality in particular is a shift
from being identified as wholly, completely and totally abnormal along a normal/
abnormal dichotomy of inclusions and exclusions, and instead being rated
along a ratio of normativities. The discourse of *tolerance* operates through this
framework. However, such neoliberal-induced tolerance has several negative
impacts on historic and mutually-supportive alliances between radical political
intervention and queer politics (Murphy, Ruiz and Surlin 2008: 5), in addition,
of course, to the downside in that neoliberal strategies do not necessarily allow
for *any* particular non-heterosexuality to be considered equitable or as favourable
as heterosexuality, leaving open the continuing capacity for discrimination,
self-deprecation, and relative codes of superiority and inferiority. This is problematic
for, particularly, queer youth for a number of reasons. Homonormativity and
the economisation of queer social life results in disproportionate access to both
material and immaterial resources (Carter 2009: 583). The idea that queer culture
requires the production of a sexual self through domesticity and consumption
(Oswin 2008: 92) does not, in other words, necessarily mean queer participation
and relative inclusion available to all persons, and particularly not to the young.
Thus, the homonormative politics that attempts to sell a 'safe' queer culture in
order to make legislative, policy and social gains does so only for a select few who
fit the homonormative criteria of white, affluent and attractive, thereby reinforcing
disadvantages and inequities *within* queer community on the basis of economic
capacity; this has the subsequent result of producing an impact on the ability of
persons to gain participation and belonging.

Homonormativity and Exclusion

What a homonormative queer culture does, then, is produce a set of exclusions
that are utilised to police the borders of queer community in order that it appear
to be palatable, desirable and profitable for wider neoliberal sociality. Conforming
to neoliberal formations of minority and a weak multiculturalism, contemporary
queer politics dislodges the inclusive, communitarian culture and politics of Gay
Liberation in favour of iterations of rights and equality, where rights are given as
'sameness with normativity' and equality as freedom for economic choice (Weiss
2008: 89, Halperin and Traub 2009: 10). What that produces for queer culture
is the establishment of new sets of norms – homonorms – in which the white,
affluent gay male consumer becomes the measure by which queer community
membership is determined (Oswin 2005: 81). Queer community as it emerged in
the mid-twentieth century has always undertaken border-policing, although this

has usually been limited to policing who was truly 'lesbian/gay' and who was not, often excluding the less categorisable and frequently rejecting bisexuality as a legitimate sexuality that could belong within queer culture (Bryant 1997: 1). As with all minority communities, disciplinary regimes come into play in the form of obligatory ways of being and expressing oneself that act as techniques of normalisation, which can include ways of dressing, ways of undertaking physical exercise, ways of desiring, attitudes and behaviours (Halperin 1995: 32), all of which are elements of subjectivity that can be adopted or adapted, but also include other ways of being which are not so easily developed: racial and ethnic norms, gender conformity, economic affluence, body types and age. For Foucault, the biopolitical and security power technologies of neoliberalism that seek to manage populations for the sake of market freedom are distinct from the disciplinarity that occurs in institutions and minority community formations. However, these do not exclude discipline, surveillance and policing, rather they subsume the sort of disciplinary power technologies that operate in smaller communities to work, through somewhat different mechanisms, on behalf of neoliberalism (Foucault 2007: 107). Thus homonormativity is more than a political accommodation into neoliberalism but, as Susan Stryker points out, something which operates also at the micropolitical community level that authorises and legitimates some queer persons and excludes other who are not seen as representative or aligned with dominant constructions of knowledge and power (Stryker 2008: 155).

There are five forms of exclusion produced through homonormativity that can be identified as impacting on queer youth generally. Many of these relate to the situational and cultural environment which makes possible the phenomenon of queer youth suicide. Firstly, racial and ethnic exclusions: homonormativity's production of the depiction of the queer citizen as an affluent, white male means that queer youth of different racial and ethnic backgrounds become not only under-represented but excluded from a full sense of belonging within queer community. This includes those who are, in wider society, perceived as the threat to the nation – increasingly today, those of Arab background, or those perceived to be 'illegal aliens' (Agathangelou, Bassichis and Spira 2008: 127). While mainstream film and television has increased its depiction of queer persons, it certainly remains difficult to see non-white queer representation, usually the result of the ways in which contemporary film and television produce queer characters as support, requiring simple and recognisable depictions only (Cover 2000). There has recently been some evidence that among queer community and youth institutions, bullying and victimisation of particular queer youth who do not conform to racial and sexual norms *by other queer youth* has been occurring (Mishna et al. 2009: 1602), replicating the forms of discrimination and exclusion that the same bullies might have experienced in wider heteronormative contexts. Thus, while queer culture itself fits within Euro-American formations of multiculturalism, this is a particularly 'white' representation of pseudo-ethnic multicultural community.

Secondly, homonormativity produces a set of norms around gender conformity, and this has significant impact on those who do not maintain contemporary norms of masculinity for men and femininity for women. Indeed, the term homonormativity was first used by transgender activists to argue that sexual orientation was not the only way in which people differ from heteronormativity and to point to the ways in which a range of gender non-conformities, transgendered persons and others are excluded from queer community political and social organising, despite the gestural 'T' in the 'GLBT' banner (Bryant 2008: 456). A certain amount of gender play is, of course, considered acceptable in homonormative queer community circles: this is not the performativity of a gender-fluid identity but the *theatrics* of effeminacy among men or masculinity among women which are enacted through recognisable codes such as campness and drag performance. This has resulted in some exclusion or marginalisation of those queer persons perceived to 'fail' in their genders and, more generally, of transgendered persons (Brown 2009: 1497). Susan Stryker (2008) has pointed to ways in which homonormativity in queer communities disparages non-gender conformity, such as masculinity in women, generally to the same extent as is experienced in heteronormative contexts; likewise the treatment of effeminacy in men is coded as an embarrassment or matter for ridicule (Padva 2002: 288–289). This has resulted in transphobia within the community (Bryant 2008: 469), and a lack of political activity around the discursive deployment of gender identity disorder concerns among children which, it has been argued, targets not homosexual children (seen as tolerable through a broad pride discourse) but 'gender non-conforming pre-homosexual children' (Bryant 2008: 464). It might be noted that there is very little reliable data on the extent to which pre-transgendered youth are at risk of suicide, as it is difficult to determine through a suicide autopsy something which may never have been disclosed, may never have involved 'evidence' such as cross-dressing, may not have involved any indication of a desire for bodily intervention or hormone treatment or may be hidden by family members due to a sense of shame over gender non-conformity.

A third exclusion emerges in the form of the physical, and relates predominantly to men and fitness. Much has been written on the idealisation and reification of the fit, masculine, tanned and toned body in queer communities (Ayres 1999, Halperin 1995: 32, Mohr 1992: 163–164, Padva 2002). The fit, perfected, idealised body in queer masculine culture operates as spectacle but also as a measure of a norm: by being one of the major images of gay men available in both mainstream media and community publications as well as in gay pornography, the image of 'what a gay male looks like' is something encountered by youth often long before one may knowingly encounter another queer person. What does that do for those who feel their bodies are not 'fit enough' or 'toned enough'? What, for the younger queer person, who feels it is impossible to produce and discipline a body that would meet the standard, and what if it is felt that this means not only being sexually unattractive but being excluded from the sociality of a queer community? These are pertinent questions around the ways in which the mediated visuality of queer homonormativity operates to exacerbate rather than alleviate a sense of isolation.

Fourthly, there is the obvious exclusion of the non-affluent, who are effectively marginalised in queer culture for a failure to conform to the stereotype of being an avid consumer or for failing to produce a sense of aesthetics through consumption. Much media depiction of queer persons circulates the notion that to be queer means to be an uber-consumer, with shopping as a favoured leisure activity and consumer aesthetics as the means by which the self is produced (Papacharissi and Fernback 2008: 363). As Brown has put it:

> In representations of urban gay life ... the affluent gay consumer is invariably a man ... assumed to be white (although this is seldom directly remarked upon), well educated, and employed in a professional capacity. He lives in the city centre, probably in a minimalist loft apartment that is largely decorated in a normatively 'masculine' style. He is well dressed, and immaculately groomed – the epitome of metrosexuality ... Much of his social life is spent in gay bars, clubs, and restaurants ... His every consumption choice confirms his identity as an urban gay man (Brown 2009: 1506).

While Brown is right to point out that this a marketing image, it is one which dominates depictions of queer masculinity both in 'mainstream' and queer community representations; there is much evidence that the homonormativity of queer consumption is taken on-board by a large number of queer persons in very conspicuous ways – as long as they have the financial advantage and capacity to do so. Again, it is important to note that this has implications for younger persons: ultimately, it presents another norm which, for a great many, cannot be met. Most younger persons (queer or otherwise) do not have an independent income, and certainly not the financial capability to produce a queer sexual selfhood through such specific forms of consumption. While it might create a certain ideal for which some might intend to strive, for others the financial requirements for being this kind of queer personage will be seen as an impossible goal. Where cohering subjectivity around a stereotype is often a necessary function for gaining recognition, and producing the intelligible self in community or categorisable belonging, the dependence on self-stereotyping is often due to the fact that queer identity is more than simply experience or expressing same-sex attractions – the production of identity in a diverse world involves all these corollaries that depend so much today on consumption. It has been argued by Brown and others that the reification of affluence and commodity consumption are not the only economies that operate in queer community (Brown 2009: 1508), although the sorts of diverse economies and sharing that are found at times in queer communities are not necessarily those which welcome youth, who tend to be excluded from consideration in such critiques.

Finally, and dovetailing with the exclusion of the non-affluent, queer youth *in general* are excluded, particularly in the homonormative politics of queer community. This is best witnessed in the gradual shift in lobbying towards gay marriage, civil unions and other rights claims that are based on domestic, coupled partnerships (Cover 2010). Such a focus on domesticity produces queer sexual identity as 'a highly privatized, monogamous and white(ned) docile subjectivity that has been decriminalized and ostensibly invited into the doors of U.S. national belonging through recent shifts in the gendered and sexual order' (Agathangelou, Bassichis and Spira 2008: 124). Again, the point should be made that youth cannot necessarily perform that particular mode of non-heterosexuality, as coupledom and domesticity are not available to the very young, nor indeed to many others. Indeed, the pressure that comes from homonormative politics to produce the self through a habitus of domestic partnership is greater through queer political representation than necessarily found today in heteronormative social contexts.

This is not to suggest that issues relevant to queer youth such as the provision of a welcoming community environment and lobbying for suicide prevention and intervention that focuses on the specificity of queerness are sidelined in queer culture in a wholesale way, but that they are politicised only within a considerably narrow reformist, legislative and lobbying agenda. Indeed, there may well be some value in such a project, noting that among the most significant risk factors for sexuality-related suicide involve concerns around self-esteem (Remafedi, Farrow and Deisher 1994: 125, Schneider, Farberow, and Kruks 1994: 108). What underpins such a linkage is, of course, the notion that legislative protections and marriage rights for queer couples will have a longer-term result of providing a more tolerant cultural environment in which self-esteem is more easily built, or is protected from the presumed ravages of legislative or public exclusion. However, the argument remains that while legislative protections, workplace relations, superannuation rights and health insurance rights may work to improve the self-esteem of a proportion of queer persons, it does little for youth. These protections serve specific 'adult' concerns and are achieved by a programme that considers adult queer needs and desires as primary.

Understanding how and why queer culture itself has not taken the 'necessary risk' of more openly incorporating issues relevant to youth (including obviously suicide and self-harm) into its array of cultural and political concerns involves acknowledging that lobby politics internationally is dominated by an approach that seeks legislative change and anti-discriminatory protections on the understanding that such reforms will invoke a trickle-down effect and alter the state of cultural marginalisation of queer youth. It is more difficult to intervene directly in areas of discursive change that do not have at least a gestural structure for dialogue or intervention, as does the political lobbying arena. However, the motivations that drive the homonormative lobby politics in queer community are not only 'middle class', but arguably also 'middle aged', rarely taking into account factors that affect sexually-diverse youth such as suicide, homelessness, a sense of cultural isolation or access to the necessary resources through which to forge identity. The funding and time of any broad-based rights movement is always finite, and some fields of intervention are inevitably ignored. Yet, as Warner points out, the international campaigns for same-sex marriage rights pours 'millions of dollars of scarce resources … into fights that most of us would never have chosen' (Warner

1999: 144). Indeed, that might include those such as younger persons who have not yet had the opportunity to participate in the community formations through which such choices are made. Thus the structure and method of queer politics governs not only the political agenda but the ways in which queer youth issues are either taken up or sidelined.

The major concern here from the perspective of understanding the conditions of subjectivity for queer youth is that queer political and cultural communities' act of buying into neoliberal assimilationism has established homonormativities of queer life that make the pinnacle of queerness the affluent, white, gender-conforming, fit, straight-mirroring, coupled male. This thereby creates the conditions that (1) make it difficult for many younger persons to transition from queer adolescence into the dominant performative codes of queer identity; (2) excludes those who would be unable to achieve a full sense of participation and belonging because they do not or cannot fulfil the racial, ethnic or body-type criteria; and (3) automatically excludes minors from representation under the GLBT banner, creating an increased gap between the 'queer haves' and the younger 'queer have-nots'. Where this relates to queer youth suicide is in the dispersal of vulnerability. That is to say, rather than viewing queer youth as always-already vulnerable *per se*, different youth will be at different levels of risk related to inclusion, shame, and available resources for identity coherence depending on the extent to which each is impacted by the range of the above exclusions that are policed by the dominance of homonormativity in contemporary queer culture.

Homornormativity, Queer Youth and Media Stereotypes

Much of the homonormative exclusionary practices I have been discussing are not necessarily hegemonic in the actual, face-to-face, social and sexual cultures of queer community even if they dominate practices, behaviours and expectations as well as the formation of contemporary queer politics. However, homonormative disciplinarity is found in its most extreme form in media representation which is very often the site through which younger persons first gain a sense or understanding of what queerness is about. Representations of identity categories that present behavioural norms, embodied with the cultural requirement to perform our identity in recognisable ways, utilise stereotypes as the means by which to communicate a package of information about the tastes, attributes and behaviours of a minority identity group. A stereotype is most likely understood as 'truth' by those who have fewer cultural resources and literacy to undo its valency such as younger, less-experienced persons. A homonormative queer culture is also understood, viewed, witnessed or otherwise becomes recognisable among younger persons who, sometimes by virtue of age alone, are too young to be physically accessing queer community and thereby able to see the extent to which diversity of attitude, taste, behaviour and lifestyle are, in fact, normative. Media of all forms rely on stereotypes to disseminate culturally-recognisable information

about personages, often for the sake of brevity and convenience (Cover 2004).
For queer persons, that results in some reductive stereotypes that are recognisable
by a broad audience but which do not reflect the reality of diverse queerness. For
younger queer persons, however, these can also act as sources of information on
'how to be' queer; that is, how to perform a non-heterosexual identity coherently,
intelligibly and in ways that are perceived to bring about community belonging
and recognition by others. Murray, for example, makes the telling remark that '[m]
any people learn that homosexuality is a possible way of life from print media. The
existence of printed material that describes homosexuality without condemning
it as inherently wrong is not taken for granted by those living in gay worlds'
(Murray 1996: 72). When, within the neoliberal framework of a homonormative
queer politics, that stereotype is required to be one which is palatable to a general
public in order to increase the capacity for tolerance and/or protections and rights,
economically, the stereotype becomes even more narrow and exclusive. It may not
be represented as negative, perhaps not even as spectacle, but it is nonetheless like
all stereotypes: exclusionary and reductive.

There are three channels by which the homonormative stereotype is encountered
by younger persons: mainstream media representations of non-heterosexuality
(i.e., film, television, journalism); queer community media (queer press,
magazines); and online sites that provide some form of service or information,
such as Chadzboys, Gaydar or Gay.com. Mainstream film and television no longer
invisibilise non-heterosexuality, although they barely combat the dominance of
heteronormative assumptions. Rather, there is considerable inclusion of lesbian
and gay persons in film and television, although these tend not only to be in line
with neoliberal homonorms, but also circulate relatively narrow stereotypes of
queer lives, behaviours, attitudes, tastes and looks. In North America, a number of
popular representations seen to appeal to wide audiences include such series and
films as *Queer Eye for the Straight Guy*, *The L Word*, *Queer as Folk* (US version)
and *Brokeback Mountain*, in addition to queer support characters in a number of
television series and films, such as *Buffy the Vampire Slayer* and *Glee*, among
many others. Murphy has characterised this new set of representations as evidence
of a reduction in intolerance and homophobia, with 'some formerly non-normative
categories of sexual identity … moving rapidly inside Rubin's "charmed circle"'
(Murphy, Ruiz and Surlin 2008: 4), which is the range of sexualities and desires
considered socially-acceptable to broad audiences (Oswin 2008: 96). Mainstream
depictions of narrow or reductive characterisations of queer persons results partly
from the need of broadcast media to rely on stereotyping to depict characters quickly
and in ways which are recognisable. However, queer community is not entirely
without responsibility in encouraging mainstream homonormative stereotypes.
Rather, organisations such as the Gay and Lesbian Alliance Against Defamation
(GLAAD) which has long acted as a watchdog over media representation and
inclusion has become increasingly professionalised, switching from a form of
media activism to one which approves and endorses a relatively narrow range
of inclusions that are built on homonormative stereotypes (Doyle 2008: 210).

Bearing in mind, then, that broadcast media is very often the site of 'first contact' with the notion or idea of any alternative to heterosexuality for the vast majority of younger persons (Cover 2000), the reliance on dominant stereotypes of white, affluent and fit homosexuals problematically invokes the representation of non-heterosexuality as exclusionary, narrow and often communicating identity as built on a set of unrealisable ideals.

Queer community media has likewise played a central role in the production of stereotypes that are homonormative in style. This is an important, although often neglected area to consider in understanding some of the processes by which younger persons come to forge a queer identity. In some previous research involving a number of in-depth interviews with younger queer persons, I found that a relatively sizeable number had purchased or subscribed to local and national queer community media publications, often self-consciously as a means by which to engage with and understand queer community long before ever meeting another queer person, venturing into a gay nightclub or joining any kind of support network (Cover 2005c). Thus queer community media is often deliberately utilised as a resource for the forging of identity (Cover 2002). However, given the ways in which the queer press operates, often within a homonormative political and cultural framework but also as a site through which stereotypes are circulated as part of a marketing strategy or dominant image regime, the use of this resource is not unproblematic and not without its own forms of exclusions.

The reliance of lesbian/gay media on 'niche-market' advertising is significant here. Although historically many lesbian/gay publications began as free and non-profit periodicals, either as disseminators of early Gay Liberationist rhetoric or distributing information about community institutions such as clubs and bars, almost all publications that fall into the category 'lesbian/gay media' are today profit-generating enterprises. For example, the American gay magazine, *Advocate*, which began as a politically-oriented 'gay rights' periodical (Altman 1982: 164, Bronski 1984: 149), was bought in 1974 by businessman David Goodstein, who re-focussed its content on the promotion of a gay culture which could be explored and accessed by affluent gay men, publishing forty pages of cultural coverage, and advertising on twenty pages (Streitmatter 1995: 183). Although there are some queer publications such as *Sydney Star Observer* in Australia that continued for longer than others to be managed as non-profit co-operatives and tend to focus more often on political news than lifestyle consumption, almost all publications are reliant on ensuring an income from advertising funds to enable wide distribution and the costs of quality staff journalists. To maintain such advertising, it is vital that the publications 'sell on' an audience to potential advertisers and sponsors. This requires deliberate acts of audience naturalisation, that being the production by a publication or media institution of an audience's sense of itself as having an affinity with that which is advertised in the publication (Moores 1993: 2). Effectively, the labour of audiences is bought by advertisers, enforcing the work to 'create the demand for advertised goods which is the purpose of monopoly-capitalist advertisers' (Smythe 1995: 222). The labour of the audience is their 'attention' or 'potential attention' sold on to the advertiser, and the act of labouring is the learning of 'appropriate' spending practices. In the case of lesbian/gay media publications, advertising executives (and most queer community publications have at least one), must ensure that the publication establishes and maintains an identifiable audience, tested through market research, that generates an affinity between advertisers and queerness. Although homonormative stereotypes of queer personage are conveyed through the authority of increasingly professionalised queer community journalism (Goddard 1996: 2), they are also disseminated in the glossy representation of happy images and groups of people in party-mode: the message being that one will be contented if that identification is made. In Valerie Jenness' words, queer community publications are not full of 'unhappy endings' (Jenness 1992: 70). Further, the fact that the gay press represents non-heterosexual persons in their own voices (Fejes 1997: 107) conveys a further sense of truth, legitimation and authority. By relying on a set of stereotypes for advertising purposes and for the production of queer consumption, queer community media gives homonormative stereotypes 'truth value' which, again, produces and reinforces forms of exclusion.

Operating similarly to queer community media, online queer sites also produce stereotypes, again through forms of homonormative representation. Internet, online communication channels and Web 2.0 environments such as social networking and YouTube's participatory culture have been enormously important in changing the ways in which younger persons develop a sense of sex and sexuality. As Hillier and Harrison have aptly put it, 'in the face of practices of exclusion in their immediate physical worlds, the Internet may provide the possibility of new and potentially liberating alternatives for ... young people' (Hillier and Harrison 2007: 83). As with queer community media only a few years earlier, there is evidence that the Internet provides a set of forums and environments utilised by young people to 'practice' sexual identity online 'in most cases before trying them out in their immediate physical worlds' and gaining confidence (Hillier and Harrison 2007: 88, 95). Resulting from the ways in which digital, online communication is narrowcast in contrast to traditional broadcast media forms, it has been increasingly possible for younger persons exploring alternatives to heterosexuality to encounter vast material on queer life online, often through basic search engine queries, but also through sites directed towards non-heterosexual youth as well as pornography and softer-core erotica.

In thinking about the role of the Internet in young queer lives, it is important not to over-rely on a distinction between the 'real world' of physical access to sociality and sexuality, and the 'digital world' of online interaction, as if they are distinct spaces of engagement. Rather, mirroring the earlier comments about the use of community media by younger queer persons as a learning tool trajecting towards a future physical engagement in queer worlds, the Internet can be seen as that same kind of resource *par excellence*, providing vast, quick and easily-accessible information for those who are approaching queer lives, a significant shift from an environment in which many once first learned of the existence of non-heterosexuality through graffiti, rumour, Christian oppositional tracts and other fleeting information (Leap 1996: 75,126–131). However, it is also important to ask about the range of diverse representations made available – not an easy task given the fact that data on how people perceive different sites, texts and acts of communication within the context of each other is not readily available on a broad scale. Given the huge numbers of sites which reference queer (25.3 million Google hits), gay (620 million), lesbian (308 million), homosexual (20.5 million) and homosexuality (13 million), it is not possible to really know the extent of diversity in representation or the numbers of sites which are anti-queer in orientation. Rather, one fact emerges in looking at some common examples. On entering the exemplary gay.com, which is a profile-based chat and networking site providing links to a number of online versions of queer community media such as *Advocate* and *Out Magazine*, the first visual engagement is with a number of profile photos of featured members, predominantly white, well-groomed, well-dressed, as well as sample pseudo-erotic photos of white, shirtless and super-fit young men. Gaydar.co.uk's opening page is, similarly, dominated by images of shirtless, toned, muscled and well-groomed young men, mostly in sexualised or romanticised coupled poses, although there is a greater racial and ethnic diversity in the images. If one undertakes a Google search on the word gay and hits images (with moderate safe-search on), the majority of photographs that appear are of shirtless, fit, young men, mostly white, amazing abdominal muscles, some wearing Speedos or underwear and a number of same from Pride Parades around the world. What this indicates is that between dedicated sites and Google searches, the possibilities of digital, online media to provide the greatest diversity and array of representations of non-heteronormative sexualities has not quite come to fruition, and rather the same homonormative stereotypes are re-circulated.

Between narrow mainstream representations of non-heterosexual persons and queer community media and online sites' reliance on stereotypes, what tends to be available as the image or resource for queer youth is the 'gay white affluent consumer' (Oswin 2005: 81). Sarah Schulman blames the mass proliferation and circulation of particular images of gay men in glossy magazines for the false representation of gay persons; she suggests there is a 'Fake, Public Homosexual' (Schulman 1995: 13). Indeed, that is certainly the case, because such media images do not represent the broad, diversity of complex persons – no stereotypes ever does. But for those who have not developed yet the cultural literacy or experience to recognise this fact, the homonormative image *appears* to be truthful. That is, for those who can identify the stereotypes, ignore the advertising, critique the choices of images and representations or understand that there is always greater diversity than found in such representations, none of this matters too much. While there is an argument that these productions of visibility across all three media forms is better than wholesale invisibility, in light of their use as a resource and as a means by which information on queer community appears as 'truth', it is important to continue asking what *sort* of visibility is produced here. Concerns around the existence of narrow stereotypes that might be read as having truth value and utilised as a resource for identity development and performativity of queer selfhood include the fact that there is a risk that intervention services delivered in community settings to queer youth might replicate these narrow perspectives. As Rosario has pointed out, research has indicating that a single program to promote a particular form of queer identity 'may not serve all youths well' and that programs must take into account and be tailored to a more diverse array of ways of being non-heterosexual (Rosario, Schrimshaw and Hunter 2008: 279–280).

Homonorms and Relative Misery

I began this chapter by remarking on the ways in which a number of writers on queer youth suicide had discussed the debilitating effects of a sense of isolation in heteronormative environments experienced by many younger queer persons, and how this has too often resulted in an understanding that once a person is old enough to access queer community in physical, geographic and social capacities, that person's risk of suicidality is thought to be mitigated significantly. This may be true for many. Certainly there is evidence of the debilitating effects of heteronormativity and the ways in which stigmatisation or exclusion of queer youth, or their relegation into non-normativity, leads to chronic emotional stress (Almeida et al. 2009: 1002). What I am arguing here, however, is that a sense of isolation produced through living in a heteronormative environment (family, home, school, small town, media representations, etc.) is not always overcome when one encounters not only queer homonormative community with its many exclusions, but also the *perception* through media forms and stereotypes of what queer community is and just who it is that might be permitted to belong to it. In that sense, there is an argument that one can be just as isolated within queer community and its representations as one might well have felt as a non-heterosexual young person existing in a significantly heteronormative environment, if not more so. Indeed, the argument here is that in being given the 'hope' that queer community is accepting and the 'answer' to isolation, anything which works to exclude a person from the promise of belonging and participation can be much *worse* than the sense of isolation or exclusion felt in being a young queer person within a heteronormatively-oriented environment, due to the what will be perceived as the failure to belong or to meet the standards required for access to that 'saving refuge'.

Recent work on suicide by James Barber has provided a useful way in which to understand the complexity of belonging and exclusion, and to overcome the idea that queer community is automatically always a saving refuge against isolation and vulnerability. Barber criticised researchers and public commentators who discuss youth suicide in terms of *generations* in crisis. He referred to this depiction as the Absolute Misery Hypothesis, the 'intuitively straightforward notion that the suicide rate of a generation is a surrogate measure of that generation's happiness. The more suicides, the greater the level of unhappiness' (Barber 2001: 49). That is, the social marginalisation, economic disadvantage or discrimination against an entire community or society had been thought previously to be a factor in a greater number of suicides. Cross-national analysis, however, indicated that this was not the case, and that instead higher rates of suicide have been associated with higher levels of psychological adjustment, happiness and affluence among groups or whole populations (Smalley, Scourfield and Greenland 2005: 138). Barber countered the Absolute Misery Hypothesis with a proposal to return to Durkheim's point that higher national suicide rates often tend to accompany good national fortune, and suggested approaching suicidality factors through what he termed a Relative Misery Hypothesis (Barber 2001: 53):

> According to the 'relative misery hypothesis', young men's predisposition to suicide is influenced by their social comparisons. When those around them are perceived to be better off than they are, the distress of vulnerable youth is magnified and their susceptibility to suicidality increased. The relative misery hypothesis would therefore predict a rise in suicide rates whenever there is a rise in the overall mood or happiness of a population, whether that rise is due to the end of war or any other event of general and positive social significance. At such times, the misery of the community's unhappiest young men will be compounded by the isolation they experience at witnessing the happiness of those around them (Barber 2001: 53).

While Barber and others who utilise the Relative Misery approach are often referring to whole national populations whereby the suicide rates among the most disadvantaged or marginalised are higher when the country is doing well, this model provides a valuable way in which to understand why queer youth suicide rates continue to be high while, in neoliberal, multicultural and homonormative terms in western countries, many queer people are much less discriminated against or socially excluded than only one or two decades ago. It is to say that *relative* to the broader queer population, some younger persons do not have the same increasing advantages, resources, finances, emotional resilience, authorised tastes or acceptable bodies, and thus are further isolated by witnessing the perceived happiness of other queer persons that they feel that may not themselves be able to achieve. Within this approach the likelihood of suicide is in fact greater (by comparison and contrast) rather than reduced (by an assumed trickle-down effect from assimilationist rights gains and the benefits received by more affluent queer adults).

In other words, where upward social comparison is a factor in psychological adjustment, the perception that one is worse off than one's lesbian or gay peers is a problem that needs to be addressed. Queer people are, indeed, doing so much better *if* the narrow homonormative depiction is seen as representative. That is, some queer persons move closer to the broad social definition of normativity and hence acceptability; but it will be the function of community discipline through representation and stereotyping which decides who those persons will be. This, then, has raised the bar for the production of queer selfhood and queer belonging, creating a greater gap and greater difficulties for integrating into queer community than existed prior to the emphasis on homonormative representations in queer politics, culture and media. The privileging of certain sexual minorities over others (Murphy, Ruiz and Surlin 2008: 5), the disciplining of queer masculinity as spectacle (Carter 2009: 605), the marginalisation of non-gender conforming persons (Bryant 2008: 456), the increasing requirement of financial capabilities and affluence for performing queer sexualities through norms of consumption (Papacharissi and Fernback 2008), the dominance of whiteness in depictions of non-heterosexuality (Mishna et al. 2009), the emphasis on fit, toned and idealised bodies (Padva 2002) and the general exclusion of younger persons from queer politics and queer political issues (Cover 2010) establish not just the risk of exclusion or isolation but social comparisons relative to the homonormativity that disciplines queer identity through community formation and that circulates even more strongly through stereotypes in mass media, queer community press and online representations. To put it another way, the gains made by homonormative and neoliberal assimilationist strategies have a *differential* impact, which increases the likelihood of rising suicide rates for those who do not benefit as much from such change and development (Cleary and Brannick 2007: 85).

It is therefore important not to assume that there is a general contentment among GLBT people that has been produced through neoliberal assimilation, nor to assume that all queer youth shift away from risk and vulnerability as such social changes become public and knowable broadly. Rather, it is necessary to see that contentment as the product of certain narratives and stereotypes of queer adulthood can, in fact, establish two elements of comparison or measurement for younger persons that produce relative misery as a causal factor in suicide; effectively a doubling of relativities. Firstly, there is the comparison between themselves and straight peers who are seen to face fewer social problems, less capacity for shame, less likelihood of discrimination and lower risk of being bullied. Secondly, there is the comparison between themselves and queer adults who appear to be doing well or at least are perceived to be happy, well-off and content. Additional to the relative misery this produces, the construction and representation of queer adults through homonormative depictions establishes norms that subsequently are found to be unrealisable, which is a known factor in the creation of self-deprecation, self-esteem deficits and the manifestation of self-destructive behaviours (Hunter and Harvey 2002: 17). Again, this is not to suggest that queer youth have not benefited from such changes, only that for those who are excluded through homonormativities in either representation, stereotype or fact, the relative misery can be much worse, putting some at greater risk than in previous social perceptions of queer community, culture and identity.

Conclusion

Changing the circumstances which produce homonormative depictions and behaviours that increase the risk of suicide through exclusion, comparison and unrealisable goals is not a task that can necessarily be undertaken solely within queer community. Indeed, the momentum towards assimilationist lobby politics is very likely unstoppable, although for activists that does not mean one stops trying. Radical activist formations such as *Queer Shame* have been energetic in critiquing the ways in which queer politics has embraced neoliberalism as a vehicle for inclusion, although producing change also means critiquing and combating neoliberalism in broader society as the structural underpinning of contemporary social relations and processes (Agathangelou, Bassichis and Spira 2008: 138), which requires then a persistent identification of the connections between queer discriminations and exclusions, the cultural environment of youth generally and other formations which produce disadvantage both social and economic.

At the same time, however, intervention and prevention techniques for non-heterosexual at-risk youth need to be more aware of the ways in which homonormativity operates and of the narrowness of the continuing stereotypical depictions in media, community press and online sites. At the most basic level, this can mean social workers and counsellors promoting the idea that 'however seemingly successful and confident their peers may be, they may also have problems and may suffer from doubts, anxieties and low mood' (Smalley, Scourfield and Greenland 2005: 139). In other words, it is important to address the existence of homonormativity in queer community and representational media by fostering the notion that queer persons are, often, far more diverse than the images a young person may have encountered. This also means actively showing that while some formations of queer community are exclusive, this is not necessarily to be seen as an individual shortcoming, failure or inability to produce the 'right' kind of sexual self.

Conclusion
Towards Liveable Lives

Life itself, as Judith Butler (2004, 2009) points out, is precarious: lives can be ended at will or by accident. The precarity of life is in that it is always relational to the lives of others, for life requires 'various social and economic conditions to be met in order to be sustained as a life' (Butler 2009: 13–14). Yet for some, the precarity of life is greater than for others, and this can include the vulnerability to self-harm or being positioned such that ending life appears to be the best and most logical option for overcoming a perceived unbearability of existence or a perception that life is unliveable. That is, for *some* subjects, the physical, infrastructural, financial and social support and protection for a life to be maintained is greater than for *other* subjects, which is not to say that these are always easily along demarcated lines of identity or recognition. For a society to take no action or demonstrate no special concern around queer youth suicide is unethical, because it fails to recognise the need for support in relationality that is endemic to all subjects. Whether the response comes from policy-makers, those trained to intervene, researchers, school-teachers, queer communities, parents or significant others in the life of a queer younger person, that response is demanded ethically because failing to respond is to discount queer lives as human lives (Jenkins 2010) or as lives which would be broadly grieved if lost (Butler 2003: 10). An ethical response, however, is more than simply developing interventionist policies, expanding counselling or engaging in social change such that queerness seems less shameful or less normal, more tolerated or more included. Rather, the nature of an ethical response is, by necessity, complex yet can lead to understanding how different responses – both pragmatic and philosophic – need to be developed outside of the normative frameworks through which queer youth suicide has generally become a policy, social or research issue.

A study of the ways in which cultural knowledges regiment subjectivity through sexual identity formation and community policing does not lead directly to intervention programmes and techniques as such, since opening questions about the contingency of identity is aimed at undoing the existing regimes through which the building-blocks of many such programmes identify and act upon risks. However, there are three ways in which an ethical response to queer youth suicidality as a social phenomenon can take careful, critical steps towards prevention which I would like to address here. Firstly, an ethical stance presents a means by which the opening up of the field of sexuality and its contingency can be undertaken in order to reduce the constraints that make a life an unliveable one. Secondly, by focusing on new ways in which sexuality and sexual identity might be thought and emerge differently for different subjects in a contemporary, digital environment, new opportunities for prevention can be developed that include new forms of perceiving community and engagement. Finally, approaching queer youth suicide from a perspective not of risk but through the simultaneous fostering and critique of resilience opens the possibility of providing solutions that aid younger persons to resist suicidality as a flight from intolerable pain without articulating the self as inviolable and thereby losing the ethical value of the recognition of vulnerability.

Ethics and Cultural Change

In her *Precarious Life* (2004), Butler argues that there is a common human vulnerability that emerges with life itself, for we are from the very beginning given over to the other and formed in relationality and the risk of violence. This leads to a demand for an ethics that responds to the fact that some lives are supported and maintained and other lives are made more vulnerable. She argues that while some lives ('us') are protected to the extent that a threat to those lives will mobilise the forces of war, other lives ('them') do not even qualify as 'grievable' (Butler 2003: 20). By that, she is arguing that for a currently-lived life to matter and to be recognised as the human life of a human subject, a subject must be recognisable as one who, if she or he ceased living, would be a loss, one of 'us' to be grieved, a life to be mourned by the community, the state and society generally. She is writing predominantly about the framework of war, whereby some lives are deemed worthy of fighting for, but the lives of those lost on the other side are not grieved by the nation built on a concept of a normative 'us'.

This ethical approach can be applied to queer youth suicide by opening the question as to whether or not young queer lives, as the non-normative 'them' in contemporary western societies, are framed as worthy of grieving in the same way as other lives. It allows us to ask from an ethical perspective if the current social perception of normativity considers queer youth lives as a loss and if, to be ethical, new ways of thinking about 'queer' and 'youth' are required in order to prevent such loss by making those lives equally as grievable. Following from the discussions in the first three chapters in this book, the lives of queer youth are – at times – depicted and understood as lives which are *expected* to be lost to suicide on the basis that they are believed to be endemically unliveable, thereby stemming opportunities for prevention. In that context, a young queer person is not considered a fully human subject due to the matrices of power that confer normativity on some sexual subjects but less legitimacy on others (even within a framework of tolerance), producing a cultural and policy environment in which we have subjects who are 'always already lost, or, rather, never "were"' (Butler 2003: 22). Normativity confers liveability, and the risk of this is that as long as contemporary cultures identify and distinguish on the basis of norms, some lives are seen as unliveable not just in social and policy terms but by the subject himself or herself struggling to live that life.

The difficulty in making a queer youth subject 'worthy' of being a life that should be saved at all costs through policy, processes, change and responsibility is due to the way in which queer subjects are persistently determined as *tolerable but non-normative* within a contemporary liberal culture that produces normativity through lists of 'acceptable' demarcations such as ethnicity, class, race, religion, sexuality and gender (Butler 2009: 138). Within a liberal ontological framework, queer youth – tenuously – can be seen as subjects worthy of living and, indeed, worth grieving, but *only* if they are added to an expanding list of possible subjects that accommodates and overcomes contemporary articulations that present queerness or, indeed, sometimes youth itself, as non-normative. As I have shown in previous chapters, neoliberalism is indeed responsible for deeming particular subjects worthy, namely those who are able to operate as the economic man, responsible both financially and personally for managing their own risks and conditions. Again, this has allowed a certain formation of queer subjectivity, as is seen particularly in recent homonormative queer community articulations of identity, in which financial affluence, self-sufficiency, whiteness and masculinity become the stereotypical markers of living a successful queer life. Most recently, such examples were communicated in a vast number of the corporate-sponsored *It Gets Better* videos, suggesting that a queer life becomes a liveable life in its articulation through financial independence, white-collar careers, conservative coupledom and other performances of sexuality that are, effectively, same-sex reorientations of heteronormativity. This, however, is neither inclusive nor guarantees that a young queer subject can recognise one's own life as liveable in such a narrow, categorical set of frameworks.

Thus while liberal and neoliberal frameworks do indeed increase the inclusivity of queer persons and thereby confer certain lives with liveability, they are not the solution to queer youth suicide as they remain built on exclusions that can exacerbate for some – not all – queer youth the unbearability of being queer. For Butler (2009: 146), such programmes do not constitute an ethical response, for they foreclose on the possibility of calling for alternative vocabularies of subjectivity and new forms of sociality. At the same time, they operate within a narrative form of progressive history in which inclusion is seen to be a natural outcome rather than critiqued in terms of the types of inclusions that make a life one deemed worthy of living (Butler 2009: 148). Because they are built on forms of normativity, such positive categorisations in tolerance risk always the possibility of exclusion that for some will make suicide the only possible escape from the unbearability of non-normativity and its more ostensible expressions (bullying, exclusion, relative misery, shame). For Butler, then, the problem is not one that is addressed by an attempt to include more people within norms or to make existing marginal categories appear 'more normal',

> but to consider how existing norms allocate recognition differentially. What new
> norms are possible, and how are they wrought? What might be done to produce
> a more egalitarian set of conditions for recognizability? What might be done, in

other words, to shift the very terms of recognisability in order to produce more radically democratic results? (Butler 2009: 6)

The key to cultural change thus involves operating outside of liberal and neoliberal frameworks, which suggests the politicisation of queer youth suicide cannot necessarily occur through the recognised methods of lobbying, queer community activism and funding. Rather, instituting the possibility of developing a contemporary sociality through which the queer youth subject is *recognisable* as a subject worthy of living, and worth grieving if lost, involves significant social change both within and outside the discourses of sexuality.

Following from her work on ethics through shared vulnerability, Butler (2009) has developed a means by which to understand how it is possible for a subject to be recognised as a subject worthy of recognition and of the responsibility of the community or sociality more broadly. How subjectivity is constituted through interpretative 'frames' is significant here, for it is this which makes a subject recognisable *as* a subject – a subject deemed worthy of living, protecting and a subject who can be grieved. Frames, likewise, deem other subjects unworthy of living and protecting, ungrievable, not viewed as genuine lives or lives which matter (Butler 2009: 163). They are that which characterise the general conditions that 'prepare or shape a subject for recognition – the general terms, conventions, and norms "act" in their way, crafting a living being into a recognizable subject' (Butler 2009: 5). Frames provide a taken-for-granted reality (Butler 2009: 12), and thereby govern what comes to be seen as natural, common-sense or familiar. In other words, they are that which confer the possibility of recognising a queer subject as a liveable life, this being not just recognition by a community but recognition by queer subjects themselves. Frames set the conditions for reactions to particular scenes, visualities, texts, images or knowledges (Butler 2009: 11), and this can include the ways in which sexual identities are categorised, formed, recognised and performed. However, frames are themselves contingent, thus there is always the possibility of attitudinal change – in this case, that includes changing how queer youth lives are perceived, developing ways in which to make those lives recognisable as grievable lives or lives which would matter if they are lost to suicide. The critical task is to show how frames, which are never wholesale or monolithic, can break with themselves such that 'a taken-for-granted reality is called into question, exposing the orchestrating designs of the authority who sought to control the frame' (Butler 2009: 12). That is, frames always risk their own undoing and the undoing of their logic, thereby making possible the collapsibility of the norms they uphold. Thus critique in its many forms from artistic expression to academic interrogation to subversions that may not necessarily seem subversive in advance are the predominant, if complex, means by which cultural change is possible, and through which queer youth can be re-figured as having lives which may be liveable and through which the unbearability that emerges from non-normativity can be stemmed.

Following queer theory and its methods of critique, the cultural change that one aims to produce is that which makes available a broader range of discourses that undo sexual identity as a fixed and innate formation necessary for subjective coherence, intelligibility and recognisability. This is to critique and disengage the hegemony of categorisations which place unnecessary pressure on adolescents to develop according to recognised normativities, to perform sexualities that may not be perform-able for some subjects, to disavow polymorphous desire and direct all erotic desire to a specific and discrete gender, and to embrace and develop an attachment to common regulatory regimes. If we are to make certain lives more liveable and less unbearable than they otherwise would be – as we are ethically bound to do – what is required is the radical subversive act of persistently re-framing sexualities and identities as contingent. This is not, as Butler (1999) has argued, to throw off the shackles of contemporary discourses of sexuality and return to a pre-nineteenth century normativity that allowed a greater range of pleasures not tied to specific identity positions, for there is no possibility of making a clean epistemological break with present regimentations of sexuality that produce desire through gendered attractions; rather it is to seek the means by which to open the space for the emergence of alternative ways in which sexuality, desire, erotics, bodies, pleasures and genders can be thought, articulated and performed. Likewise, it is to be wary of the force of identity politics and identity-based preventative measures that foreclose on or invisibilise existing and unanticipated diversities for the gains that benefit only a few (and, rarely, queer youth).

Throughout this book, I have pointed to the fact that the categorisation of sexual subjects along the dichotomy produced by the hetero/homo binary is both historical and, despite the deeply-felt attachment of many people to such identity categories, disavows the contingency and constructedness of sexual desire. Often unsuspectingly, such categorisation enacts a violence on younger persons. Sometimes this is through the demand to categorise oneself as heterosexual or homosexual before one is ready to do so, a demand that might even be expressed unwittingly through a comment or a joke. Sometimes this violence is enacted through the well-meaning but problematic structure of suicide intervention techniques whereby a subject, one who may not be able to produce an attachment to one or other category of sexuality, is thought to be simply having difficulty coming to terms with being homosexual and encouraged to affirm an impossible or incompatible queerness (Cover 2011). Sometimes this violence occurs surreptitiously, through the shame that is accorded non-normativity and by the complex array of factors through which a queer subject may find he or she is living a life that is marked by shame, despite the efforts to turn sexual shame into identity pride. Sometimes this violence is through the unwitting exclusion by queer community of a queer subject who feels that he or she may not live up to those glossy, happy images as expectations of a coherent, intelligible and – indeed – well-adjusted queer self. And this is where a demand for an ethical perspective comes in. For Butler, we are all formed in violence against our will, and often through categorisations which confer intelligibility or recognisability. However, the ethical responsibility that emerges from her perspective is 'not to repeat the violence of one's formation', not to reconstitute the violent matrix of power that formed us in the first place (Butler 2009: 167). What this implies is that the framework of identity politics as the model through which claims are made on behalf of queer youth is not always the best or most ethical means by which arguments for cultural change can be made, because it is founded in the violence of inclusion and exclusion (Murphy 2011: 578) and the violence of refusing contingency (Jenkins 2010: 102–103). Thus an ethical position on queer youth suicide demanding that our world pay attention to the problem in a way which embraces its complexity is one that calls for looking *beyond* sexual categorisation, and that can mean the ethical demand is a demand for the undoing of the foundations of sexuality and sexual minority status themselves.

At the same time, an ethical perspective on queer youth suicide here is one which rejects the over-valuation of queer suicide statistics, even though these have been remarkably useful in motivating the development of policy, funding of intervention and prevention techniques and the development in health sciences of new methods of counselling, for example. An ethics does not emerge from the force of statistical numbers generated through a biopolitical measurement as to *how many* lives need to be lost before change is required. The biopolitical framework of governmentality that frames and determines the recognisability of lives on the basis of statistical figures and measurements is incapable, as scholars following Foucault have shown, of presenting a singular life as valuable (Fassin 2009: 52). With that in mind, existing policy frameworks will not necessarily be the means by which responding to queer youth suicide as a social problem will be possible, even with the support of statistics, for making lives grievable in order to make them liveable is not compatible with the forms through which biopolitics produces the concept of living, such as through demography, epidemiology, public health and planning. Although ethics that focus on the individual, such as particular religious perspectives which make claims that every individual is valued, are often very difficult and complex to put forward and, in this case, to apply to the field of queer youth suicide, it remains the case that such an ethics as I have been articulating it is one which looks not to the need for prevention of queer youth suicide *because* the numbers are statistically higher than those of non-queer youth who self-harm. Rather, it looks to the singularity of youth who seek out suicide *because* they are non-heterosexual, non-normative, at a distance from the norm on a curve of normalities, or because the processes of normative sexual becoming have made life unbearable. Numbers, then, are much less the target of this claim that the violence of normativities.

Finally, the ethical demand for broad social action on queer youth suicide and, as I maintain, for looking to the complexity of the relationship between subjectivity, normativity, community and suicidality in the queer youth suicide formation, is a demand which struggles against the violence of *doing nothing*. It is a demand for action that can take many forms for the development of prevention, but in order for that demand to be recognised – in order for the queer subject to be recognised as worthy, grievable and vulnerable differentially from other subjects – the starting point is the undoing of the frames that produce queer subjects through the notion that vulnerability is endemic to queer youth rather than a common, human, corporeal and shared attribute of humanity in relationality. Change that brings about a sociality and forms of relationality that can apprehend the vulnerability of some queer youth and thereby respond ethically to queer youth suicide is not something which can be known in advance. However, as Butler (2009: 22–23) suggests, grasping the precariousness of embodied life as not just a feature of some lives but as a generalised condition (a generality that can be denied some subjects by failing to recognise those lives as grievable and worthy of living) is a means by which a critical and ethical perspective can lead towards social change. The commonality of life's precarity and the certainty of death is one of the available possibilities for undoing the cultural valuation of subjects along the lines of sexual norms. By working towards a commonality that undoes difference and the distance from others through, as Butler suggests, recognising the vulnerability of the other calls for a new politics that puts the vulnerable ahead of queer rights claims.

Prevention

It is not always obvious how such a radical position can be understood to benefit subjects specifically or address a problem in ways which can be applied pragmatically. Indeed, queer theory has frequently been the subject of such criticism, although this is often wrongly thought of as being the result of a critical theory which is 'out of touch' with lived realities. However, critique does have value for opening the possibilities for realities to be lived differently and, in the case of this topic, for finding ways in which unliveable realities can be transformed into those which are liveable. Addressing cultural change is thus a necessary element in prevention. For Rosario and colleagues (2008: 280), for example, this can be practical while still grounded in critically engaging with the larger social context in which a broad range of queer youth come to know themselves in shame or exclusion or in other ways which make life unliveable. There are various existing measures and programmes aimed at preventing youth suicide generally, and it pays to ask where these fit within an ethical framework that seeks to undo the violence of categorisation as the existing means of defining sexual identity. Non-pharmacological treatments focus on the social environment of younger persons, and include outreach programmes that attempt to educate the public about suicide and suicide risk, frequently through the everyday work of medical practitioners, school-teachers and counsellors and youth service personnel dealing with children and adolescents (Kloos et al. 2007: 92). Others operate to train those working with younger persons to identify risk specific to queer youth through various screening measures. However, such attempts at early identification, while important as a means of intervention, are problematic not only because it is difficult to determine at younger ages who is queer and who is not (unless that information is volunteered) but, more importantly, the attempt to identify even in queer-affirmative frameworks puts added pressure on those very subjects in ways which can lead to unbearability of living as outlined in Chapter 4.

In that sense, certain means of interventional prevention occurring today through schools, medical centres, counselling services and youth groups – while well-intentioned and undoubtedly successful for some number of subjects – may not necessarily be ethical as they repeat that violence of categorisation. Where help is deliberately sought through an act of articulating sexual minority status it is, of course, a different story, although strategies designed to encourage suicidal individuals to seek help are known to be ineffective in capturing the broader range of attempted suicides (Smalley, Scourfield and Greenland 2005: 146). At the same time, this is not to suggest that pharmacological and therapeutic intervention is unnecessary or without value, for it should be borne in mind that queer youth, like many others, can suffer from mental health problems which may lead to suicide (McAndrew and Warne 2010: 93). Again, an ethical responsiveness to the issues faced by queer youth requires not assuming that all queer youth who are suicidal are suffering from mental health issues, for some suicides can indeed be the rational choice or the only choice available for those who, in sociality, find life unliveable or unbearable while for others clinical depression or other mental health concerns may be causal of suicidality without necessarily having anything to do with subjective queerness in the first instance. To fail to make a categorical judgment, to fail to intervene, would from this perspective be to act without ethics of responsibility.

Within the framework of responding to an overall queer population and a broader queer youth suicide problem, a number of writers have recently argued that direct preventative measures can occur effectively today through the use of online media. It has been argued that suicidal younger persons are better able to seek help online than in person, although it has also been suggested that risks of suicide can increase through this medium as a result of the inability for professionals to intervene directly through online communication in cases where this is warranted (Martin 2006: 3). Outreach programmes have been trialled online with the view that the Internet and social networking offers a novel opportunity to reach queer youth who may be making use of it as a resource for other developmental concerns and for socialisation (Silenzio et al. 2009: 459). Indeed, as a site in which subjects can share their experiences without fear of retaliation has been posited as an important benefit of online communities (Tyler 2009: 92), although it does have to be asked if this is achievable without categorisation, without repeating other forms of violence and without risking the additional injurability and suicidality that can come through the prevalence of cyberbullying online (Gerrish 2011, Hinduja and Patchin 2010). Given the vast power the Internet gives to young people to organise, network and articulate creatively and critically, it is perhaps this site which has the strongest potential for emerging preventative measures. For these to be effective, they must be developed collaboratively and coalitionally between youth representing very broad sexualities and practitioners open to understanding emerging youth cultural perceptions of sexuality rather than relying on older models.

Resilience

Having argued for broad cultural change in a way that is impossible to know the outcome in advance and, similarly, having argued that forms of prevention on the whole are not always enough or are not always deployed in ways which ethically address the constitutional problems of queer youth suicide, it may appear that there is an impasse in terms of practically dealing with queer youth suicide as a social phenomenon in general. However, one element that combines both the ethical demand for cultural change and the urgent requirement for new ways of thinking and undertaking prevention is to return to Ritch Savin-Williams' (2001) argument that we should worry less about queer youth suicide risks and vulnerability and, instead, consider what it is that makes some youth more resilient against suicide than others, and advance this possibility broadly.

Resilience here can mean the capacity to find effective alternatives to taking the decision to end life as an escape from unbearable pain. The overall ethos of the *It Gets Better* site, as discussed in Chapter 3, argued that school bullying frequently made life intolerable but that hope for a time beyond bullying (after graduation) must be maintained in order for queer youth to be resilient enough to resist suicide. However, as I argued in Chapter 6, such optimism is not available to *all* subjects, in that the hope for a happy, tolerable existence as an adult is not something which is equally available to everyone and, for many, the pain of exclusion not only dashes such hope but can add further to the unbearability of living through comparison of rates of exclusion leading to the suicide risk factor of relative misery. In pragmatic terms, resiliency factors have been identified among queer youth, and these include contact with supportive individuals, supportive schooling environments and self-efficacy (Crisp and McCave 2007: 406). In the case of the first but taken in light of the arguments above around the violence of categorisation, it can be said that supportive networks need not necessarily be queer networks but simply the networks of family, peers and significant others who provide the emotional and social scaffolding necessary for life not to be – or at the very least not to *feel* – so precarious. Supportive schools is an obvious area for ongoing prevention, given these are the sites at which heteronormativity is so regularly articulated both ostensibly through bullying and surreptitiously through curriculum. For these to be the site instead for fostering resiliency may, however, mean more than just the development of protective policies but a wholesale transformation of schooling in general. Certainly there are many other reasons why such a transformation is desperately required.

The third factor of resilience through self-efficacy is more complex, for there is a need not to assume that this is the private responsibility of individuals to manage, as in neoliberal frameworks, rather than an issue for social welfare and sociality in general. The sort of resilience I am considering here is not grounded in hope nor in claims of strength or the development of a stance of nonchalance against the social dynamics which can exclude, de-normalise or induce shame for a queer subject. Rather, attributes of resiliency involve an awareness of the contingency and constructedness of current situations, positions, environments, sensibilities and feelings such that at the particular piqued moment in which life comes to seem wholly unliveable, alternatives emerge through which life can be perceived otherwise. In some ways, this is to recognise the self in its contingency, multiplicity and dynamic complexity as a way of overcoming the sense that there is no pathway for ending intolerable emotional pain except suicide. Finding alternatives through the self-efficacy of hope or life opportunities may be effective for many, but where shame, the impossibility of identity coherence or relative misery may be the primary factors for a young queer person in becoming suicidal, this requires understanding shame as something not indelible, understanding identity as contingent and understanding community exclusion as cultural. In other words, resiliency is through bearing witness to the cultural constructedness of the situation of the self as constituted in discourse and the historicity and contingency of identity and sexuality. This is prevention through critique whereby deconstruction rather than affirmation is the tool to forging resilience.

At the same time, it should be said that for resilient subjects to be ethical subjects requires not self-efficacy as a posturing of inviolability, even though the term resiliency often comes to mean this. Frequently it is presented through the claim that one must be strong, stand up to bullies and face discrimination with a stoic front. Not only has this proven ineffective in combatting suicidality, but it is to fail to take note of the value in recognising one's own vulnerability and thereby the vulnerability that is common to humanity. It is possible to be resilient, indeed, through embracing the precarity of life itself rather than through claims or performances of inviolability. By understanding the precariousness of life in general, by understanding the contingency of the meaning of subjectivity and sexuality themselves, a queer life can, indeed, be re-figured as a liveable life.

Post Script: Jamey

Very soon after completing the main body of this book, I was told of the suicide that occurred in September 2011 of fourteen year-old Jamey Rodemeyer of Buffalo, New York. One might imagine that after having been immersed for some time in reading, thinking and writing about queer youth suicide in both the abstract of theory and in the study of many specific cases and stories, that one would become immune to the subjective disturbance of hearing yet another story, but that is definitely not the case. Jamey's story has both similarities to and differences from those I have been discussing and thinking about, reinforcing and yet also demanding an expansion of the stance I have taken on prevention and cultural change. Jamey was the second student to have committed suicide in his school since 2010, and had been seeing a social worker and a therapist (Tan 2011). He had been bullied at school for some time, and for the year prior to his suicide had also been the recipient of anti-queer bullying from anonymous posters on his online Formspring account; a fact which puts at least partly into question the wholesale common hope that the Internet will be a site of tolerance, help-seeking and through which new formations of sexual subjectivity might be developed. Posts directed at Jamey included statements such as: 'Jamie [sic] is stupid, gay, fat annd [sic] ugly. He must die!' and 'I wouldn't care if you died. No one would. So just do it :) It would make everyone WAY more happier' (Tan 2011). These acts of anonymous bullying are authorised by existing knowledges that frame queer youth as suicidal and articulate the interpellative force that seeks to declare a life as unliveable.

However, Jamey routinely discussed bullying in a range of online forums and was known to have been highly active in the defence of other recipients of bullying in his school. What makes this suicide even more notable than some of the other tragic situations I have discussed is the fact that, in May 2011, he had posted a video on the *It Gets Better* website, chronicling his experience of being bullied but also speaking of his highly supportive friends, the public support of gay community figures and celebrities such as Lady Gaga. He went on to discuss just how widespread that support had been before encouraging others likewise to have hope for a better, personal future: 'People I don't even know online – I know that sounds creepy, but they're so nice and caring and they don't ever want me to die, it's just so much support for me. So, just listen here: it gets better – look at me!' (http://www.youtube.com/watch?v=-Pb1CaGMdWk). His death reinforces the point that it does *not* get better; not while the existing frames that codify norms of sexuality persist. As with other suicidal subjects who find life unliveable in the despair of an over-exposure to the abyss of truth or the loss of a 'deep and reassuring ground' (Caputo 1993: 239), Jamey came to understand that bullying is merely the visible and obvious expression of power formations that render a subject at an unliveable distance from the norm. Hope for change through an end to bullying is, then, both fleeting and futile; waiting for life to become less unbearable is not something on which we can rely as a preventative measure for addressing queer youth suicidality.

Equally as disturbing in this case is the fact that Jamey's death did not stop the bullying. It was widely reported that at a homecoming dance held by his school immediately after his wake and attended by his sister, students chanted in memory of Jamey 'You're better off dead!' and 'We're glad you're dead!' (Stump 2011). While the suicide of a young queer person might be a disturbance that demands an ethical response from some, for others the force by which queer lives are framed as non-lives is so rigid that the end of that life is not only ungrievable but un-recognisable as death. That the bullying continues beyond death indicates that the temporal moment of a death that is recognised and gives subjectivity the status of human life in temporality is not recognisable to those who perpetrate the bullying; those who are authorised to bully by virtue of Jamey's distance from a recognisable norm. The power relations that give context and meaning to norms, life and liveability must thereby be the target of prevention, the site of intervention and engagement.

In re-thinking queer youth suicide from the perspectives of culture and identity, then, it is important to note that Jamey is not representative of the male queer youth stereotype of someone who is closeted, isolated, lonely and un-supported. Rather, the infrastructure of support appears to be stronger and greater than ever before: through counselling, the other videos on the *It Gets Better* site, his involvement in online communities and a highly supportive network of peers. What this terrible suicide of such a young person reveals, then, is the unbearable force of *normativity* in contemporary culture, enacted through bullying but also through so many other (perhaps positive) representations, statements and articulations. Much like the case of Tyler Clementi, one can discern here the unbearability of existence in the persistence of being made to feel non-normative through the very structuration in contemporary culture of sexuality along demarcated proximities and distances from codes of normality. Despite support, despite tolerance, and despite efforts to combat shame or proffer positive identity formation, it is that which makes, even for those who appear resilient and active in combatting discrimination and harassment, a life unliveable. From this perspective, it is made even more clear that the task of making young queer lives liveable will not be achieved through personalised or group-based intervention and existing preventative measures, nor will it occur in the hope that positive inclusion, representation and connectedness will achieve that goal in the longer term. Rather than *intervention* along existing categorical lines in which risk is determined by categories of sexuality, preventing the ongoing phenomenon of queer youth suicide requires *engagement* with the problems that occur under existing regimes whereby identity is produced in the conventional terms of sexual choices. Making queer lives liveable is a task that will be long, complex, multi-faceted and focused on the culture and meaning of sexuality itself.

Bibliography

Aarons, L. 1995. *Prayers for Bobby: A Mother's Coming to Terms with the Suicide of Her Gay Son*. San Francisco: HarperCollins.

Adam, B. D. 2009. How might we create a collectivity that we would want to belong to? in *Gay Shame*. Edited by D. M. Halperin and V. Traub. Chicago and London: The University of Chicago Press, 301–311.

Agathangelou, A. M., Bassichis, M. D. and Spira, Tamara L. 2008. Intimate investments: Homonormativity, global lockdown, and the seductions of empire. *Radical History Review*, 100, 120–143.

Ahmed, S. 2004. *The Cultural Politics of Emotion*. Edinburgh: Edinburgh University Press.

Almeida, J., Johnson, R. M., Corliss, H. L., Molnar, B. E. and Azrael, D. 2009. Emotional distress among LGBT youth: The influence of perceived discrimination based on sexual orientation. *Journal of Youth and Adolescence*, 38(7), 1001–1014.

Altman, D. 1971. *Homosexual Oppression and Liberation*. 2nd Edition, 1993. New York: New York University Press.

Altman, D. 1982. *The Homosexualization of America, The Americanization of the Homosexual*. New York: St. Martin's Press.

Anderson, B. 1983. *Imagined Communities: Reflections on the Origins and Spread of Nationalism*. 2nd Edition. London: Verso.

Argent, S. 2010. Mother and (gay) son. *Blaze*, 29 July. http://blaze.gaynewsnetwork.com.au/feature/shelley-argent-mother-and-gay-son-003911.html, accessed 28 February 2011.

Ashcraft, C. 2003. Adolescent ambiguities in *American Pie*: Popular culture as a resource for sex education. *Youth & Society*, 35(1), 37–70.

Attwood, F. 2006. Sexed up: Theorizing the sexualization of culture. *Sexualities*, 9(1), 77–94.

Ayres, T. 1999. China doll – The experience of being a gay Chinese Australian, in *Multicultural Queer: Australian Narratives*. Edited by P. A. Jackson and G. Sullivan. New York and London: Haworth Press, 87–97.

Barber, J. G. 2001. Relative misery and youth suicide. *Australian and New Zealand Journal of Psychiatry*, 35(1), 49–57.

Battin, M. P. 1995. *Ethical Issues in Suicide*. Englewood Cliffs, N.J.: Prentice-Hall.

Beattie, D., Cunningham, S., Jones, R. and Zelenko, O. 2006. 'I use online so the counsellors can't hear me crying': Creating design solutions for online counselling. *Media International Australia*, 116, 43–52.

Beck, A. T., Weissman, A., Trexler, L. and Lester, D. 1974. The measurement of pessimism: The Hopelessness Scale. *Journal of Consulting and Clinical Psychology*, 42(6), 861–865.

Becker, R. 2006. Gay-themed television and the slumpy class: The affordable, multicultural politics of the gay nineties. *Television & New Media*, 7(2), 184–215.

Belkin, L. 2010. Suicide and the internet. *New York Times*, 30 September. http://parenting.blogs.nytimes.com/2010/09/30/suicide-and-the-internet/, accessed 10 November 2010.

Bell, V. 1999. Performativity and belonging. *Theory, Culture & Society*, 16(2), 1–10.

Benn, S., Todd, L. R. and Pendleton, J. 2010. Public relations leadership in corporate social responsibility. *Journal of Business Ethics*, 96(3), 403–423.

Bennett, T. 1983. Texts, readers, reading formations. *Literature and History*, 9(2), 214–227.

Berry, C. and Martin, F. 1998. Queer'n'Asian on the net: Syncretic sexualities in Taiwan and Korean cyberspaces. *Inqueeries*, June, 67–93.

Bersani, L. 1995. *Homos*. Cambridge, Mass.: Harvard University Press.

Blood, R. W. and Pirkis, J. 2001. Suicide and the media: Part III: Theoretical issues. *Crisis*, 22(4), 163–169.

Blow, C. M. 2009. Two little boys. *New York Times*, 24 April. http://blow.blogs. nytimes.com/2009/04/24/two-little-boys/, accessed 28 February 2011.

Bronski, M. 1984. *Culture Clash: The Making of Gay Sensibility*. Boston: South End Press.

Brown, G. 2009. Thinking beyond homonormativity: Performative explorations of diverse gay economies. *Environment and Planning A*, 41(6), 1496–1510.

Bryant, K. 2008. In defense of gay children? 'Progay' homophobia and the production of homonormativity. *Sexualities*, 11(4), 455–475.

Bryant, W. M. 1997. *Bisexual Characters in Film: From Anaïs to Zee*. Birmingham, NY: Harrington Park Press.

Buchbinder, D. 1997. *Performance Anxieties: Re-producing Masculinity*. St Leonards, NSW: Allen & Unwin.

Butler, J. 1990. *Gender Trouble: Feminism and the Subversion of Identity*. London and New York: Routledge.

Butler, J. 1991. Imitation and gender insubordination, in *Inside/Out: Lesbian Theories, Gay Theories*. Edited by Diana Fuss. London: Routledge, 13–31.

Butler, J. 1993. *Bodies that Matter: On the Discursive Limits of 'Sex'*. London and New York: Routledge.

Butler, J. 1997. *The Psychic Life of Power: Theories in Subjection*. Stanford, CA: Stanford University Press.

Butler, J. 1999. Revisiting bodies and pleasures. *Theory, Culture & Society*, 16(2), 11–20.

Butler, J. 2003. Violence, mourning, politics. *Studies in Gender and Sexuality*, 4(1), 9–37.

Butler, J. 2004. *Precarious Life*. London: Verso.

Butler, J. 2005. *Giving an account of Oneself.* New York: Fordham University Press.

Butler, J. 2009. *Frames of War: When is Life Grievable?* London and New York: Verso.

Caplan, S. E. 2003. Preference for online social interaction: A theory of problematic internet use and psychosocial well-being. *Communication Research*, 30(6), 625–648.

Caputo, J. D. 1993. *Against Ethics: Contributions to a Poetics of Obligation with Constant Reference to Deconstruction*. Bloomington and Indianapolis: Indiana University Press.

Carter, J. 2009. Gay marriage and pulp fiction: Homonormativity, disidentification, and affect in Ann Bannon's lesbian novels.' *GLQ*,15(4), 583–609.

Case, S-E. 1995. The student and the strap: Authority and seduction in the class(room), in *Professions of Desire: Lesbian and Gay Studies in Literature*. Edited by G. E. Haggerty and B. Zimmerman. New York: Modern Language Association of America, 38–46.

Cass, V. 1979. Homosexual identity formation: A theoretical model. *Journal of Homosexuality*, 4(3), 219–235.

Castells, M. 1997. *The Information Age: Economy, Society and Culture Volume II: The Power of Identity*. Oxford: Blackwell.

Chapman, A. L, Specht, M. W. and Cellucci, T. 2005. Factors associated with suicide attempts in female inmates: The hegemony of hopelessness. *Suicide & Life-Threatening Behavior*, 35(5), 558–569.

Cleary, A. and Brannick, T. 2007. Suicide and Changing Values and Beliefs in Ireland. *Crisis* 28(2), 82–88.

Cloud, J. 2005. The Battle Over Gay Teens. *Time Magazine*, 2 October. http://www.time.com/time/magazine/article/0,9171,1112856,00.html, accessed 10 November 2010.

Cohen, A. P. 1985. *The Symbolic Construction of Community*. London: Ellis Horwood and Tavistock Publications.

Commonwealth of Australia. 2008. *Life is for Everyone Framework: Research and Evidence in Suicide Prevention*. Canberra, ACT: Department of Health and Ageing.

Cover, R. 2000. First contact: Queer theory, sexual identity, and 'mainstream' film. *International Journal of Gender and Sexuality*, 5(1), 71–89.

Cover, R. 2002. Re-Sourcing queer subjectivities: Sexual identity and lesbian/gay community media. *Media International Australia (incorporating Culture & Policy)*, 103, 109–123.

Cover, R. 2004. Bodies, movements and desires: Lesbian/gay subjectivity and the stereotype. *Continuum: Journal of Media & Cultural Studies*, 18(1), 81–98.

Cover, R. 2005a. Political suicide: GLBT politics, human rights (to life), and the politicization of queer youth suicide. *Journal of Intergroup Relations*, 31(4), 25–44.

Cover, R. 2005b. Queer subjects of suicide: Cultural studies, sexuality and youth suicide research/policy in New Zealand.' *New Zealand Sociology*, 20(1), 76–98.

Cover, R. 2005c. Engaging sexualities: Lesbian/gay print journalism, Community belonging, social space and physical place. *Pacific Journalism Review*, 11(1), 113–132.

Cover, R. 2010. Politicising queer issues and activism: Disciplinarity, biopolitics and the means by which activist issues enter the public sphere. *Reconstruction: Studies in Contemporary Culture*, 10(3), http://reconstruction.eserver.org/103/Cover_01.shtml

Cover, R. 2011. The chasm & the abyss: Queer theory and the socialities of queer youth suicide. *Interalia: Journal of Queer Studies*, 6, 1–22.

Creed, B. 1995. Lesbian bodies: Tribades, tomboys and tarts, in *Sexy Bodies: The Strange Carnalities of Feminism*. Edited by E. Grosz and E. Probyn. London and New York: Routledge, 86–103.

Crisp, C. and McCave, E. L. 2007. Gay affirmative practice: A model for social work practice with gay, lesbian, and bisexual youth. *Child Adolescent Social Work Journal*, 24(4), 403–421.

Curran, J. 2002. *Media and Power*. London: Routledge.

Curtis, M. 1999. Growing up Bent. *The Age*, 3 August, T1.

D'Emilio, J. 1992. *Making Trouble: Essays on Gay History, Politics and the University*. New York and London: Routledge.

Davis, M. 1997. *Gangland: Cultural Elites and the New Generationalism*. St. Leonards, NSW: Allen & Unwin.

Davis, T. S, Saltzburg, S. and Locke, C. R. 2009. Supporting the emotional and psychological well being of sexual minority youth: Youth ideas for action. *Children and Youth Services Review*, 31(9), 1030–1041.

Day, G. 1990. Introduction: popular culture – The conditions of control? in *Readings in Popular Culture: Trivial Pursuits?* Edited by Gary Day. New York: St. Martin's Press, 1–13.

de Lauretis, T. 1989. Queer theory: Lesbian and gay sexualities: An introduction. *Differences*, 3(2), iii–xvii.

Dorais, M. 2004. *Dead Boys Can't Dance: Sexual Orientation, Masculinity, and Suicide*. With S. L. Lajeunesse. Translated by P. Tremblay. Montreal and Kingston: McGill-Queen's University Press.

Doyle, V. 2008. 'But Joan! You're my daughter!': The Gay and Lesbian Alliance Against Defamation and the politics of amnesia. *Radical History Review*, 100, 209–221.

Drummond, W. 1997. Adolescents at risk: Causes of youth suicide in New Zealand. *Adolescence*, 32(128), 925–934.

Duggan, L. 2002. The new homonormativity: The sexual politics of neoliberalism, in *Materializing Democracy: Toward a Revitalized Cultural Politics*. Edited by R. Castronovo and D. Nelson. Durham, NC: Duke University Press, 175–194.

Durkheim, E. 1952. *Suicide: A Study in Sociology.* Translated by J. A. Spaulding and G. Simpson. London: Routledge and Kegan Paul.

Dyer, R. 1993. *The Matter of Images: Essays on Representations.* London and New York: Routledge.

Edwards, W. J. 1996. A sociological analysis of an in/visible minority group: Male adolescent homosexuals. *Youth & Society*, 27(3), 334–355.

Emslie, M. 1996. Ignored to death: Representations of young gay men, lesbians and bisexuals in Australian youth suicide policy and programs. *Youth Studies Australia*, 15(4), 38–42.

Epstein, S. 1990. Gay politics, ethnic identity: The limits of social constructionism, in *Forms of Desire: Sexual Orientation and the Social Constructionist Controversy.* Edited by E. Stein. New York and London: Gardland, 239–293.

Eribon, D. 2004. *Insult and the Gay Self.* Translated by M. Lucey. Durham and London, Duke University Press.

Erwin, K. 1993. Interpreting the evidence: Competing paradigms and the emergence of lesbian and gay suicide as a 'social fact'. *International Journal of Health Services*, 23(3), 437–453.

Espelage, D. L. and Swearer, S. M. 2008. Addressing research gaps in the intersection between homophobia and bullying. *School Psychology Review*, 37(2), 155–159.

Farquhar, C. 2000. Lesbian in a post-lesbian world? Policing identity, sex and image. *Sexualities*, 3(2), 219–236.

Fassin, D. 2009. Another politics of life is possible. *Theory, Culture & Society*, 26(6), 44–60.

Fejes, F. 1997. Reviews of E. Alwood, *Straight News: Gays, Lesbians and the News Media* and R. Streitmatter, *Unspeakable: The Rise of the Gay and Lesbian Press in America.' Journal of Homosexuality*, 34(1), 105–110.

Fenaughty, J. and Harré, N. 2003. Life on the seesaw: A qualitative study of suicide resiliency factors for young gay men. *Journal of Homosexuality*, 45(1), 1–22.

Flowers, P. and Buston, K. 2001. 'I was terrified of being different': Exploring gay men's accounts of growing-up in a heterosexist society. *Journal of Adolescence*, 24(1), 51–65.

Foderaro, L. 2010. Teen violinist dies after student internet lark. *The Age*, 1 October. http://www.theage.com.au/world/, accessed 1 October 2010.

Foucault, M. 1988. The ethics of the care of the self as a practice of freedom, translated by J. D. Gauthier, in *The Final Foucault.* Edited by J. Bernauer and D. Rasmussen. Cambridge, Mass.: MIT Press, 1–20.

Foucault, M. 1990. *The History of Sexuality: An Introduction.* Translated by R. Hurley. London: Penguin.

Foucault, M. 1994. *Ethics, Subjectivity and Truth.* Edited by P. Rabinow, translated by R. Hurley et. al. New York: New York Press.

Foucault, M. 2004a. *Abnormal: Lectures at the Collège de France, 1974–1975.* Edited by V. Marchetti and A. Salmoni, translated by G. Burchell. New York: Picador.

Igartua, K., Thombs, B. D., Burgos, G., and Montoro, R. 2009. Concordance and discrepancy in sexual identity, attraction, and behavior among adolescents. *Journal of Adolescent Health*, 45(6), 602–608.

Italie, L. 2010. Gay community send YouTube video message: It gets better. *The Age*, 8 October. http://www.theage.com.au/digital-life/, accessed 9 October 2010.

Jagose, A. 1996. *Queer Theory*. Carlton South, VIC.: Melbourne University Press.

Jaworski, K. 2008. 'Elegantly wasted': The celebrity deaths of Michael Hutchence and Paula Yates. *Continuum: Journal of Media & Cultural Studies*, 22(6), 777–791.

Jenkins, F. 2010. Judith Butler: Disturbance, provocation and the ethics of non-violence. *Humanities Research*, 16(2), 93–115.

Jenness, V. 1992. Coming out: Lesbian identities and the categorization problem, in *Modern Homosexuality: Fragments of Lesbian and Gay Experience*. Edited, by K. Plummer. London and New York: Routledge, 65–74.

Kalliotis, P. 2000. Bullying as a special case of aggression: Procedures for cross-cultural assessment. *School Psychology International*, 21(1), 47–64.

Karasawa, M., Asai, N. and Tanabe, Y. 2007. Stereotypes as shared beliefs: Effects of group identity on dyadic conversations. *Group Processes & Intergroup Relations*, 10(4), 515–532.

Kelly, P. 2001. Youth at risk: Processes of individualisation and responsibilisation in the risk society. *Discourse: Studies in the Cultural Politics of Education*, 22(1), 23–33.

Kendall, C. N. and Walker, S. 1998. Teen suicide, sexuality and silence. *Alternative Law Journal*, 23(5), 216–221.

Kim, Y. S. and Leventhal, B. 2008. Bullying and suicide. A review. *International Journal of Adolescent Medical Health*, 20(2), 133–154.

King, M., Semlyen, J., Tai, S. S., Killaspy, H., Osborn, D., Popelyuk, D. and Nazareth, I. 2008. A systematic review of mental disorder, suicide, and deliberate self harm in lesbian, gay and bisexual people. *BMC Psychiatry*, 8(1), 70–86.

Kinz, R. 1998. Email to *GLB-News Listserv*, 5 January 1998.

Kloos, A. L., Collins, R., Weller, R. A. and Weller, E. B. 2007. Suicide in preadolescents: Who is at risk? *Current Psychiatry Reports*, 9(2), 89–93.

Kral, M. J. 1994. Suicide as Social Logic. *Suicide & Life-Threatening Behavior*, 24(3), 245–259.

Kulkin, H. S., Chauvin, E. A. and Percle, G. A. 2000. Suicide among gay and lesbian adolescents and young adults: A review of the literature. *Journal of Homosexuality*, 40(1), 1–29.

Latham, R. 2002. *Consuming Youth: Vampires, Cyborgs, and the Culture of Consumption*. Chicago and London: University of Chicago Press.

Leap, W. L. 1996. *Word's Out: Gay Men's English*. Minneapolis: University of Minnesota Press.

Lebson, M. 2002. Suicide among homosexual youth. *Journal of Homosexuality*, 42(4), 107–117.

Lester, D. 1997. The role of shame in suicide. *Suicide & Life-Threatening Behavior*, 27(4), 352–361.

Lloyd, H. M. 1958. *On Shame and the Search for Identity*. New York: Harcourt, Brace and Company.

Luders, M. 2008. Conceptualizing personal media. *New Media & Society*, 10(5), 683–702.

McAndrew, S. and Warne, T. 2010. Coming out to talk about suicide: Gay men and suicidality. *International Journal of Mental Health Nursing*, 19(2), 92–101.

McBee-Strayer, S. M. and Rogers, J. R. 2002. Lesbian, gay, and bisexual suicidal behavior: Testing a constructivist model. *Suicide & Life-Threatening Behavior*, 32(3), 272–283.

McDaniel, J. S., Purcell, D. and D'Augelli, A. R. 2001. The relationship between sexual orientation and risk for suicide: Research findings and future directions for research and prevention. *Suicide & Life-Threatening Behavior*, 31(1), 84–105.

McDermott, E., Roen, K. and Scourfield, J. 2008. Avoiding shame: Young LGBT people, homophobia and self-destructive behaviours. *Culture, Health & Sexuality*, 10(8), 815–829.

Macdonald, R. and Cooper, T. 1998. Young gay men and suicide: A report of a study exploring the reasons which young men give for suicide ideation. *Youth Studies Australia*, 17(4), 2–27.

McKinley, J. 2010. Suicide put light on pressures of gay teenagers. *New York Times*, 3 October. http://www.nytimes.com/2010/10/04/us/, accessed 10 November 2010.

Maira, S. and Soep, E. 2004. United states of adolescence? Reconsidering US youth culture studies. *Young: Nordic Journal of Youth Research*, 12(3), 245–269.

Martin, G. 2006. Editorial: On Suicide and Subcultures. *Australian e-Journal for the Advancement of Mental Health*, 5(3), 1–5.

Mehra, B. and Braquet, D. 2006. A 'queer' manifesto of interventions for libraries to 'come out' of the closet! A study of 'queer' youth experiences during the coming out process. *LIBRES: Library and Information Science Research Electronic Journal*, 16(1).

Meyer, J. 1996. Sexuality and power: Perspectives for the less powerful. *Theory & Psychology*, 6(1), 93–119.

Miller, D. N. and Eckert, T. L. 2009. Youth suicidal behavior: An introduction and overview. *School Psychology Review*, 38(2), 153–167.

Mills, S. 1997. *Discourse*. London and New York: Routledge.

Mishna, F., Newman, P. A., Daley, A. and Solomon, S. 2009. Bullying of lesbian and gay youth: A qualitative investigation. *The British Journal of Social Work*, 39(8), 1598–1614.

Mohr, R. 1992. *Gay Ideas: Outing and Other Controversies*. Boston: Beacon Press.

Mokros, H. B. 1995. Suicide and shame. *The American Behavioral Scientist*, 38(8), 1091–1101.

Moon, J. 2009. Gay shame and the politics of identity, in *Gay Shame*. Edited by D. M. Halperin and V. Traub. Chicago and London: The University of Chicago Press, 357–368.

Moores, S. 1993. *Interpreting Audiences: The Ethnography of Media Consumption*. London: Sage.

Morrison, L. L. and L'Heureux, J. 2001. Suicide and gay/lesbian/bisexual youth: Implications for clinicians. *Journal of Adolescence*, 24(1), 39–49.

Muehrer, P. 1995. Suicide and sexual orientation: A critical summary of recent research and directions for future research. *Suicide and Life-Threatening Behavior*, 25(s1), 72–81.

Mulvey, L. 2006. *Death 24x a Second: Stillness and the Moving Image*. London: Reaktion Books.

Munt, S. 2007. *Queer Attachments: The Cultural Politics of Shame*. Aldershot: Ashgate.

Murphy, A. V. 2011. Corporeal vulnerability and the new humanism. *Hypatia*, 26(3), 575–590.

Murphy, K. P., Ruiz, J. and Surlin, D. 2008. Editors' Introduction. *Radical History Review*, 100, 1–9.

Murphy, T. F. 1997. *Gay Science: The Ethics of Sexual Orientation Research*. New York: Columbia University Press.

Murray, S. O. 1996. *American Gay*. Chicago and London: University of Chicago Press.

New Zealand Ministry of Health. 2000. *Suicide and the Media: the Reporting and Portrayal of Suicide in the Media*. http://www.moh.govt.nz, accessed 3 January 2005.

Nicholas, J. and Howard, J. 1998. Better dead than gay? Depression, suicide ideation and attempt among a sample of gay and straight-identified males aged 18 to 24. *Youth Studies Australia*, 17(4), 28–33.

Nip, J. Y. M. 2004. The relationship between online and offline communities: The case of the Queer Sisters. *Media, Culture & Society*, 26(3), 409–428.

Nungesser, L. G. 1983. *Homosexual Acts, Actors, and Identities*. New York: Praeger.

Olson, E. D. and King, C. A. 1995. Gay and lesbian self-identification: A response to Rotheram-Borus and Fernandez. *Suicide & Life-Threatening Behavior*, 25(s1), 35–39.

Orlando, J. 2000. Homosexuality is a risk factor for teen suicide, in *Teen Suicide*. Edited by T. L. Roleff. San Diego, CA: Greenhaven Press, 19–23.

Oswin, N. 2005. Towards radical geographies of complicit queer futures. *ACME: An International E-Journal for Critical Geographies*, 3(2), 79–86.

Oswin, N. 2008. Critical geographies and the uses of sexuality: Deconstructing queer space. *Progress in Human Geography*, 32(1), 89–103.

Padva, G. 2002. Heavenly monsters: The politics of the male body in the naked issue of *Attitude* magazine. *International Journal of Sexuality and Gender Studies*, 7(4), 281–292.

Padva, G. 2004. Edge of seventeen: Melodramatic coming-out in new queer adolescence films.' *Communication and Critical/Cultural Studies*, 1(4), 355–372.

Papacharissi, Z. and Fernback, J. 2008. The aesthetic power of the Fab 5: Discursive themes of homonormativity in *Queer Eye for the Straight Guy*. *Journal of Communication Inquiry*, 32(4), 348–367.

Piers, G. and Singer, M. B. 1971. *Shame and Guilt: A Psychoanalytic and a Cultural Study*. New York: W. W. Norton & Company.

Pirkis, J. and Blood, R. W. 2001. Suicide and the media: Part II: Portrayal in fictional media. *Crisis*, 22(4), 155–162.

Plöderl, M., Kralovec, K. and Fartacek, R. 2010. The relation between sexual orientation and suicide attempts in Austria. *Archives of Sexual Behavior*, 39(6), 1403–1414.

Plummer, K. 1995. *Telling Sexual Stories: Power, Change and Social Worlds*. London and New York: Routledge.

Probyn, E. 1996. *Outside Belongings*. New York and London: Routledge.

Probyn, E. 2000. Sporting bodies: Dynamics of shame and pride. *Body & Society*, 6(1), 13–28.

Probyn, E. 2004. Everyday Shame. *Cultural Studies*, 18(2–3), 328–349.

Probyn, E. 2005. *Blush: Faces of Shame*. Minneapolis: University of Minnesota Press.

Quigley, R. 2011. What do I have to do for people to listen? Boy, 14, kills himself after 'gay' taunts and thanks Lady Gaga in his final post. *Daily Mail*, 21 September. http:// http://www.dailymail.co.uk/news/article-2039801/, accessed 28 October 2011.

Remafedi, G. 1994. Introduction: The state of knowledge on gay, lesbian, and bisexual youth suicide, in *Death by Denial: Studies of Suicide in Gay and Lesbian Teenagers*. Edited by G. Remafedi. Boston: Alyson Publications, 7–14.

Remafedi, G., Farrow, J. A. and Deisher, R. W. 1991. Risk factors for attempted suicide in gay and bisexual youth. *Pediatrics*, 87(6), 869–875.

Remafedi, G. Farrow, J. A. and Deisher, R. W. 1994. Risk factors for attempted suicide in gay and bisexual youth, in *Death by Denial: Studies of Suicide in Gay and Lesbian Teenagers*. Edited by G. Remafedi. Boston: Alyson Publications, 123–137.

Roberts, R. 1996. School experiences of some rural gay men coping with 'countrymindedness', in *Gay and Lesbian Perspectives III: Essays in Australian Culture*. Edited, by G. Wotherspoon. Sydney: Department of Economic History, University of Sydney, 45–69.

Rofes, E. E. 1983. '*I Thought People Like That Killed Themselves': Lesbians, Gay Men and Suicide*. San Francisco: Grey Fox Press.

Rosario, M., Schrimshaw, E. W. and Hunter, J. 2008. Predicting different patterns of sexual identity development over time among lesbian, gay, and bisexual youths: A cluster analytic approach. *American Journal of Community Psychology*, 42(3–4), 266–282.

Rosello, M. 1998. *Declining the Stereotype: Ethnicity and Representation in French Cultures:* Hanover, NH: University Press of New England.

Rotheram-Borus, M. J. and Fernandez, M. I. 1995. Sexual orientation and developmental challenges experienced by gay and lesbian youths. *Suicide & Life-Threatening Behavior*, 25(suppl.), 26–31.

Russell, S. T. 2003. Sexual minority youth and suicide risk. *The American Behavioral Scientist*, 46(9), 1241–1257.

Russo, V. 1981. *The Celluloid Closet: Homosexuality in the Movies*. New York: Harper & Row.

Rutter, P. A. and Soucar, E. 2002. Youth suicide risk and sexual orientation. *Adolescence*, 37(146), 289–299.

Ryan, C., Huebner, D., Diaz, R. M. and Sanchez, J. 2009. Family rejection as a predictor of negative health outcomes in white and latino lesbian, gay, and bisexual young adults. *Pediatrics: Official Journal of the American Academic of Pediatrics*, 123(1), 346–352.

Saulnier, C. F. 1998. Prevalence of suicide attempts and suicidal ideation among lesbian and gay youth, in *Violence and Social Injustice Against Lesbian, Gay and Bisexual People*. Edited by L. M. Sloan and N. S. Gustavsson. New York: Haworth Press, 51–68.

Savin-Williams, R. C. 1996. Self-labeling and disclosure among gay, lesbian and bisexual youths, in *Lesbians and Gays in Couples and Families: A Handbook for Therapists*. Edited by J. Laird and R-J Green. San Francisco: Jossey-Bass, 153–182.

Savin-Williams, R. C. 2001. A critique of research on sexual-minority youths. *Journal of Adolescence*, 24(1), 5–13.

Saxey, E. 2008. *Homoplot: The Coming-Out Story and Gay, Lesbian and Bisexual Identity*. New York: Peter Lang.

Scheff, T. 1994. Emotions and identity: A theory of ethnic nationalism, in *Social Theory and the Politics of Identity*. Edited by C. Calhoun. Oxford: Blackwell, 277–303.

Scheff, T. J. and Retzinger, S. M. 1991. *Emotions and Violence: Shame and Rage in Destructive Conflicts*. Lexington, Mass.: Lexington Books.

Schneider, S. G., Farberow, N. L. and Kruks, G. N. 1994. Suicidal behavior in adolescent and young adult gay men, in *Death by Denial: Studies of Suicide in Gay and Lesbian Teenagers*. Edited by G. Remafedi. Boston: Alyson Publications, 107–122.

Schulman, S. 1995. Gay Identity and the Media Blitz. *Lambda Book Report*, 4(8), 12–14.

Sedgwick, E. K. 1990. *Epistemology of the Closet*. London: Penguin.

Sedgwick, E. K. 1993a. Queer performativity: Henry James's *The Art of the Novel*. *GLQ*, 1(1), 1–14.

Sedgwick, E. K. 1993b. *Tendencies*. Durham: Duke University Press.

Sedgwick, E. K. 2003. *Touching Feeling: Affect, Pedagogy, Performativity*. Durham and London: Duke University Press.

Shaffer, D., Fisher, P., Paides, M. and Gould, M. 1995. Sexual orientation in adolescents who commit suicide. *Suicide & Life-Threatening Behavior*, 25(s1), 64–71.

Shannon, C. E. and Weaver, W. 1949. *The Mathematical Theory of Communication*. Urbana: University of Illinois Press.

Shneidman, E. 1985. *Definition of Suicide*. New York: John Wiley & Sons.

Siebers, T. 2009. Sex, shame, and disability identity, with reference to Mark O'Brien, in *Gay Shame*, ed. D. M. Halperin and V. Traub. Chicago and London: The University of Chicago Press, 201–216.

Silenzio, V. M. B., Duberstein, P. R., Tang, W., Lu, N., Tu, X. and Homan, C. M. 2009. Connecting the invisible dots: Reaching lesbian, gay, and bisexual adolescents and young adults at risk for suicide through online social networks.' *Social Science & Medicine*, 69(3), 469–474.

Sinfield, A. 1996. Diaspora and hybridity: Queer identities and the ethnicity model. *Textual practice*, 19(2), 271–293.

Skidmore, C. W., Linsenmeier, J. A. W. and Bailey, J. M. 2006. Gender nonconformity and psychological distress in lesbians and gay men. *Archives of Sexual Behavior*, 35(6), 685–697.

Smalley, N., Scourfield, J. and Greenland, K. 2005. Young people, gender and suicide: A review of research on the social context. *Journal of Social Work*, 5(2), 133–154.

Smythe, D. 1995. The audience commodity and its work, in *Approaches to Media: A Reader*. Edited, by O. Boyd-Barrett and C. Newbold. London: Arnold, 222–228.

Spivak, G. C. 1999. *A Critique of Postcolonial Reason: Toward a History of the Vanishing Present*. Cambridge, Mass.: Harvard University Press.

Streitmatter, R. 1995. *Unspeakable: The Rise of the Gay and Lesbian Press in America*. London and Boston: Faber and Faber.

Stryker, S. 2008. Transgender history, homonormativity, and disciplinarity. *Radical History Review*, 100, 145–157.

Stump, S. 2011. 'Teen's parents: After suicide, he's still being bullied.' *MSNBC Today.com*, 27 September. http://today.msnbc.msn.com/id/44684938/ns/today-today_people/t/, accessed 29 October 2011.

Suicide Prevention Resource Centre. 2008. *Suicide Risk and Prevention for Lesbian, Gay, Bisexual, and Transgender Youth*. Newton, MA: Education Development Center, Inc.

Talburt, S., Rofes, E. and Rasmussen, M. L. 2004. Introduction: Transforming discourses of queer youth and educational practices surrounding gender, sexuality and youth, in *Youth and Sexualities: Pleasure, Subversion, and Insubordination In and Out of Schools*. Edited by M. L. Rasmussen, E. Rofes, and S. Talburt. New York: Palgrave Macmillan, 1–13.

Tan, Sandra (2011). Teenager struggled with bullying before taking his life. *BuffaloNews.com*, 27 September. http://www.buffalonews.com/city/schools/article563538.ece, accessed 28 October 2011.

Tefft, L. M. 2000. Many factors put teens at risk of suicide, in *Teen Suicide*. Edited by T. L. Roleff. San Diego, CA: Greenhaven Press, 66–69.

Terranova, T. 2009. Another life: The nature of political economy in Foucault's genealogy of biopolitics. *Theory, Culture & Society*, 26(6), 234–262.

Thompson, K. 1982. *Emile Durkheim*. London: Tavistock Publications.

Tomkins, S. S. 1962. *Affect, Imagery, Consciousness*. New York: Springer.

Toscano, A. 2007. Vital strategies: Maurizio Lazzarato and the metaphysics of contemporary capitalism. *Theory, Culture & Society*, 24(6), 71–91.

Tremblay, P. and Ramsay, R. 2004. The changing social construction of western male homosexuality: Association with worsening youth suicide problems. http://www.youth-suicide.com/gay-bisexual/construction/, accessed 12 April 2011.

Troiden, R. R. 1988. *Gay and Lesbian Identity: A Sociological Analysis*. Dix Hills, NY: General Hall.

Tyler, I. 2009. Against abjection. *Feminist Theory*, 10(1), 77–98.

Vaid, U. 1995. *Virtual quality: The Mainstreaming of Gay and Lesbian Liberation*. New York: Anchor.

Vanasco, J. 2010.'New gay student suicide adds to national tragedy. *365Gay*, 21 October. http://www.365gay.com/news/, accessed 30 October 2010.

Walls, N. E., Freedenthal, S. and Wisneski, H. 2008. Suicidal ideation and attempts among sexual minority youths receiving social services. *Social Work*, 53(1), 21–29.

Walton, G. 2006. H-cubed: A primer on bullying and sexuality diversity for educators. *Professional Development Perspectives*, 6(2), 13–20.

Warner, M. 1999. *The Trouble with Normal: Sex, Politics, and the Ethics of Queer Life*. New York: The Free Press.

Warner, M. 2009. Pleasures and Dangers of Shame, in *Gay Shame*. Edited by D. M. Halperin and V. Traub. Chicago and London: The University of Chicago Press, 283–296.

Warren, C. A. B. 1974. *Identity and Community in the Gay World*. New York: Wiley.

Weiss, M. D. 2008. Gay shame and BDSM pride: Neoliberalism, privacy, and sexual politics. *Radical History Review*, 100, 87–101.

White, J. 2009. *Research to Practice: Doing Youth Suicide Prevention Critically: Interrogating the Knowledge Practice Relationship*. British Columbia: Federation of Child and Family Services of British Columbia.

Widdicombe, B. 1997. Can We Catch Our Falling Stars? *OutRage Magazine*, 174, November, 52–56.

Williams, R. 1976. *Keywords*. Glasgow: Fontana.

Williams, R. 1981. *Culture*. Glasgow: Fontana.

Zhao, Y., Montaro, R., Kgarua, K. and Thombs, B. D. 2010. Suicidal ideation and attempt among adolescents reporting 'unsure' sexual identity or heterosexual identity plus same-sex attraction or behavior: Forgotten groups? *Journal of the American Academy of Child & Adolescent Psychiatry*, 49(2), 104–112.

Filmography

A Beautiful Mind (dir. Ron Howard, 2001).
A Single Man (dir. Tom Ford, 2009).
An Early Frost (dir. John Erman, 1985).
Another Country (dir. Marek Kanievska, 1984).
Boys in the Band (dir. William Friedkin, 1970).
But I'm a Cheerleader (dir. Jamie Babbit, 1999).
Butterfly Kiss (dir. Michael Winterbottom, 1995).
Come Undone [*Presque Rien*] (dir. Sébastien Lifshitz, 2000).
Consenting Adult (dir. Alan J. Pakula, 1992).
Hannibal (dir. Ridley Scott, 2001).
Heathers (dir. Michael Lehmann, 1989).
Prayers for Bobby (dir. Russell Mulcahy, 2009).
Silence of the Lambs (dir. Jonathan Demme, 1991).
Stonewall (dir. Nigel Finch, 1995).
The Opposite of Sex (dir. Don Roos, 1998).
This Special Friendship [*Les Amities Particulieres*] (dir. Jean Delannoy, 1964).
Totally Fucked Up (dir. Gregg Araki, 1993).
Trevor (dir. Peggy Rajski, 1994).
Wonder Boys (dir. Curtis Hanson, 2000).
Zee and Co (dir. Brian G. Hutton, 1972).

Index